little man, what now?

Der Stürmer

Nürnberger Wochenblatt zum Kampfe um die Wahrheit

HERAUSGEBER: JULIUS STREICHER

| Nummer 10 | Nürnberg, im März 1932 | 10. Jahr 1932 |

Die Weltpest

Deutscher Christ hab' acht

Das gelobte Land / Die Hand Juda / Der Fluch des Nazareners / Judas und Pilatus Auf Golgatha / Christlicher Judenschutz Judenhaß gegen alles Christliche Werde Nationalsozialist

Seine Ahnung

Wie lange werd's dauern, dann wenn mer hier in Deutschland auch bloß hinter Gitterstäben zu sehen sein

Aus dem Inhalt

Die Kundgebung der 28 000
Ende des roten Massenbetruges
Der Schillingsfürster Landfriedensprozeß
Wie sind die Kläger
Soll es so bleiben?

Die Juden sind unser Unglück!

HIS SUSPICION. "How long will it be before we too will be seen here in Germany only behind bars?" *The title involves a pun: "Ahnung" also refers to "Ahnen," or "ancestors."*

Little Man, What Now?
Der Stürmer in the Weimar Republic

Dennis E. Showalter

ARCHON BOOKS
1982

First published 1982 as an Archon Book,
an imprint of The Shoe String Press Inc.,
Hamden, Connecticut 06514

Printed in the United States of America

Library of Congress Cataloging in Publication Data

Showalter, Dennis E.
   Little man, what now?

   Bibliography: p.
   Includes index
   1. Antisemitism—Germany.   2. Stürmer.   3. Streicher, Julius, 1885–1946.
4. Germany—Politics and government—1918–1933.   5. Germany—Ethnic
relations   I. Title
DS146.G4S47   305.8'924'043   82-6640
ISBN 0-208-01893-X   AACR2

Contents

Preface

    This book began when, during a research trip to the Hoover Institution, I encountered a handsomely bound set of *Der Stürmer*. While paging through the volumes, I realized that the paper, even more than its editor Julius Streicher, had become an almost mythical bogey, the sort of thing not exactly better forgotten, but not worth soiling a scholar's hands and mind. The student of *Der Stürmer* does not have the satisfaction of dealing with horror on a cosmic, cathartic scale. His are documents not of destruction, but of petty malices and petty grievances—the unpleasant underside of daily life. The reaction of my friends and colleagues when I proposed doing a monograph on the subject was uniformly one of disgust. "How can you stand it?" I was asked time and again. This book is the answer.

    The thesis that someone must clean out history's sewers is open to criticism. It can be argued that a book focusing on *Der Stürmer*'s contents, by dredging up and discussing ancient scandals and false accusations, dignifies slander by footnotes. It can be suggested that it is impossible to determine the appeal and impact of such a newspaper from the perspective of a half-century. It can be asserted the *Der Stürmer* was the hobby of a Nazi leader considered repulsive even by many of his party comrades, a manifestation of an individual's pathologies, and a correspondingly unsuitable source for generalizations about National Socialist anti-Semitism. All three objections involve the same question. Can a book on *Der Stürmer* be anything but an exercise in academic sensationalism?

Preface

Der Stürmer certainly was Streicher's personal plaything. It also was, and has remained, a major symbol of the homicidal, genocidal anti-Semitism that continues to make the name of Nazi Germany a synonym for evil. Anti-Semitism was vital to National Socialism. It was the cornerstone of a messianic ideology based on biological racism. Whatever minor variations existed, the National Socialist world view is best described as an interpretation of history as a binary struggle between Good, as incorporated in the Aryan/German community, and Evil, as embodied in international Jewry. Hitler regarded himself as chosen by destiny for the task of saving the historical process from a people biologically impelled to undermine that process because of their inability to wage the struggle for existence fairly.[1]

This does not necessarily mean that *Mein Kampf* incorporated a blueprint, however disguised, for the Final Solution. In part this reflects the fact that Hitler and his party had few clear positive political concepts. National Socialism knew better what it was against than what it supported, and the movement's chaotic internal structure did not lend itself to projecting any calculated program systematically. It is nevertheless certain that long before 1933 the National Socialists planned to establish legal and extralegal systems designed to exclude Jews from every sphere of German life, to give them no protection against "healthy public opinion."[2]

The concept of exclusion was itself a form of Final Solution to the Nazi true believer. If in fact one accepted the premise, basic to National Socialist ideology, that the Jew was a parasite, incapable of creating his own culture, surviving only by secretly exploiting unwary host peoples, then isolating him from his host organism would bring about his destruction as surely as would this process with any other parasite.

This emphasis on the inherent racial worthlessness of the Jew can be used to reconcile the contradictory images of Jews in Nazi propaganda. On one hand he was the omnipotent and omnipresent adversary. On the other, he was vermin, presenting the petty threat of the seducer, the cheat, or the bad neighbor. In National Socialist terms, the Jew's instinctive need to insure his survival by destroying the societies on which he preyed meant that no means were too petty, no achievements too small. A girl seduced, a Gentile insulted, a bill unpaid—all contributed to the final end, just as did a country undermined or a people demoralized at one fell swoop.

Instrumentally, this dichotomy was a particularly effective propaganda device. It enabled cosmic evil to be presented in comprehensible, manageable proportions. It also offered a means of bridging National Socialism's intellectual gaps, of rationalizing blatant contradictions in the movement's political, social, and economic goals. The protean style of Nazi politics enabled appeals to the interests, hopes, and commitments of a wide variety of Germans. It generated a corresponding risk of falling among stools, of being dismissed as simple opportunism. The Jew, however, could be used to explain the hostility between labor and capital. He could be described as the cause of both agricultural poverty and industrial unemployment. The connection might be shaky, but it was enough to satisfy the increasing number of Germans who heard what they wanted to hear in Nazi speeches and promises.[3]

Scholarly opinions on the general impact of Nazi anti-Semitism continue to vary widely—not least because of the impossibility of expressing it in quantitative terms. Lucy Dawidowicz considers anti-Semitism central to Hitler's rise. Golo Mann presents it as one ingredient in a poisonous stew of misery and hatred. Sebastian Haffner argues that Hitler's "homicidal Jew-phobia" alienated even other anti-Semites.[4] Regional, sexual, and generational case studies agree that anti-Semitism was seldom a significant positive element in the Nazi appeal.[5] On the other hand, anti-Semitism is an identifiable factor in all of the groups so studied. Perhaps the most important point in the debate is not that Germans were receptive to Nazi anti-Semitism, but that they were not sufficiently repelled by it to reject other elements of the movement's appeal.[6] And since *Der Stürmer* more than any other Nazi institution focused on the Jew, directly and as a symbol, its contents can at least be used to indicate the kinds of anti-Semitic arguments the National Socialists thought would be effective.

Der Stürmer is a useful subject of study for still another reason. George Mosse has argued for the importance of popular culture in creating and sustaining the images of anti-Semitism whatever their objective relevance.[7] And *Der Stürmer* is one of the few institutions whose mention draws reactions from virtually every German who reached maturity between 1923 and 1945. The usual response is some variant of "oh yes, that horrible paper and its disgusting cartoons. I used to walk by its displays, but of course I paid no attention." The paper's propaganda value is similarly dismissed on the grounds that its accusations were too extreme to be taken seriously by any but the most confirmed racists or the simplest minds.

This position demands some qualification. Popular culture still remains in the stage of description as opposed to analysis. Most of these descriptions, however, manage to agree that popular culture is by its nature incomplete. It employs general situations and formula plots, conventions and stereotypes, all presented to be filled in by the individual consumer.[8] For this reason, since the days of Henry Nash Smith, popular culture has generally been considered a reasonable positive gauge of popular sentiments.[9] This involves a commonsense assumption. Popular culture is a consumption culture, essentially designed to sell. Therefore it must presumably incorporate the feelings and faiths of its purchasers—or at least, not challenge them drastically. Intellectual historians likewise assume direct correlation among ideas, attitudes, and behavior. The existence of popular anti-Semitism in nineteenth-century Germany, for example, is frequently presented as a direct prefiguration of Auschwitz.

An increasing number of scholars deny that popular culture is an accurate guide to public attitudes on any given subject. Entertainment forms and leisure-time activities are not incarnations of basic values. Students of popular culture must concentrate instead on the impact of that culture. They must study the effect of formula plots and stereotyped characters on consuming audiences sharing varied networks of social and cultural relationships.[10]

This theory is technically impossible to apply directly to a newspaper which ceased publication over three decades ago and whose tone was such that very few people today will admit reading it except as a piece of youthful folly. A profile of the typical *Stürmer* reader can no longer be constructed—except in a special sense. Works of popular culture rarely demand high degrees of concentration or commitment for extended periods. On the other hand, popular culture is pervasive. To avoid exposure to it demands deliberate, consistent effort. Popular culture may not embody some pseudo-Jungian version of collective un-consciousness. It is likely to reflect a minimum acceptable de-nominator of its consumers' attitudes. Specifically, it is reason-able to suggest that those who purchased or read *Der Stürmer* between 1923 and 1933 were not so disgusted by its message that Julius Streicher, anti-Semitism, and National Socialism became by extension equally repulsive. Nor did the well-publicized ex-istence of such a newspaper deter Germans of finer sensibilities from cheering and voting for the Hitler movement.

This study of *Der Stürmer* is confined to the *Kampfzeit*, the years of the Weimar Republic, when a marketplace of ideas still existed. After the Nazi seizure of power, *Der Stürmer* enjoyed a privileged status and a generally—though not entirely—free hand in its accusations. A subscription to it could easily be seen as part of an insurance policy. Under the Republic, however, the paper had to make its way commercially. It could and did face a broad spectrum of legal and extralegal action initiated by its vic-tims. In this context the present book evaluates not only a specific Nazi newspaper, but also the limits of freedom in a democratic society. By operating on the edge of these limits, *Der Stürmer* helped determine the points where free speech legally became license in Weimar Germany. Evaluating the paper's legal posi-tion can also illustrate the attitudes behind the laws which per-mitted it to exist—a more complex spectrum than is generally recognized.

Concentrating upon the contents of a paper like *Der Stürmer* poses certain moral and intellectual problems. Streicher's audience was not living in a vacuum. The events re-ported in *Der Stürmer* were often subjects of articles in other newspapers, discussed in political speeches, or items of general information. Alternative viewpoints, corrections, and emenda-tions, were available naturally, almost automatically. A mono-graph focusing on *Der Stürmer*, however, inevitably exists in at least a partial vacuum, particularly because Streicher depended heavily for credibility upon plausibility. This element of popular culture, aptly dubbed the Fleming effect after the creator of

James Bond, involves using concrete information to balance a story's fantastic or imaginative elements.[11] Incidents reported in *Der Stürmer* could be freely invented. They could be extensively embroidered. Or they could have happened substantially as they were reported. The important point, which will be developed in the body of this book, is that more of them *might* have happened than one would wish to concede. Particularly in its everyday material *Der Stürmer* did not always tax reader credulity to its limits. Similarly, few of the letters in Streicher's file suggest hoaxes. They were submitted by everyone from prosperous businessmen to unemployed day laborers. Most of them seem to have been composed by people unused to the process. The handwriting ranges from difficult to illegible. The orthography is frequently highly individual. The stationery includes torn sheets of notebook paper and reverse sides of advertisements. While the writers' perceptions may by highly dubious, their sincerity is much less questionable.

This makes it particulary tempting even at this distance in time to correct Streicher's falsehoods and exaggerations. I finally, however, decided against attempting to condemn most *Stürmer* errors and distortions. On one level this would involve reconstructing dozens of sexual encounters, business deals, and traffic incidents, then determining the difference between consent and seduction, or between hard bargaining and dishonesty. On another, such an effort would be the equivalent of arguing the sparrow's innocence in the death of Cock Robin, or attempting to prove that Jack did not really kill the giant by cutting down the beanstalk. It is a process insulting alike the author's integrity and the reader's intelligence.

This approach has its dangers. In contending that *Der Stürmer* was more than undifferentiated ranting produced by and appealing to disturbed minds, the present work risks imitating the defense attorney in Stanley Kubrik's classic film *Judgment at Nuremberg*. To secure the acquittal of his Nazi client, he forcefully presents alternative interpretations of individual events—interpretations just plausible enough to distort the underlying truths of the Third Reich. Repeating *Stürmer* accounts unverified from independent sources also seems to disregard the possibility of elaborate hoaxes, or sincere beliefs influenced by emotional disturbance or simple misunderstanding. The numerous "sole survivors" of the Alamo or of Custer's last stand frequently told stories believable in themselves. Nor is the material in such modern sheets as the *National Enquirer* usually accepted at its face value.

Der Stürmer, however, worked to establish an alternative psychic reality for its readers. The paper's self-proclaimed mission was to set the record straight, to expose the conspiracy behind seemingly unrelated events. It illustrated and embodied the politics of myth and paranoia which lay at the heart of National Socialism. Presenting such material with limited embellishment enables sections, pages, and paragraphs of the following work to give the sense and flavor of *Der Stürmer's* points as they might have been taken by committed Nazis, by the semi-converted, and by general readers before the Holocaust. The value of writing history forward instead of backward outweighs the risks mentioned above. It does not obviate the need for mentioning them.

A related difficulty involved dealing appropriately with *Der Stürmer's* crudely pejorative, often grossly inaccurate, use of the word "Jew." To let it stand is to risk giving old lies new life. To sprinkle the text with ironic quotations or qualifying adjectives like "alleged" again insults both author and reader. To determine the exact ethnic heritage and confessional status of every one of Streicher's journalistic victims is impossible at this distance. It also credits *Der Stürmer* by systematically attempting to refute its attacks on the Jewish community and on individual Jews. Wherever possible I have omitted names from the text. Most exceptions involve items of general news, as opposed to private scandals. *Stürmer* articles frequently feature the names of individuals accused of Streicher-defined offenses against Germany. These names have been replaced by dashes in the footnotes wherever this was consistent with accurate documentation.

I have also chosen to delete most names of the *völkisch* correspondents in Streicher's files. To give the author of some unprinted fifty-year-old piece of tavern anti-Semitism or office gossip can hardly be said to serve the cause of scholarship. The date and contents of a given letter make it easily recoverable in an individual file of Streicher's *Nachlass*. To do more seemed an open invitation to keyhole history. And I have no wish to emulate Julius Streicher by embarrassing anyone beyond his deserts.

Der Stürmer cannot be interpreted in isolation. The paper touched peripherally or extensively, on a broad spectrum of themes and events contributing to the growth of National Socialism. For this reason the notes include a relatively large number of general references designed to help the reader integrate *Der Stürmer* into the history of the Weimar Republic and the Nazi movement. *Stürmer* references themselves almost always represent a cross-section of the articles on a given subject, chosen on the basis of their content and their dates of publication.

One somewhat more technical point also required a decision. Streicher's rich vocabulary of insult seemed to be best to sustain its impact when translated into current idiom. Only the uniquely Bavarian epithet of "sow" defied this process. Finally I let it stand as written or uttered—partly because of memories of growing up in a German and German-Polish community where "sow" was an ultimate insult, certain to initiate a playground fight. It was one of the few pleasant emotions evoked during the research and writing of *Little Man, What Now?*

ACKNOWLEDGMENTS

The writing of this book involved support from many institutions and individuals. Colorado College provided funds for travel and subsidized the photocopying of some material. The staffs of the Hoover Institution on War, Revolution, and Peace, the *Bundesarchiv Koblenz*, the *Staatsarchiv Nürnberg* and the *Stadtarchiv Nürnberg* facilitated my work with advice and assistance. In Nürnberg, Manfred Rühl took time from a busy schedule to share his insights into *Der Stürmer*'s place in the history of National Socialism. Professor Jay Baird of Miami University offered comments on Streicher's political testament. My colleague Professor Armin Wishard provided assistance with Bavarian idioms. And Departmental Secretary Judy McClow added the typing of revisions and corrections to her crowded schedule.

Once again the reference staff of Colorado College's Tutt Library did the work of a university library with the resources of a small college, and with a professional competence in which any institution of higher learning can take pride. Their good humor in the face of endless requests for obscure material and their unfailing ability to produce that material within a few days alike evoke my admiration. For hours of work saved, I express my deepest thanks.

Without Helen Foster, this book would never have appeared. A working historian in her own right, she translated barely-legible hieroglyphics into a neatly-typed manuscript while offering valuable suggestions on the organization and presentation of the material. Her combination of friendship, professional expertise, and technical skill contributed more than even she realizes to the intellectual and literary structure of *Little Man, What Now?*

No acknowledgment, however fulsome, could offer appropriate credit to my family. Clara Kathleen and John delighted in rearranging note cards and rewinding microfilm reels. Clara Anne facilitated the project's completion by refusing to take it too seriously. They helped me keep my priorities in order; the dedication is to them, with love.

I

Der Stürmer's

Matrix

The purpose of this section is to fit *Der Stürmer* into its context as a National Socialist local newspaper. Chapter one presents an overview of the situation facing the paper's major potential readers: Bavarians, Franconians, and Nürnbergers. While social, economic, or psychic malaise is no guarantee that a sheet like *Der Stürmer* will find an audience, circumstances did offer Julius Streicher opportunities for establishing a favorable reception for his paper. Chapter two concentrates on Streicher and his rise to prominence as an anti-Semitic politician and the leader of the Nazi movement in Franconia. Chapter three focuses on *Der Stürmer* itself, its place in the context of the German and National Socialist presses, and its specific editorial and commercial policies.

1 | The Audience

Der Stürmer eventually became a newspaper of national and international significance. Its primary contexts, however, were regional and local: Bavarian, Franconian, and *Nürnbergisch*. Bavaria had and retains for many intellectuals, particularly those of north German extraction, an image similar to that of the South in American culture—rustic, religious, benighted, obstinately hostile to whatever passes as truth elsewhere. Extremists of every sort found shelter everywhere in Germany during the Weimar years, but it was Bavaria which offered Hitler official and unofficial protection. After his release from Landsberg, Franconia, and specifically Nürnberg, became the new center of the scatttered *völkisch* movement. Before the political takeoff of 1930, it was the Franconian vote that made National Socialism something more than just another crackpots' association. It is logical at least to ask whether Bavaria and its society have some tragic flaws unique even for Germany. Psychologically, too, the most objective scholar can hardly be criticized for wondering just what kind of people would vote for a movement whose dominant local figure was a man like Julius Streicher.

The modern state of Bavaria is a conglomerate of lands which the House of Wittelsbach increased substantially by annexing bits and pieces of territory during the Napoleonic Era. After 1815, the government had worked energetically and successfully to superimpose a spirit of Bavarian nationalism on a set of strong local and regional loyalties. A Bavarian might be, as Bismarck was once alleged to have declared, a cross between a human being and an Austrian, but the hybrid was vital enough to preserve Bavaria's federal position in the Second Empire. Domestically, Imperial Bavaria was characterized by less class conflict than her neighbor north of the Main. The aristocracy dominated neither the army nor the bureaucracy. The industrial proletariat was relatively small, and many wage workers regarded themselves as petty bourgeoisie. The Social Democratic Party, while active and well-organized, was too weak numerically to encourage a Bavarian version of *Sammlungspolitik*. Even major strikes were commonly received by the middle classes with the opinion that paying too much attention only encouraged malcontents.

Politics south of the Main was not a process of good spirits and *Gemütlichkeit*. The Peasant Leagues of the 1890s demonstrated a growing willingness on the part of the small farmer to challenge existing authority structures. In the Landtag, bitterness between the Catholics and the liberals made both groups willing to form temporary alliances with the Socialists. On balance, however, the internal tensions which were coming ever closer to paralyzing Prussia were not fully developed in Bavaria before 1914. State and society were still functioning without talk of putsches or emergency legislation.[1]

A system able to stand the strains of peace proved unequal to the added friction of war. From the beginning public opinion was influenced by the stories of men on leave: talk of massive losses, poor food, and haughty treatment by incompetent Prussians. Systems of rationing, requisitioning, and distributing scarce resources—specifically food—irritated people without intimidating them. The bureaucracy failed to check unauthorized purchasing and hoarding. By the war's fourth year the government was unable either to cope with multiple crises on its own or to mobilize support from the political parties. It collapsed at the first halfhearted challenges from its disgruntled subjects.[2]

Any generalizations about Bavaria must be modified when applied to Franconia. Before 1803 this region had been a cartographer's nightmare, and its unity was still more administrative than substantive. Geographically and politically Franconia tended to see itself as a bridge between Munich and Berlin. Bavarian particularism involved centralization on Munich, which to most Franconians meant favoring the historic Bavarian provinces at the expense of the new. Internally, the region was divided religiously and economically. The proportion of Protestants was higher than elsewhere in Bavaria. Catholic and Protestant communities were mixed in a haphazard fashion reflecting Franconia's checkered political history, and confessional tempers were traditionally intense. Economically Nürnberg was the industrial heart of Bavaria. Regional political centers like Ansbach and Bayreuth and religious centers like Bamberg and Eichstätt had high percentages of officials, administrators, and other white-collar workers. Central and Upper Franconia, the area that was to become "Streicher country," were regions of farmers and forest workers. Many of these sought additional income from home industries: toy- and basket-making and textile work, often done for low wages and sold to Nürnberg wholesalers.

Voting patterns were correspondingly mixed. Since 1871, the liberal parties had been stronger in Franconia than anywhere else in Bavaria. The conservatives were influential in rural areas, particularly those bordering industrial regions like Nürnberg. Social Democracy attracted an increasing number of urban workers. The Catholic parties controlled the Catholic vote in the countryside and dominated such cities as Bamberg. The practical result of this political fragmentation is best indicated by the Reichstag elections of 1912. Of the eleven electoral districts in Central and Upper Franconia, five sent Social Democrats to Berlin. Three voted for the Center Party. The Conservatives won two seats, the National Liberals one.[3]

The Württemberg ambassador to Bavaria in 1922 praised Franconia as a land of small farmers who wanted only peace to work their fields. It seems more appropriate to describe it as a region so divided within itself that a party emphasizing the politics of transcendence could conceivably attract a disproportionate number of voters in a hurry.[4] A propaganda line stressing the sterility of existing party divisions and the futility of existing conflicts among Germans might well have been developed with Franconia in mind. The approach was to prove successful from the beginning of its application by the Nazis.

The city of Nürnberg had its own complex past and present. Once among the wealthiest imperial free cities, it suffered economic decline and political eclipse, was annexed by Bavaria in 1806, then utilized the railroad to become a major industrial center. Toymaking and pencil manufacturing, metal working and machine tool construction, gave Nürnberg a flexible economy. By 1914 the city was heavily involved in bicycle manufacturing. The infant auto industry also established itself in a city which had an increasing reputation for hospitality to innovation.

Politically Nürnberg had long been a center of middle-class liberalism. The Bavarian Progressive Party, opposed to militarism, socialism, and protectionism, favorable to Bismarck's vision of German unity, polled over 90 percent of the votes cast for the first national Reichstag. A rival force emerged as Social Democracy survived years of persecution to increase its voting strength steadily. The party's ideological center was the *Fränkische Tagespost*, the best and strongest socialist sheet in Bavaria, second in quality and influence only to the *Vorwärts* itself. In practice, however, Nürnberg Socialists were committed to compromise and reform—an attitude culminating in 1914 when the Socialists and the Progressive Party combined to elect Otto Gessler as mayor and to give Nürnberg a functional two-party system. Extremists in both camps who argued that politics should be based on rigidly defined class conflict found relatively few adherents. Confrontation tended to involve rhetoric instead of action.

The outbreak of war badly strained the city's structure. Much of Nürnberg's economy depended on other countries and regions for markets and raw materials. War brought shortages, unemployment, and sharp declines in living standards. By 1917, the Socialists had split into Majority and Independent factions. When the Bavarian Republic was proclaimed on November 7, 1918, and workers' and soldiers' councils formed spontaneously in Nürnberg, the two parties acted jointly to take control of the local revolution. Beyond that, however, they were unable to proceed. Mayor Gessler promptly declared that the city administration would work with the new system. Most of the socialists, whether old-line party members or freshly-minted members of the councils, favored maintaining and modifying the existing order as opposed to initiating radical reforms.

This decision was more logical in Nürnberg than in many industrial cities of Germany. The typical revolutionary from the working classes was a soldier who wanted to go home, or a defense worker who wanted stable employment and a full stomach. Socialists served on the city council. Socialists trusted Gessler's good will. Gradualism seemed a feasible approach to Nürnberg's problems—at least temporarily.[5]

2

It has become almost a cliché to describe the eventual collapse of the Weimar Republic in terms of its failure to "complete" the revolution of 1918. In another sense, however, Friedrich Ebert, Philipp Scheidemann, and their regional and local counterparts had a clearer sense of the political possibilities in 1918 than do their academic critics. Historians concentrating on the structural weaknesses of Imperial Germany have lost sight of an overrriding point. German society before 1914 embodied no significant irreconcilable elements. The interest groups competing in parliament, in the administration, and in public life generally were not interested in destroying the machine. They sought rather to control it for their own purposes. The Germany so frequently described as being on the verge of disintegration by 1914 withstood and surmounted four years of wartime pressure greater than anything faced by France or Britain. Home front and fighting front alike held together in the face of shortages, bureaucratic inefficiency, international isolation, and a numerically and materially superior enemy. Even the alleged military dictatorship of Hindenburg and Ludendorff depended for domestic success primarily on negotiation and compromise rather than brute force.[6] And this in turn implied a social consensus still strong enough to accept compromises in the interest of victory. Once that hope was dashed the consensus collapsed, but the collapse itself proved temporary. Unlike the situation existing in revolutionary Russia, well over half of the German people counted themselves as belonging to the middling sort, whatever their class position might be in a Marxist-based analysis. For a new government, born in the climate of a defeat many Germans regarded as incomplete, to attempt a top-to-bottom reconstruction of society and politics would have represented an all-or-nothing attempt to do something of whose desirability even many revolutionaries were unconvinced.

The revolution which swept over Germany and Bavaria in the fall of 1918 was more turnout than turnover. Existing symbols were removed, but discontent with existing social patterns was not strong enough to break through the forces favoring stability—at least not on a long-term basis. The behavior of many of the men and women caught up in the revolution was such a departure from their previous patterns of conduct that it was almost bound to be temporary. Once individuals and interest groups realized that the old order was strong enough to resist the amount of pressure most Germans were willing to apply, they needed reasons to explain or justify their recent actions.

In Bavaria, an obvious alibi was the perceived behavior of Kurt Eisner's regime and its bizarre successors. The Bavarian revolution was not the exclusive work of Munich intellectuals and assorted cranks. But the lunatic fringe was able to give the movement a style which frightened and alienated conventional elements in Bavarian society. Eisner and his associates made even handier scapegoats for the workers and soldiers, officials and peasants, who had briefly supported the revolution but by the spring of 1919 were repenting of their actions. What better explanation could a Bavarian wish than that decent people had been temporarily led astray by an unholy set of radicals, traitors, and crackpots? It had just enough truth to be plausible. No extraordinary mobilization of psychological defense and denial mechanisms were required to accept it. It absolved anyone willing to denounce the "outside agitators." And it contributed to the radical right's audience because their orators proved among the loudest in attacking the "November criminals."[7]

On a more concrete level, Rainer Hambrecht attributes the growth of National Socialism in Franconia to three conditions: economic and political uncertainty generated by depression, a dominant *Mittelstand*, and a strong Protestant community conscious of its nationalist and anti-Catholic traditions. The Franconian Nazis found their first supporters among the urban lower middle class. Around 1929, they began attracting the peasant vote. Franconia's Catholics remained generally immune to Nazi appeals. Nor did the National Socialists make major breakthroughs among the workers, though the percentage of proletarians who voted Nazi in Franconia was higher than elsewhere in

9

Germany. After 1930, however, other parties and organizations were swept away on a tide that even before the general *Machtergreifung* had made the Nazis the real rulers of broad sections of Franconia.[8]

The success of the Nazis in Nürnberg has been interpreted in similar terms. Nürnberg, so this argument runs, was an industrial city which retained a large number of small businesses, making it a center of the "old *Mittelstand*," the merchants and free professionals. As early as 1924, this section of the polity had been so badly demoralized by the war and its aftermath that it was vulnerable to the hatred, fear, and demagoguery which were to be Julius Streicher's stocks in trade. The inflation of the early 1920s, rather than the Great Depression, turned the middling people of Nürnberg away from the republic and made them unusually receptive to a vulgarian like Streicher. In this sense he was Nürnberg's version of contemporary television's Archie Bunker—a respectable man's *doppelgänger*, an intellectual's nightmare, embodying and articulating feelings that most people usually submerged beneath business suits and white collars.[9]

Some patterns of statistical analysis support this interpretation. Comparison of election results in Nürnberg shows that National Socialism drew much of its support from the voter reservoir of the middle-class parties. The Nazis' biggest successes came in districts where the bourgeois parties were heavily represented in proportion to the Socialists and Communists. Industrial workers were not completely immune to the Nazi appeal. This has been described as reflecting the fact that many voters may have worked in the city, but retained a "peasant outlook"—they voted Socialist when times were good, National Socialist when times were bad.[10]

Martha Ziegler provides another approach to the nature of National Socialist voting support in Nürnberg through her use of stepwise multiple regression analysis, a means of simultaneously evaluating the relationship among a set of independent variables and the relationship between those variables and a dependent variable. Her dependent variable is the proportion of the votes received by a political party in each precinct of Nürnberg for selected local and national elections. She lists twenty-seven independent variables. Two are political: the change in the number of votes and the proportion of eligible voters. Fifteen involve occupational categories—a sophisticated breakdown designed to eliminate the careless use of such vague terms as "working," "middle," or "upper" classes. The remaining ten involve sexual balance, population changes, and the uses made of buildings in the precincts: private residences, businesses, rental properties, and similar property distribution.

When applied to the National Socialist vote, the highest proportion of positive variables fit Ziegler's category of "Mid-Level White-Collar Employees"—medium-rank officials, independent merchants and managers. Second on the list are the small-scale self-employed businessmen, craftsmen, owners of small stores, and similar occupations. Less important were lower- and upper-class white collar workers, pensioners, professionals, and widows. Once the Nazis began expanding their electoral support, they drew votes from so many occupational groups that it is easier to discover the groups that did not vote Nazi, specifically the skilled and unskilled workers, than to determine those that did.

Ziegler's computer work confirms the general impression left by examining soft data. After 1928, the NSDAP in Nürnberg expanded its support among all occupational groups which had provided voters before 1928. Since the percentage of eligible voters casting ballots remained constant, it also seems clear that the Nazis gained their votes at the expense of other parties, as opposed to tapping the non-voting section of the population. As in Franconia as a whole, the Blacks and Reds resisted the tide. Bourgeois, Protestant Nürnberg, however, was voting, if not necessarily thinking, National Socialist.[11]

The world-view and the mind-set of the modern German bourgeoisie have found few spokesmen. French- and English-speaking scholars and critics deride them as lukewarm and timid, unwilling to commit themselves to party politics, sacrificing liberalism to nationalism at every turn from 1848 to 1933. Within Germany, conservatives and radicals alike despise them for being what they are—people in the middle, strongly committed neither to old traditions nor new ideas. Theorists present fascism as the kind of political system the "little man" can be expected to develop when left to his own devices. Aesthetes condemn his taste. Psychiatrists criticize his sex life. And the proven fact that

11

National Socialism drew much of its support from this unpopular sector of the German population gives the bourgeoisie's critics apparently irrefutable justification for their charges.

Hermann Glaser asserts that the tone and content of most Nazi propaganda fit the life style and ideology of German's petty bourgeoisie so well that it struck the proper chords automatically. The German burgher sought superficial happiness, peasant-style good health, and a contented everyday life, all presented with an overlay of *kitsch*. The elementary schools contributed to this process by presenting the illusion of education. Their poorly trained teachers, cursed with dreams beyond their station in life, were barely able to bring their pupils up to the intellectual level of vulgar periodicals like *Ostara*, while at the same time encouraging them to believe that this was true culture. More specifically, Glaser argues, the repressed dreams and fantasies of these beer mystics tended to focus on the "Orient." Nineteenth-century popular literature presented the "East" as a place of abnormalities, where slave girls were flogged and pepper rubbed into their wounds. By the end of the century, this approach had evolved into a kind of soft-core pornography paving the way for *Der Stürmer*—a pornography presenting the "oriental" Jew as a contrast to Aryan cleanliness, order, and morality. Arguments on similar lines could be multiplied to no purpose. If accepted, they all suggest the same point: Julius Streicher and *Der Stürmer* mirrored the worst attitudes of the German bourgeoisie.[12]

However accurate this mass psychoanalysis may be, emotions still had to be translated into political action. War, economic depression, and anxiety combined after 1918 to produce new attitudes in the *Mittelstand*. Whether small businessman or free professional on one hand, manager or white-collar employee on the other, the new breed tended to demand results rather than rhetoric from its elders and betters. Its members perceived themselves crushed between big labor and big business, overlooked by big government, and derided by big intellectuals. They shifted votes, switched party allegiances, and voiced grievances. They viewed themselves as the real victims of economic and political rationalization, the people everyone overlooked until it was time to pay taxes. The accuracy of this self-evaluation is debatable. Psychic realities, however, are not usually vulnerable to statistical analysis and rational refutation.[13]

The theory that this amorphous group might have been voluntarily "socialized" and integrated into a left-liberal progressive front, whether before 1914 or during a fleeting opportunity missed sometime after November, 1918, is at best an exaggeration. Such a process would have involved major changes on the part of *Mittelstand* and Social Democrats alike. The socialists tended to demand overt conversion on the part of the bourgeoisie. To Marxist ideologues it was necessary to put off the old man and put on the new, to be born again in the spirit of *Das Kapital*, in order to enter the kingdom of Karl. This mind-set was hardly attractive to the many *Mittelständler* who regarded themselves as independent thinkers. Small shopkeepers and artisans, white-collar workers and farmers, continued to hope for independence and were correspondingly reluctant to submerge themselves in what they regarded, however wrongly, as a mass movement of mass men. They were equally reluctant to abandon the patriotism and nationalism generally regarded as representing integration into the German community. *Mittelstand* organizations, moreover, often incorporated a significant anti-Semitic element. Long before National Socialism, these groups had discovered the uses of a more or less polite anti-Semitism as a cement holding together a collection of people proud of their individuality.[14]

It is at least questionable whether any mass-based *Mittelstand* party could have been organized along the political lines developed in Bismarck's Reich and continued under Weimar. There were simply too many overlapping and contradictory interests for interest-group politics to be strongly sucessful. It is also true, however, that the self-defined leaders of the *Mittelstand* were consistently unsuccessful in overcoming this handicap. One of the major weaknesses of middle-class political parties was the arrogance of their leadership. The German Democratic Party (DDP), founded in 1918, has often and aptly been described as a party of leaders without followers. Its rapid loss of voting support—a process beginning as early as 1919—reflected at least partly the inability of its leading men to become politicians as opposed to political schoolmasters. The party had too many men for whom democratic and republican ideals were practical or desirable things to be presented to willing and obedient followers. Hermann Luppe, Nürnberg's great mayor during the Weimar years, delighted in chastising Germany and Nürnberg for a long catalogue of social, economic, and political sins. His observations may have been reasonably accurate, but his hectoring tone was unlikely to find a significant echo among Nürnberg's reeling middle classes. It was scarcely remarkable that organizations like the *Jungdemokraten* could not keep bourgeois youth away from Nazi meetings. At least the sermons delivered there were not designed to make their auditors do constant penance.

As the DDP lost touch with its potential following, the numerous regional splinter groups attempting to revitalize the "dying middle" proved even less successful. None of them took the Nazis particularly seriously. Hitler and his followers were ultimately too sweaty and vulgar to deserve consideration as political rivals. It was an error of arrogance that cost Germany dearly. The Nazis' politics of transcendence, of overriding the class and caste differences of Germany by an appeal to a community of blood, did prove acceptable both as a last resort and the fulfillment of a cherished dream.[15]

In this context *Der Stürmer* can be presented as an unpleasant manifestation of the only movement purporting to speak effectively for a "middle" which as events showed was more disoriented than moribund. In a sense this middle projected many of its own values onto National Socialism. Specifically, Streicher could be seen by Franconian voters as a man who carried sound ideas to an extreme. His speeches and his newspaper alike could be taken the way a cat takes a pill embedded in hamburger. By a process known only to cats, he swallows the meat and rejects the medicine. Relevant too is Bavarian socialist Wilhelm Hoegner's evaluation of his countrymen's hostility to government authority and their unwillingness to accept unpleasant situations without complaint. According to Hoegner, the local leaders were likely to be the loudest complainers.[16] The career of Streicher and the success of *Der Stürmer* offer corroboration of the thesis that Bavarians under the Weimar Republic took full advantage of their constitutional rights to free speech, and admired those who went even further. The argument's content was less important than its tone, as long as the tone was shrill.

Anti-Semitism was the essence of Julius Streicher's political message, and here too he did not operate in a vacuum. Yet despite the many detailed studies of German anti-Semitism, it remains an elusive phenomenon. Since at least the Middle Ages, negative images of the Jew had permeated Christian myths, liturgies, and literature. Medieval frescoes and carvings portrayed Jews in unflattering or threatening fashions. Depictions of Christ's circumcision, for example, frequently showed male Jews brandishing huge knives over an Infant whose mother vainly sought to protect Him. The blood libel, originating in the Roman Empire, found firm footing in medieval Germany. It was accompanied by numerous legends of sacrificed or murdered children.

Attitudes believed long dead came to life once more under the stresses that produced the Weimar Republic. In Bavaria Catholic youth movements in 1919 were discussing a pamphlet *Judas, der Weltfeind*, by the same author who later wrote for *Der Stürmer* under the name of "Heimdal." North German evangelical pastors and pampleteers delighted in similar forms of Jew-baiting. Institutional Christianity failed to take even a neutral position against the increasingly rabid offensive mounted against the Jewish minority in Germany during the Weimar years. And theological subtleties were likely to have limited effect on the casual churchgoer who knew what he saw, or what he sang, or, with growing frequency, what he heard from the pulpit.[17]

Legal emancipation in the nineteenth century did little to diminish the marginal position of German Jews. Their economic position was not the sole reason for continued anti-Semitism. It was, however, a sine qua non. Jewish concentration in certain occupations and professions created an image of disproportionate economic strength which was often a reality. In cities as far apart as Frankfurt am Main and Breslau, Jews paid proportionally higher taxes than either Catholics or Protestants. The German Jews' role in the expansion of capitalism was particularly significant in that they applied what might be called "capitalistic" principles of advertising and competition to small businesses frequently ill-equipped to cope with these developments.

Economic hostility was reinforced by intellectual anti-Semitism. On one level it was theological, fostered by what seemed to many Christian writers a willfully stubborn refusal to respond to legal emancipation by religious assimilation. On another, it reflected the increasing hostility broad sections of German society felt for the modern era.[18] Fritz Stern presents this as a Peter Pan approach to life—an attitude held by emotional and intellectual children who refused to grow up.[19] The anti-modern value system is not quite so simply dismissed. The ugliness, the pace, the attitudes of a rapidly industrializing society could inspire legitimate disgust and legitimate rejection. Nor was there any reason why Germans should not have sought alternatives to liberalism on one hand and Marxism on the other. This hostility, however, tended to seek a visible, tangible enemy, and found it in the city. In particular, the 1890s witnessed an explosion of *Heimatliteratur*, a form of romantic poetasting asserting that the German's true home was the countryside and stressing rural ideals in the hope of making them a reality. This emphasis on the nobility of horse manure, the virtues of the simple life, and the joys of open-air copulation was not inherently dangerous. Nostalgia became a social problem only when these rural romantics began linking their hostility to city life with anti-Semitism. Writers of this school attacked the "Jewish spiritual proletariat," spreaders of socialism and decadence, whose spirit dominated the large cities and made them hotbeds of revolution and centers of a rootless fourth estate. Germans must become aware, the argument ran, of the "Jewish-oriental" influence in politics and finance, department stores and theaters, advertising and sex lives. The horsemen of the Apocalypse attacking the German soul had Jewish faces.[20]

Cultural anti-Semitism also deepened as more and more Germans grew familiar with neighbors who seemed like them in so many ways, yet different in enough areas to generate a nightmare effect. A society where old and new overlapped in an almost random fashion, a society where no one could quite be sure who he was, where he was, or where he stood in relation to those around him, contributed to a general atmosphere of insecurity. Paradoxically, the stresses within Imperial Germany might have been less if the country had had one or two clearly visible minorities against which to unite, one or two groups bearing some clearly identifiable mark of Cain. But unlike the United States, Germany had no blacks, no Indians, no Mexicans. Instead her society's minorities could only be distinguished with an effort. Jews, Poles, or Alsatians, socialists or capitalists, professors or *Wandervögel*—any and all could be and were objects of suspicion and dislike to each other and to those "Germans" who longed to be part of a mainstream they were never quite able to find.

Here the issue of the so-called *Ostjuden* was disproportionately important. In the course of the nineteenth century Jews, some from eastern Europe, and some German citizens from Posen and West Prussia, began settling in other parts of Germany. They were businessmen, craftsmen, students, and would-be emigrants to the United States who changed their minds; by 1914, approximately ninety thousand "foreign Jews" were registered as German residents. They were a focal point of suspicion and hostility, both public and private. Neither in terms of statistics nor attitudes could they be described objectively as an unassimilable minority. They were, however, the closest Imperial Germany came to an outcaste, a subculture of untouchables.[21]

For all its sound and fury, for all its roots in the modern German experience, anti-Semitism before 1914 was not a significant political force. Political anti-Semitism depended heavily, if not exclusively, on local leaders and local issues. The parties organized on such a basis tended at best to be ephemeral splinter groups. By 1914 they had little more than a shadow existence—a Reichstag deputy or two, a local newspaper, and a set of adherents who could most charitably be described as marginal members of their respective communities. Certainly the Germany of Wilhelm II had nothing comparable to the Christian Social Party of Hapsburg Austria.[22]

World War I significantly influenced the development of anti-Semitism. Kaiser Wilhelm's civil truce was threatened from the beginning by accusations of Jewish profiteering, shirking, and cowardice. By 1916 the complaints led the High Command to issue a general order requesting the exact numbers of Jews serving in combat positions compared with those in combat support and on the lines of communication. The results of the survey meant little compared to its implication that Germany's Jews were a collection of shirkers, seeking safe jobs instead of taking the risks of fighting for a society offering them security and prosperity as Jews, and full acceptance at what seemed to many Gentiles the nominal price of conversion to Christianity.

This notorious order emanated from the imperial establishment. Grassroots anti-Semitism was fostered by two other war-related factors. The German army was recruited territorially, but the high casualties of modern war made it difficult to maintain units entirely from their local areas. Moreover, as the war progressed, the high command grew increasingly concerned over the reliability of its conscripts from Prussian Poland and Alsace-Lorraine. The result was a tendency to make a virtue of necessity by assigning Poles and Alsatians as reinforcements to units whose own depots could not keep them up to strength. Certainly not all of these men were Jews, but some of them were. And Jew or Gentile, the men of a draft from Posen posted to a battalion recruited in Württemberg or Hanover were initially certain to be treated as outsiders. When differences of culture and dialect were added, the General Staff's fears could be perceived as reality at the company level.

Soldiers who spent time on the eastern front often encountered an even deeper form of cultural shock. Adolf Hitler's reaction to his first sight of a Galician Jew in prewar Vienna appears to have been duplicated for many Gentile German soldiers encountering the *shtetl* culture between 1914 and 1918. The poverty-stricken Polish and Russian Jews tended to regard the German and Austrian armies as potential customers, if not actual liberators. Would-be contractors, people seeking connections, *Luftmenschen* of all sorts, flocked to occupation headquarters offering to transact business, dubious and legitimate. Veterans who later wrote *Der Stürmer* describing their disgust at Jewish living conditions, or their revulsion at Yiddish-speaking pimps touting red-light districts that made Hamburg's *Reeperbahn* look sanitary, were less likely to be hard-core anti-Semites than soldiers fed up, far from home, and quick to condemn anything not done in quite the same way as within the sound of their own streetcars or church bells.[23]

For a variety of reasons, therefore, World War I provided opportunites for anti-Semitism to assume virulent forms and develop direct faces. In such a climate it seemed logical for the secretary of the newly founded German National Peoples' Party (DNVP), in civil life a *Privatdozent* in ancient history, to suggest to party leader Count Cuno von Westarp that the DNVP had no chance of success in the twentieth century unless it became a mass party. And the best way to become a mass party was to foster hatred. Use rapes, real or invented, of German women by aliens. Stress the shaming of young girls by Poles and blacks. Produce hack films and hack literature stressing a racist party line. A shocked Westarp replied that he was sufficiently old-fashioned to believe that successful agitation could depend only on provable deeds.[24] The Nazis were not so particular.

2 | The Editor

It is safe to say that no major leader of the National Socialist movement, from its beginnings in the 1920s to its official end on the gallows and in the prison cells of its conquerors, has aroused such universal execration as Julius Streicher. As gauleiter of Nürnberg, as editor of *Der Stürmer*, and as a human being, he emerges as a man without significant redeeming qualities. Contemporaries inside and outside of Germany portrayed him as a monster. His codefendants at Nürnberg shunned him. Historians most frequently mention him in negative comparisons: to suggest that another person was not quite so bad, or that another set of policies were not quite so repulsive. The best he has received is the suggestion that his trial and execution at Nürnberg were based on what he was rather than what he did.[1] But if Streicher is hardly likely to be the subject of revisionist studies, an outline of the man's background and career are nevertheless necessary to present *Der Stürmer* in context.

1

Streicher's early career in many respects reflects the social dynamics of the Kaiser's Germany. He was born in 1885, in Fleinhausen in Bavarian Swabia. Like Hitler and other Nazi leaders, he was alleged to have Jewish and Gypsy ancestors—a thesis Streicher may have encouraged by saying at one point that in order to hate Jews properly, one needed a good share of Jewish blood in one's own veins. However, the self-hate and self-doubt often cited as factors in Hitler's anti-Semitism played at best a minor role in Streicher's development. The statement, if he did make it, was likely a reflection of his pleasure in shocking people rather than the revelation of a dark family secret.

Streicher was the youngest of nine children, six of whom were still living in 1926. His father was a village schoolmaster. Two of his brothers and a sister followed that career; two of his sisters also married elementary teachers. Streicher's boyhood remains lost in the mists of triteness. In later life he was fond of saying that his mother often told him that he was the kind of bad boy who was sure to land in jail. This, however, is hardly worth taking seriously. Growing up in Fleinhausen he seems to have done no more than exhibit the behavior patterns of a younger sibling who developed an aggressive approach to life. His choice of a career was not original. Opportunities for the son of a village teach to get a university education were distinctly limited in turn-of-the-century Germany. Instead Streicher attended an institution for training primary school teachers, completing its course with a set of average grades and then becoming a substitute. In rural Bavaria, this meant moving from village to village replacing ill or absent teachers. Despite a minor clash with one pastor, he received regular promotions and good efficiency reports, passed his final examinations, and completed his military service as a one-year volunteer, with the comment in his records that he was not a good candidate for promotion.[2]

Streicher was disciplined for insubordination. But punishment for this offense was common in the German army, particularly for one-year volunteers who fell into disfavor with noncommissioned officers. Men of Streicher's social and educational background were not generally regarded as officer material even in Bavaria. Nor was every one-year volunteer automatically appointed a noncommissioned officer of the reserve on discharge. By itself Streicher's experience cannot be taken as a manifestation of abnormal behavior or a significantly undisciplined mind.[3]

A year after his return to civil life, Streicher became involved in another disagreement with a supervising priest. At this stage the Ministry of Education still could simply have dismissed him. He was, however, regarded as a good teacher, a man who could inspire his classes. The ministry also had little sympathy with what it regarded as excessive clerical interference in its classrooms. Then a solution emerged from an unexpected quarter. Konrad Weiss, school supervisor of Nürnberg, had been instrumental in promoting a new kind of primary school. The common school brought together Catholic and Protestant children, separating them only for religious instruction. Finding experienced teachers, however, was a continuing problem. A man like Streicher was just the type Weiss sought: outspoken, competent, with a reputation as an anticlerical—and with nowhere else to go. As a Catholic, he could hardly teach in a Protestant confessional school. To assign him to another Catholic school was to invite another conflict with another priest. Nürnberg offered him professional opportunities he was unlikely to receive anywhere else in Bavaria.[4]

Streicher started at the bottom, teaching first and second grade girls from working-class neighborhoods. He lived among his students and learned at first hand the economic problems of proletarian families in a newly industrialized city. His promotions and salary increases came on schedule. His supervisors and his students made no complaints about his work. Streicher's personal life also moved upwards. He met a baker's daughter, Kunigunde Roth. While a primary school teacher might rank a cut or two below an independent businessman, Streicher was handsome, assertive, and ambitious. The two married in 1913, and moved into an apartment in a middle-class district of Nürnberg.

Then came Sarajevo. Streicher, assigned to the Sixth Bavarian Reserve Infantry, was noticed during the first days of mobilization for his ability to hearten other reservists, most of whom were leaving families behind. Once the shooting started, he proved from the beginning a good soldier and a lucky one. He earned the Iron Cross in 1914 and by 1917 had established such a formidable combat record that he was commissioned lieutenant in a Mountain Machine Gun Detachment, one of the army's elite formations.

He served in the Caporetto offensive, then was transferred back to Lorraine in the closing weeks of the war. Unlike the soul-numbing hammering of Passchendaele, or the materiel battles of Cambrai and Amiens, these theaters featured a good amount of open warfare. Dash and energy displayed by a junior officer could still count for something. Streicher finished the war with the Bavarian Military Service Order and the Iron Cross, First Class—both earned the hard way, in the face of the enemy. He also finished the war with a spotless service record. Its only negative comment involved Streicher's attempt—a vain one—to avoid being sent through an army delousing station in Salzburg.[5]

The man who returned to Nürnberg at the end of the war was short and stocky, with a thick neck and a chin sufficiently prominent to be listed as his main distinguishing feature in a police report. One of Streicher's biographers describes him as an average man until his demobilization.[6] This point can be debated, if for no better reason than the unlikelihood of an average man's winning Streicher's collection of medals and surviving the war to wear them. But if Streicher's combat career was remarkable, it was not unusual. Thousands of junior officers brought similar records from the western front. If Streicher felt that fate had spared him for a purpose, this too was an attitude common among returning veterans of all armies. Streicher's behavior on returning to Nürnberg does indicate that he, like many of his erstwhile comrades and former enemies, was seeking outlets for energies developed during four years of war. If he had been an average man before 1914, he was average no longer in at least one respect. He had learned the value of action properly applied. It had kept him alive. It had brought him recognition, tangible and intangible, from superiors and fellow soldiers alike. This was an approach difficult to abandon overnight.

Streicher's postwar political activity began almost by accident. He was not a complete novice. In 1911 he had delivered election speeches for the Progressives in Nürnberg. He had belonged to the *Jung-Fortschritt-Nürnberg*, and in May, 1913, had even been elected to that group's executive committee.[7] Nevertheless, when he began attending veterans' meetings on his return from the war, he was probably seeking fellowship rather than followers. Opposition to the Bavarian Republic led him to the *völkisch* League for Defense and Defiance (*Schutz-und Trutzbund*), and to less formal meetings of other right-wing groups. Streicher quickly made enough of an impression as a tavern orator in these circles to expand his sphere of action. Early in 1919 Streicher started appearing at Socialist and Communist meetings and speaking in their discussions.

At this stage he appeared still strongly motivated by a combination of a desire for excitement and a wish to show what he could do before a wider audience. The excitement was usually forthcoming. In his later career Streicher was fond of describing situations in which the audience cheered him until he was shouted down by Jewish-Marxist claques. It is more realistic to accept the hypothesis that Streicher, for the first time since his own school days, found himself outmatched. As a teacher and an officer, he had grown accustomed to giving orders and enforcing his decisions through a combination of official authority and force of character. In a Marxist-organized meeting these qualities were not likely to keep Streicher from being tied into logical knots by men who had read books of which he had never heard.[8]

Apparently Streicher found enough of these opponents to wound his vanity to the point of desperation. Simple frustration may help explain his sudden emergence as an anti-Semite. Streicher's public account of his conversion was that one night after another humiliation, he was returning home when an unknown man pressed a copy of Theodor Fritsch's *Handbuch zur Judenfrage* into his hand. Streicher read it and found his light on the road to Damascus. In his political testament written in 1945, he credited anti-Semitic orator Karl Maerz with opening his eyes to the Jewish question. While specifics may be debated, this material, with its pseudo-intellectual structure and pseudoscientific arguments, almost certainly acted as a catalyst.[9]

The doctors and psychiatrists who examined Streicher in 1945 as he went on trial for his life concluded that he was not insane but suffered from an obsessive neurosis manifested in anti-Semitism. The difficulties involved in developing psychiatric diagnoses even of cooperative defendants at Nürnberg are well established, and Streicher was anything but a willing subject.[10] Given his values and behavior, however, the temptation to apply psychological evaluations proved irresistible for contemporaries as well as historians. As early as 1924, the Landsberg prison doctor described Streicher as having "psychopathic characteristics," and his political opponents soon learned that the surest way to drive him into a rage was to question his sanity. An accompanying tendency has been to interpret Streicher's life before 1919 as manifesting certain pathological or pre-pathological tendencies.[11]

The process is handicapped by the dearth of information on Streicher's childhood and adolescence compared even to Adolf Hitler, to say nothing of such subjects of major psychobiographies as Martin Luther or Mahatma Gandhi. The admittedly limited available records of Streicher's pre-*völkisch* career do not indicate a personality manifesting significant defects of integration. The possibility that Streicher suffered some form of neurological or psychological trauma during the war cannot be ruled out but must remain conjecture. The work of George Vaillant, however, offers an alternative approach. In *Adaptation to Life*, he argues that adult relationships and adaptive patterns developed over periods of years are as important to personality development as the adjustments and experiences of childhood and adolescence.[12] This model can be applied effectively, if generally, to Streicher's career. Whatever the roots of his increasing uncontrollability, it definitely reflected Streicher's proportionate awareness of the absence of restraints strong enough to counterbalance the psychic and political rewards of his behavior. His egocentricity similarly grew with reinforcement. But while Streicher derived important emotional support from his public following, this following developed as a result of his behavior as well as his ideas. It was not a ready-made audience demanding radical anti-Semitism from its leaders.

Streicher's fanatical obsession with anti-Semitism was the product of an intellectual process. Nothing in his early life or career, even his own retrospective musings, indicates the presence of either significant anti-Jewish behavior or—unlike Hitler —significant contact of any kind with Jews. Now, confronted with a set of interpretations that seemed to make sense of a confusing world, Streicher lived up to his self-image as a man of intelligence and learning. He investigated the issue. He read widely, ranging from such anti-Semitic esoterica as Johann Eisenmenger's eighteenth-century *Entdecktes Judentum* to a variety of contemporary Jewish publications. He built a library of Judaica and pseudo-Judaica which donations and confiscations eventually swelled to over eight thousand volumes. He could season his lectures and essays with quotations from Jewish writings, most of them acquired at second hand, but presented convincingly enough to convince several courts of his expertise in Jewish studies. Audiences cheered him. But apart from their applause Streicher was convinced that the Jewish question was indeed the key to world history.

This does not mean that Streicher himself believed everything he said and published. Nor does it mean that his anti-Semitism was not a reflection of personal pathologies hitherto undemonstrated or unrecorded, but now allowed to flourish. But if before 1919 Streicher had been a man of action, for the rest of his life he was to live by a single idea—and its consequences. Julius Streicher was greedy, power-hungry, and cynical, but until the day of his execution he insisted that he was a racial anti-Semite from reasoned conviction. His friends, his enemies, and his judges believed him. To deny the possibility of such a belief is to restrict a definition of ideas to those concepts generally acceptable morally as well as intellectually to the academic community.[13]

During the immediate postwar years, Streicher cultivated the vanity that distinguished him during his political career. He became meticulous in his dress, fond of checking his appearance in mirrors, punctilious about matters of etiquette. He wrote verses that rhymed, dabbled in watercolors, and enjoyed presenting himself as a man of taste and judgment in the arts. His opinions on painting, drama, and literature provided much amusement for his enemies, personal and political, but reflected his own belief in himself as a sensitive, cultured man forced by circumstances into politics. And for short periods at least, he was able to sustain the image effectively. For example, a Swedish explorer with long experience in Germany wrote in 1937 that instead of the brute he had expected to meet, Streicher proved a cultivated man and a charming host whose palatial home was decorated more tastefully than orthodox National Socialist views on art might lead one to expect.[14]

Streicher's enemies and opponents frequently described him as sexually perverse, accusing him of everything from participating in a gang rape to receiving female visitors clad only in bathing trunks. During the Weimar years, however, his amatory behavior seems to have been more direct than perverse. He simply propositioned any woman who took his fancy. He received his share of indignant rejections, but there were also enthusiastic acceptances. Streicher enjoyed variety. It was a public joke in Nürnberg that after the Nazi seizure of power, golden party insignia—the sign of an Old Fighter—appeared on the breasts of teachers at a prestigious girls' school, telephone operators, and even the cleaning woman at the city hall. Streicher's wife, highly regarded by her neighbors, regarded her appropriate place as in the home, three steps behind her husband. This kind of person is often able to ignore or deny flagrant infidelities for long periods of time. Even outside of *völkisch* circles, Streicher's image was enhanced by his open and successful womanizing. It was a style calculated to inspire admiration, if not always emulation, among the little men who were so important to the success of National Socialism.[15]

2

During 1919 Streicher grew increasingly dissatisfied with what he considered the limited goals and excessive intellectualism of the League for Defense and Defiance. By this time a number of small right-wing groups, conservative, nationalist, and *völkisch*—anti-Versailles, anti-capitalist, and anti-Semitic—had established themselves in Nürnberg and its environs. In 1920 Julius Streicher joined one of them, the *Deutsche Sozialistische Partei* (DSP), and rapidly became the leader of its Nürnberg branch and editor of its party paper, the *Deutscher Sozialist*. The paper's initial editorial line was a mixture of socialism and anti-Semitism. Streicher, however, argued that "socialism" could mean anything and everything in *völkisch* circles. A writer or speaker using it as a main theme could easily find himself in a set of semantic traps. Anti-Semitism, on the other hand, lent itself well to polarization, to establishing a set of simple blacks and whites. It was a useful way of separating allies from enemies within the *völkisch* movement. It was also a concept whose essentials were easily grasped. This made it, in Streicher's opinion, a useful means of reaching the masses. As yet, however, this viewpoint reflected more faith than experience. Certainly his party comrades were increasingly critical of an anti-Semitism they regarded as harmful both to the DSP's credibility and to its respectability.

By 1921 personal and ideological conflicts within the DSP led Streicher to join the Augsburg-based *Deutsche Werksgemeinschaft der Abendlandischer Bundes* (DWG). Initially he may have hoped to emerge as leader of a united Bavarian *völkisch* movement. He was thwarted partly by the continued refusal of Adolf Hitler's Munich-based Nazis to consider merging with other parties, and partly by his inability to establish firm control over even the DWG. Constant public conflicts among the leadership diminished confidence among the rank and file to a significant degree. And this in turn meant that the Nazis, who at least seemed to know where they were going, began attracting first listeners, then members, from the DWG. Streicher weighed his options and opened negotiations with Hitler.[16]

Streicher and Hitler were not natural allies, but each man had cards to play. Hitler was well aware that Streicher was supposed to have described the Nazi führer as a salon revolutionary who drove through Munich in an automobile accompanied by women smoking cigarettes.[17] Streicher had also been openly hostile towards any organized Nazi activity in Nürnberg. From Hitler's perspective it nevertheless made sense to try to win Streicher's support rather than attack him directly on his home ground. Streicher's conflicts within the DSP and the DWG had focused on his violent oratory and his anti-Semitism—characteristics likely to make him interesting to Hitler. He embodied in his own person the traditional anti-Semitism of the *Mittelstand*, the more ruthless version accepted by postwar *völkisch* elements, and the adjustment problems of returning veterans. By this time too Streicher had evolved into a popular speaker with a strong base of listeners. He cultivated the common touch. He enjoyed, or gave the appearance of enjoying, simply sitting down at a table in a *Gasthaus* or beer garden and discussing crops, life, the war, and politics with anyone willing to stay for the monologue —often spicing his narrative with stories of narrow escapes from political enemies, Jews, and communists. The combination was not one to be rejected out of hand.

In the final analysis, Streicher seems to have impressed

Hitler as the kind of person who could be handled, if not manipulated. His driving activism and ruthless energy were accompanied by a limited focus. The Jewish issue was his ideological and intellectual mainspring. Apart from this, his dreams were regional. He saw himself as more Bavarian than German and more Franconian than Bavarian. Hitler was suspicious of Streicher as the two men began negotiations. But it was the suspicion a feudal lord might feel for a potentially overmighty vassal, rather than the hostility of a führer towards a potential rival.[18]

Streicher for his part had ample reason to consider seriously the prospects of joining the NSDAP. He was beginning to suffer from diminishing tangible assets. His followers tended to admire his style rather than his ideas and were correspondingly willing to change allegiance. He needed cash to meet debts and fines. But even after he formally entered the Nazi Party on October 8, 1922, Streicher tended to maintain his independence. His activity on behalf of the movement was undeniable. In public, he described Hitler as the key to Germany's future. Institutionally, however, Streicher from the beginning worked to establish personal control over the local party machinery. The resulting infighting, culminating in a mutiny of the SA, brought National Socialism in Nürnberg to the verge of self-destruction by the summer of 1923. Hitler's eventual decision to support Streicher and expel his opponents from the party reflected both the close personal relationship that had developed between the two men and available information that a majority of Nürnberg Nazis supported Streicher. But Hitler also made plain his unhappiness at the continued feuding in Nürnberg—and at its institutionalization in Streicher's latest journalistic venture.[19]

On April 20, 1923, *Der Stürmer* made its first public appearance. Its initial targets were neither Jews nor "November Criminals," but Streicher's local party enemies. Even by the standards of the *völkisch* movement, Streicher went for the groin. One foe was described as "overambitious," a second as an embezzler of party funds, and a third as looking like a bastard and acting like a psychopath. These men, Streicher declared, had been bribed and misled by Jews in order to weaken the anti-Semitic forces in Nürnberg.[20] Despite Hitler's misgivings, *Der*

Stürmer stumbled along until its editor's attention was distracted by a more practical political problem.

Streicher's behavior during the Beer Hall Putsch finally overcame any lingering mistrust Hitler may have felt for his strong-minded subordinate. When summoned to an "important conference" in Munich on November 8, Streicher left Nürnberg immediately and played a sufficiently prominent role in the succeeding events to be promptly arrested and imprisoned on his return to Nürnberg. He was almost as promptly released by authorities sympathetic to his cause and afraid of mass demonstrations on his behalf. Not until January was he rearrested and tried. He was confined for two months in Landsberg Prison—a sentence qualifying him definitively for admission to the Nazi pantheon and Hitler's personal inner circle. Certainly the experience did nothing to deter him from announcing his candidacy for the Bavarian Landtag and resuming his self-defined role as leader of the *völkisch* movement in Nürnberg.[21]

Frustrated upward mobility was an important element encouraging stable committment to the Nazi movement. A high proportion of the gauleiters, for example, were men with secure positions who had either risen above their parents' social status or maintained the same level while perceiving themselves suited for better things.[22] Men feeling themselves blocked or unrecognized by more traditional sectors of Weimar society could find more than psychic comfort in the emerging alternative society of the NSDAP. Particularly in the 1920s, it offered virtually unlimited opportunities for even the moderately talented. The party had nowhere to go but up. At thirty-nine, Streicher was an ex-officer suspended because of the Putsch from a teaching career at best unlikely to take any startling turns until eventual retirement. His political future seemed far brighter, even in the aftermath of the Putsch. For every polite suggestion that he had a duty to discipline his rowdier followers, there were a dozen declarations that the longer he spoke the better his audience would enjoy it, offers to pick him up at the station and take him out to dinner, and reports that "everyone" in a given community anxiously wanted to know if Streicher would "really" be at a meeting. When Streicher appeared on a platform, he could count on applause and waving handkerchiefs. When he opened his morning mail, he could reasonably expect to find a letter telling him that a previous speaker had been a colossal failure, and only Streicher's personal intervention could save the *völkisch* movement in Einöddorf.[23]

The reports of Streicher's speeches submitted by police agents consistently stressed the importance of his delivery over content. He and his message were becoming part of a subculture. If his meetings and rallies were surprisingly orderly, at least by the standards of Weimar Germany, this was not only a reflection of the presence of uniformed stormtroopers, Anyone who attended a Streicher speech was likely to know generally, if not exactly, what to expect. Streicher was no more prone to introduce significant variations into his act than any successful public performer. His speeches increasingly resembled modern rock concerts: crowds arriving early, Streicher making a spectacular entrance, a lesser Nazi light opening the performance, then Streicher himself taking the podium, starting slowly and reaching his full stride halfway through the session. Like any superstar, Streicher had his share of off nights, when his rhetoric was "of the usual kind and brought nothing new." One police reporter sounded more like a drama critic than a guardian of order when he described Streicher as "not quite in form" and delivering a "dismal" speech. But such failures had little effect on audiences who saw these meetings as a ritualized means of participation in a new political liturgy.[24]

Paradoxically, Streicher's very success as a speaker encouraged him to revive and develop *Der Stürmer*. The newspaper, after a four-month hiatus, reappeared in Nürnberg in March, 1924. In a movement stressing verbal and visual propaganda, *Der Stürmer* could be interpreted as an idiosyncratic ego reinforcement for a man whose eccentricities—to use the kindest possible word—from the beginning made him remarkable even in a party whose concept of leadership encouraged all forms of preening and posturing. But Streicher by mid-1924 was finding himself in an increasingly restrictive double bind. At its best the Nazi movement at this period had relatively few good speakers. Any outsider with talent was hardly likely to be welcomed by Streicher in territory he regarded as a personal fief.[25] On the other hand, Streicher's local entourage by this time consisted chiefly of imitation Streichers—men who did little more than copy his style and manner as far as they were able. Any organization sponsoring one of these men knew they were getting the party's second string. The problem was made worse by Streicher's administrative inefficiency. He seemed to have constant trouble answering his mail. Groups or individuals would request his presence two or three times without a reply, then receive a polite put-off. Streicher's cavalier attitude never provided significant resentment. On the contrary, his very aloofness seems to have inspired greater and greater eagerness to have the master himself appear in one's home town. In this context, *Der Stürmer* had incalculable value as a surrogate Streicher. The paper could convey its editor's message on a weekly basis, whetting readers' appetites for his appearance in the flesh.

The question was where Streicher's activity was leading him. As a paramilitary revolutionary movement, National Socialism was finished after November 9. Behind the scenes, however, the Franconian Nazis engaged in still another faction fight. On January 1, 1924, the *Völkischer Block*, or *Deutsche Arbeiterpartei*, had been formed as a combination of successor to the banned NSDAP and covering organization for similar *völkisch* groups. As a member of the *Block*, Streicher won election to the Bavarian Landtag in April. He rapidly became, however, one of its *enfants terribles*. He had lost none of his anti-Semitism, and now combined it with an increasingly left-slanted oratory, emphasizing eight-hour days and lowered rents for workmen. Any German of any party, Streicher declared, was welcome in the fight against Germany's real enemy—the Jew.

Streicher's anti-Semitism by itself disturbed relatively few. Those splinter *völkisch* elements adhering to the National Socialist movement were also strongly anti-Semitic. Their leaders were critical of Jewish banks and Jewish department stores. Their newspapers contained articles and letters worthy of *Der Stürmer* at its worst.[26] The problem was personal. Streicher might be popular among rank and file party members, but his aggressive, bullying tactics and crude personal behavior had alienated most of the leaders. His new proletarianism was also alien even to those labor Nazis like Gregor Strasser, who wanted to bridge the gap between propertied and unpropertied—not use it to divide Germany even further.

On July 21, 1924, Streicher was expelled from the DAP.

Four days earlier he had founded a Nürnberg branch of the *Grossdeutschen Völksgemeinschaft* (GVG). This organization, originally established by Alfred Rosenberg as a south Bavarian cover for the NSDAP, had begun spreading north with at best limited success. In Franconia it was little more than a synonym for Streicher and his friends. Streicher declared that he decided who could climb on the train, and he alone blew the whistle.[27]

Officially the GVG demanded the right to follow an independent path while Hitler was in prison. Its actual behavior, particularly in Nürnberg, was far more modest. Though Streicher fought a long and desperate rear-guard action, his political activity and his anti-Semitism finally brought about what amounted to his permanent suspension from the classroom, with a small pension replacing the salary that was still his principal income. The police were beginning to investigate his private life a bit more closely than he found comfortable. His political enemies had made public suggestions that his associates included known criminals, and that he had "immoral associations" with the wife of a doctor in Ipshitz. To the first charge the police turned up a few men convicted for minor crimes, with no evidence that Streicher's association with them went beyond politics. As for Streicher's love life, his visits to Ipshitz were ostensibly in the name of maintaining contacts with a "close party friend." They certainly were not legally actionable.[28] Nevertheless, though Streicher might temporarily have a firm grip on a party strong enough to elect six of its members to the Nürnberg city council, his long-term prospects needed improvement by the end of 1924.

Streicher turned increasingly to Adolf Hitler. He described Hitler's writings as necessary for mental and physical health. More significantly, he insisted that once released from prison, the führer should be free to make any decisions he saw fit. *Der Stürmer's* criticism of the "shameless" *völkisch* leaders who tried to bind Hitler to a predetermined program struck responsive chords in Landsberg.[29]

3

On March 2, 1925, Hitler was the featured speaker at three

separate rallies in Nürnberg. Approximately forty-seven hundred people paid a mark to cheer Hitler and Streicher to the echo and to hear Hitler reward Streicher's loyalty by appointing him gauleiter of Franconia. Streicher's disruptive behavior remained a subject of concern. In the final analysis, however, Hitler accepted the principle that made each Nazi agent supreme in his own sphere. This decision reflected Hitler's own commitment to the concept. It reflected his belief in Streicher's personal loyalty. It reflected the fact that the newly organized NSDAP was numerically stronger in Franconia than anywhere else. Given Hitler's continuing uncertain relationship with the northern wing of the party, Franconia might be a bridge between the Munich and Strasser factions.

Streicher also had his public uses. Hitler was frequently banned from speaking in public. Even when he was available, the party warned its local groups that Hitler could only attend meetings and rallies where large crowds were certain. He was "not a wandering propaganda speaker, but the leader of the movement." And a man like Streicher, who could fill the Nürnberg Coliseum at a mark a head, who could be described as the most popular Nazi speaker in Thuringia next to Hitler himself, and who could be requested to speak in Bremen because he was well-known in north German *völkisch* and Marxist circles, was too valuable as a table-setter to be driven from the party because of his personality.[30]

Streicher had come far since 1923. "Psychopaths, to Work" was the title of a *Stürmer* article that set the tone for his renewed political activity.[31] Despite the constant involvement in libel cases which distracted Streicher from his political role, he made speech after speech throughout Franconia. If official party membership remained low, Streicher collected enough in admission fees to make his *Gau* one of the financial bulwarks of National Socialism. If an increasing number of party leaders despised Streicher, Hitler continued to allow him the familiar form of address. *Der Stürmer* contained an increasing amount of party news—columns announcing meetings, speeches, and rallies. And what was to be made of an ad for a Bavarian May Dance, featuring waltzes, schottisches, and polkas, and organized by the social committee of the NSDAP?[32] It is little wonder that a police report of March 23,1927, described the political situation in Nürnberg as "quiet."[33]

"Quiet" did not mean dead. Streicher could still draw crowds when lecturing on the threat to German working girls from Jewish bosses, or the demoralizing effects of *Fasching*.[34] But by 1927 he was fully established both as a Nazi leader and a local character. Then geography furnished him with another opportunity for favorable national publicity. Hitler announced that the annual Nazi party conference would be held in Nürnberg. Modern railway connections and medieval history alike spoke for the city as a location. The presence of a strong Nazi party helped the decision. And finally, Streicher himself could be counted on for a good show. His influence in the party was at its peak. His support from Hitler was so strong that rumor alleged Streicher had some sort of incriminating evidence against the führer—a suggestion Streicher affirmed by not denying it. In 1927, however, Hitler could not have chosen a better man to host the convention that was intended to mark the rebirth of National Socialism as a party and a movement.

By Streicher's standards as printed in *Der Stürmer*, the rally was a huge success, replete with blowing trumpets and bright eyes, displays of manly chests and shouts of "Heil!" The Nürnberg police dryly reported that the attendance was "good enough," though less than Streicher expected. Official figures stated that around 9,000 people participated in the parades; anywhere from 15,000 to 20,000 were otherwise involved as participants and observers. The same report, however, also noted increasing stress in the Nürnberg party.[35]

"Stress" was a mild word for what was happening behind the scenes in Nürnberg. The local SA refused to regard itself any longer as Streicher's bodyguard. Streicher was also careless, to say the least, with party funds. In the fiscal year 1926/1927 alone, around thirty-six thousand marks entered the Nürnberg party coffers, but Streicher refused any open accounting and intimidated the official bookkeepers. In the aftermath of the 1927 rally, Streicher was openly accused of pocketing party funds. When Munich ignored these charges, Streicher's enemies turned on his lieutenant, Karl Holz, accusing him of using party funds to visit a lover in Bayreuth. Streicher's alleged response was that

Hitler too had women, and no one made a fuss over the fact.[36] But he considered the situation serious enough in the fall of 1927 to begin expelling his rivals from the NSDAP on his own authority and filing complaints with SA headquarters about the behavior of the local stormtroopers. SA leader Franz Pfeffer von Salomon responded, with Hitler's approval, that the SA was an independent organization of the party; any attempt to found a rival group would be met with expulsion.[37]

Whether Streicher actually planned to organize his own storm troop is debatable. What is certain is that this reproof encouraged his local enemies to organize an *NSDAP Ortsgruppe Nürnberg Mitte* on December 2, 1927. Its leader, retired city official Ludwig Käfer, hoped to isolate Streicher by attracting his enemies within the party. But on December 15, Adolf Hitler informed Käfer that his organization was to be disbanded immediately. The NSDAP told Nürnberg's newspapers that there was only one *Ortsgruppe* in the city and Käfer's splinter group had no right to use the party name. At the same time, Streicher's public meetings were better attended than ever before. Käfer's drew small crowds, including many Streicher supporters looking for and finding trouble.[38]

As the conflict sharpened, local groups of the party began asking Munich for advice. The Nazis of Forchheim, for example, declared that they knew there was tension in the Franconian movement. They were aware of the charges Käfer made against Streicher and found them unbelievable. On the other hand, Käfer was known as an eager and committed adherent of National Socialism and Adolf Hitler. Who was to be believed? More significantly, what were Hitler's views? What did he want done?[39] These were the kinds of questions Hitler had been awaiting. The issue in Franconia was no longer "what does Streicher think?" but "what does Hitler think?"[40] On May 18, he gave his answer by appearing at Streicher's side and publicly shaking his hand during an election rally in Nürnberg. The opposition was destroyed as a political force.

Streicher's victory confirmed his position in Nürnberg. The SA received a new commander, one whom Streicher found congenial. The opposition was expelled from the NSDAP. At the same time, Streicher lost much of his official control over the

Ortsgruppen in northern Bavaria, finding himself reduced to the leader of *Untergau* Nürnberg-Fürth. Official decisions, however, were seldom decisive in the Nazi organization. Streicher's influence as a speaker and an editor remained, but he seems to have learned that he depended on Hitler's support for his place in the Nazi organization. For the first time in his career as a Nazi Streicher had been outmaneuvered—not by his local opponents, but by Hitler. Simply by doing nothing, the führer had placed Streicher at a significant disadvantage. He had fought this battle as he had fought others, but this time he had had to keep one eye on Munich, on the man who could break him with a word or make him with a handshake. By February, 1929, he was restored as leader of the two *Untergauen* Nürnberg-Fürth and Central Franconia, his traditional hunting grounds. But he was restored to this position; he did not retake it.[41]

In 1929 Streicher reshuffled the organization of his *Gau*. Those local leaders who had risen independently of Streicher had by this time largely either left the party or abandoned Franconia. An assortment of new names whose only common denominator was their loyalty to, and dependence on, Streicher began making their appearance simultaneously in police and party records. The bureaucratization of National Socialism made few strides in Streicher's territory. He preferred to run things himself with the support of a clique whose criminal records made them unique even among the Nazis. Local groups saw their dues-paying membership shrink to a handful and found themselves spending as much time selling *Der Stürmer* as engaging in direct political activity.[42] Streicher himself, however, remained a guaranteed attraction. His loyal followers would stop any real disturbance before it began. He could hold crowds in a state of excitement for four hours at a stretch. From the remote villages in the Franconian hinterland he continued to receive requests to appear himself, or to send copies of *Der Stürmer* for distribution as recruiting and propaganda material.[43]

His own successes led Streicher to develop a theory of propaganda. It was a mistake, he declared, to depend on unknown speakers to sustain meetings. A man without a reputation could not count on drawing an audience, and the experience of almost a decade indicated that failure bred failure. Streicher went on to describe in detail the way meetings should be advertised, structured, and orchestrated—with the spotlight always on a star performer. And more than many of his party comrades, including Hitler, Streicher emphasized the importance of a strong party press. Particularly in the countryside, he argued, assemblies were not enough. The farmers received no continuous information about the movement; the impact of a speaker tended to sink to that of a traveling circus. What was needed, Streicher said, was consistent marketing of three papers: the party daily, the *Völkischer Beobachter*; the Nazis' national illustrated weekly, the *Illustrierter Beobachter*; and of course, the local "fighting sheet" —in Franconia's case, *Der Stürmer*.[44]

Streicher's emphasis on star speakers and on the importance of the party press was designed to fatten his pocketbook and enhance his reputation. During 1929, police records indicate that Streicher averaged three to five speeches weekly. *Der Stürmer* too reached towards a wider public by everything from congratulating generals on their birthdays to describing the economic prosperity and the peace of mind to be gained by following Hitler's teachings. Streicher even began emerging as an advice columnist. "A German girl" wrote that she was sixteen and a Nazi at heart, but she was forbidden to join the party by her father. The father was a Social Democrat to please his Jewish employer and told her that she could not be an active Nazi. Streicher's response was one to gladden the heart of the stereotypical German parent. The family bread, he declared, could not be endangered. Be patient; the day will come when you and your father can both wear your colors without fear.[45]

If *Der Stürmer*'s tone grew relatively avuncular, Streicher continued to force potential rivals out of the party or out of Franconia. His increased control of his own *Gau* was bought at the price of an increasing number of resignations during the spring and summer of 1930. Rumors credited Hitler with a desire to distance himself from Streicher and similar disreputable old fighters in order to improve the party's image in the eyes of the respectable bourgeoisie. Yet as the Nazis prepared for the Reichstag elections in 1930, Streicher continued to maintain his position and most of his image.[46]

Hitler's continued support for Streicher still involved

POISON GAS OVER GERMANY. "Just wait, fellow, we'll put a stop to your dirty tricks." *The theme of a Jew using poison gas on Germans is frequent in Nazi propaganda.*

adherence to the leadership principle and dislike for abandoning old comrades. Streicher's negative image among party leaders also counted in his favor. If Gregor Strasser wanted Streicher's political head, that was all the more reason for Hitler to leave it on his shoulders. Nor should *Der Stürmer*'s influence be overlooked. Hitler's growing personal fondness for the paper, especially the cartoons, is well-documented. The sheet's virulent Jew-baiting reflected both National Socialism's ideology and Hitler's tactical use of anti-Semitism as a means to connect goals and proposals otherwise appearing mutually exclusive. It might be a temporary drawback to a party seeking respectability; nevertheless, the motivating force behind *Der Stürmer* was also the motivating force behind National Socialism. It could not be lightly abandoned or altered.

Franconia's Nazis did not approach the national elections on September 9, 1930, with unusual optimism. In Nürnberg and Franconia the party had campaigned aggressively. Its rural meetings were well-attended. In Nürnberg a series of well-publicized brawls with the Communists served to keep the National Socialists in the news. The audiences, however, had shown no significant interest in voting Nazi, as opposed to watching Streicher's performances. *Der Stürmer* expressed the surprise many party members and officials felt at the victory which returned 107 National Socialist deputies to the Reichstag. It reported Nürnberg's "greatest Nazi assembly," with—according to Streicher—over fifty thousand stormtroopers cheering Adolf Hitler. More concretely, between September and November, 1930, *Gau Mittelfranken* registered 1,245 new members—an increase of 30 percent.[47] Streicher was riding high. The Nazi landslide had made him something of a national figure. The Berlin police even took enough notice of him to ask the Nürnberg authorities for detailed information. The answer reflected Streicher's local image. He was described as having a decisive influence on Franconia's Nazis, and being "now as ever *the Frankenführer* of the NSDAP."[48]

Streicher's major direct influence was probably on those voters who admired, respected, or were willing to accept a brutal, forceful political style. "We are charging forward" proclaimed *Der Stürmer*. A "Drumfire over Franconia" was crushing all opposition, right, left, or center. "The *Volk* was deciding" the issue, and the Nazis were striding to victory over the political corpses of the "system" and its supporters.[49] In fact the Nazis were able to put an increasing number of their members in public positions and provide an increasing number of customers for sympathetic businessmen. The growth of the party, however, could not be entirely traced to Streicher. The Nazi breakthrough in Franconia reflected a complex combination of factors, including cooperation by non-Nazi conservatives: judges and clergymen, small businessmen and farmers. But it was a breakthrough rather than a breakdown. The process is clearly reflected in contemporary police reports.

4

The police of Franconia and Nürnberg have generally been described as sympathetic to emerging National Socialism. The reality is more complex. Under the Empire, police officials regarded themselves as symbols and representatives of a system which was for the people, but not necessarily of or by them. They drew their ultimate authority from that system, finding no need for anything more than negative public support, the kind of support that left them free to do their jobs. The Republic was based on an entirely different theory of state-citizen relations, laudable in principle but difficult at best to translate into practice. And as the Republic polarized, instead of citizens passively watching officers execute the law, policemen in cities, towns, and villages faced actual or potential mobs. Increasingly they tended to regard any kind of political meeting by any group whatsoever as nothing but another opportunity for would-be politicians to attack officials in performance of their duty.[50]

Among the most common causes of trouble was the deliberate scheduling of simultaneous rallies by National Socialists and the SPD's *Reichsbanner*. Whatever its behavior during the actual *Machtergreifung*, the *Reichsbanner* at this time was at least as determined as the Nazis to control the streets and beer halls of Franconia. Particularly when the rival groups were closely matched in numbers, a constable or two who kept their heads could provide an excuse to avoid a fight by making judicious threats of arrest. This was not always enough.

The Ministry of the Interior was free with good advice, informing the local police that they should begin intervening when they knew trouble would start instead of waiting for someone to throw a punch or a bottle.[51] In practice the men on the spot could not always move to keep rival factions apart without violating accepted constitutional rights of speech and assembly. What, for example, were village gendarmerie to do when Nazi vendors tried to distribute back numbers of *Der Stürmer* at a *Reichsbanner* excursion? The courts had frequently upheld the National Socialists' right to distribute old newspapers as part of their propaganda machine.[52]

An increasing number of district administrations were banning an increasing number of Nazi meetings by the summer of 1931. This, however, was no real solution to the problem of political violence. It was, as *Bezirksamt Rothenburg* put it, necessary for local authorities to maintain the confidence of all citizens in these troubled times. This could not be done by deliberately harrassing a party which, at least in the Rothenburg district, had gained members and sympathizers including a large number of respectable citizens.[53] A year later, *Bezirk Neustadt* went a step further. The Republicans in the district, the authorities declared, could not legitimately complain of Nazi "terror." The alleged "terror" simply reflected new facts. Neither Social Democrats nor Communists could maintain their once-strong positions in the face of a National Socialist movement which had won the support of 60 to 70 percent of the district's population. The street-corner and tavern arguments endemic to small towns had taken on a different set of dynamics. It was always to be regretted when a woman seven months pregnant was jostled in such a dispute. These and similar incidents, the Neustadt authorities argued, smacked less of politics than of family feuds or beer-fueled quarrels. Now, however, if those involved were either of rival parties or had just recently become politically "awakened," such affairs were presented, depending on the views of the newspapers involved, as signs of an incipient breakdown of public order or as part of an ongoing struggle for the renewal of Germany under Hitler.[54]

The reports from *Bezirk Neustadt* cannot be dismissed out of hand as the special pleading of Nazified bureaucrats. Another set of police reports and eyewitness statements from that summer set a revealing scene. The event began in a tavern when two parties, one including three soldiers, another composed mostly of socialists, began singing at the same time. The rival choristers rapidly began attempting to drown out each other. A soldier yelled "pfui" at the conclusion of a song he felt insulted his uniform. The troopers then sang a song which, in the crowded, noisy atmosphere, sounded like the "Horst Wessel Lied"—although they later swore it was merely a barracks tune using the same melody. As the atmosphere grew tenser, an older—or soberer—man seized a few moments of silence to strike up a popular folk tune. With what can be presumed some relief, since both groups included women and children, everyone joined in singing first that song, then another.

The incident might have ended there, but just before closing time, men of each group resumed their argument at the urinal trough, then took it outside. By this time it had dwindled to a word exchange. Then another nearby *Gasthaus* also closed its doors at the legally prescribed hours. This tavern had been dispensing free beer all evening. The policy was a popular way for proprietors to draw customers in neighborhoods where many regular drinkers were out of work or underemployed. For free or reduced-price beer, even the most loyal of men were likely to desert their *Stammlokal*. The other results of the policy became apparent when the new crowd reached the street. An evening of serious drinking combined with the first shock of fresh air and the sight of an argument to produce results familiar to any neighborhood patrolman. Words flew, then fists, rocks, and anything else usable as a weapon. The resulting lacerations, arrests, and fines certainly owed something to politics. They owed a good deal more to alcohol, to the desire of three young soldiers to cut a figure for their girls, and not least to the sanitary arrangements of German *Gasthäuser*.[55]

For Streicher such incidents were part of the march of the "Brown Battalions" whose "tireless efforts" were "restoring faith in Germany" once more. As I looked through the party papers, wrote one sixteen-year-old, I saw only mutual libels. As I read books I saw that they were written by Jews. I may be too young to join the Nazi movement, but I can work for it. "A crippled veteran" declared that the time had come to destroy the whole "party pigsty" and begin anew. A Franconian who had moved to Hamburg boasted of his success at using *Der Stürmer* to convert acquaintances in that red stronghold.[56] The impression of revolution around the corner was so strong that in October, 1931, the Nürnberg police declared that Streicher was becoming more reserved in his speech, and was trying to avoid disturbances of the peace by his followers. Why run unnecessary risks?[57]

By January, 1932, the official morale of Franconia's Nazis had reached a peak. *Der Stürmer's* features and cartoons took on a new tone of confidence, greeting Hitler's announcement of his candidacy for the presidency by proclaiming his success inevitable. Optimism extended so far that the Franconian SA and SS were put on alert before the election in the expectation that Hitler's victory would spark reaction by the Socialist and Communist paramilitary groups, in turn offering an excuse for the storm troopers, hopefully in cooperation with the police and the army, to make a final end of their rivals.[58]

Hitler's percentage of the presidential vote in *Mittelfranken* was 43.5— a 20 percent gain over 1930—and taken in isolation, a substantial triumph. Compared to expectations, it was a setback. Even *Der Stürmer* was taken aback. Any hopes entertained by non-Nazis or anti-Nazis that this defeat might sober the new National Socialists proved, however, vain. Within weeks Streicher was enthusiastically describing "the second assault"— the presidential runoff election of April 10, which brought Hitler even more votes in Franconia, almost 50 percent in *Mittelfranken* alone.[59] In Nürnberg, the Nazis counted over a hundred thousand votes while the other parties combined reached only a hundred and forty thousand.

In the aftermath of the April elections, Streicher emphasized the party's triumph in his *Gau*. But Franconia was the key to Germany in more ways than one. Like the Nazis generally, Streicher now faced a demographic problem. Analysis of the National Socialist vote in *Mittelfranken* indicated that the movement was most successful among rural Protestants and urban *Mittelständler* who feared loss of their jobs and status. Group dynamics also proved a significant factor. Religiously or occupationally homogeneous communities seemed relatively more susceptible to Nazi influence than did mixed election districts. But the number of such closed communities was limited. Streicher's newspaper and his speeches had reached most of them. The percentage of increase in the Nazi vote between March and April was lower than the average for Germany.

Streicher also confronted growing election fatigue. In April, only two weeks after the second presidential election, Bavaria held its *Landtag* elections. Communal elections were scheduled during the same period. On July 31 came new elections for the *Reichstag*. The Franconian Nazis had their share of successes, particularly on a local level, but the absolute number of Nazi voters continued to decline. Even *Der Stürmer* was showing the strain. For every column describing the movement as "A Hundred Meters from the Finish Line"; for every article treating Hitler's heroic flights over Germany; *Der Stürmer* ran two appeals for funds to an increasingly jaded audience. Gimmicks such as a memorial coin for the elections of July 31—"the last parliamentary election in the Germany of the November crime"—were juxtaposed with simple encouragements to give what one had left in this last round. Subscriptions to the party press were dropping. Using a technique he preferred to ascribe to Jewish department stores, Streicher went so far as to offer a rebate of eighty pfennigs monthly to anyone subscribing to the *Völkischer Beobachter* at full price.[60]

By winning, the National Socialists appeared to be losing. The July elections more than doubled their representation in the *Reichstag*, but their base of support was by no menas as solid as any of the leaders, whether in Germany or in *Mittelfranken*, wished. The dissolution of the *Reichstag* in September meant a fifth major election campaign. This one was described by the Nürnberg police as the quietest of the year, probably because all the parties were out of funds. There was simply no money for parades and placards.[61]

The check to National Socialist hopes in 1932 gave Streicher's enemies, new and old, a fresh lease on life. Wilhelm Stegmann, a successful landowner, had developed in the late 1920s into an agitator and speaker second only to Streicher himself. In the summer of 1930, he was appointed head of the Franconian SA. Unlike Streicher, he knew how to make friends; by 1932 Stegmann was probably the most genuinely popular Nazi in Franconia. Streicher saw both Stegmann's personality and his official position as a threat to his own status as *Frankenführer*. Stegmann for his part resented Streicher's constant attempts to assert direct control over the SA, and apparently had grown to despise Streicher as a human being. By this time, too, a new breed of men was rising to the top in the Bavarian party. Seven of the eight Bavarian gauleiters were under forty. Streicher, at forty-five, was beginning to appear a bit shopworn. He had been on the political scene for a decade. He had had no new ideas since the Munich putsch. His constant emphasis on the Jewish question was increasingly regarded by the party's young Turks as a symbol of dangerous inflexibility. Streicher, in short, seemed more vulnerable than at any time since 1924.

Streicher fought this battle with cash as well as words, by refusing to support the Franconian SA beyond an irreducible minimum. This fit a general pattern of conflict among party organizations for scarce funds. The SA troopers, who understood only that they were expected to finance an increasing proportion of their activity from their own limited resources, began protesting to their local leaders, who in turn took their complaints to Stegmann. Stegmann attempted to obtain satisfaction from Streicher. Rebuffed, he turned to Hitler, who demanded that as the younger and junior man, he should mend his fences with Streicher. Stegmann promptly resigned as SA leader.

This did not save him from continued attack in speeches and in *Der Stürmer*. Nor had Stegmann lost his personal following in the SA. A group of angry stormtroopers demonstrated against Streicher himself in Nürnberg. Then Hitler again intervened. He met personally with Stegmann. With a combination of threats, promises, self-pity, and bizarre behavior, he convinced him to end his campaign of opposition. By this time, however, the SA had the bit in its teeth and filed bitter complaints about the treatment of Stegmann and barely veiled threats of mass defections if Streicher remained the head of the political organization.

The SA had spent a long, hard year of marches, fights, and traveling. All three activities were beginning to fray tempers—

particularly when the trips to other cities had to be financed by collecting money for gas from the men themselves. The Nürnberg SA's actual fatal casualties during the entire *Kampfzeit* were only five—including one man run over by a streetcar and another who died of pneumonia ostensibly caught during an open-air rally. But enough men had been injured, enough men had lost sleep and money, that Streicher's announcement that the Nürnberg *Ortsgruppe* was going to build a *Hitlerhaus*, a miniature replica of the Brown House in Munich, inspired particularly lively protest. Only the *Machtergreifung* defused the situation by giving the SA a set of tasks more to their liking.[62]

Between January and March, 1933, Nürnberg and Franconia saw its Nazis behave as though they already possessed the power they had so long sought. The incidence of Nazi-inspired riots grew weekly as the police virtually suspended any counter-activity. *Der Stürmer* and Streicher reached new heights of denunciation, openly warning anti-Nazis to stay home and sing small. The structural factors discussed earlier combined with a virulent anti-Communist campaign and a certain bandwagon effect finally to bring the Nazis over 50 percent of the Franconian vote in the elections of March 5. Voting Nazi in this particular election was, however, no indication of long-standing permanent support for the movement. A list of party members in *Gau Mittelfranken* submitted to the *Reichsleitung NSDAP* in April 1934 —a year after the seizure of power—illustrates this point. Despite thirteen months for the accretion of "March violets," fellow travelers, and opportunists, membership figures are almost shockingly low. Less than 3 percent of Nürnberg's population carried party cards. In Erlangen, the university town, slightly over 4 percent of the residents belonged to the NSDAP. Gunzenhausen, the setting for so many rallies and meetings, had 7 percent Nazis. In the villages, percentages were often significantly higher. Twenty-seven of Sonnersdorf's 126 residents were party members. In Brunst, the figures were 57 of 226; in Brunn, 68 of 460—illustrations of the collective communal mentality mentioned earlier. Such communities, however, were far outnumbered by villages who had one or two Nazi inhabitants, or none at all. Most of the *Gemeinde* in Streicher's *Gau* could not count over 5 percent of their population in the party rolls. Nor were any of the districts significant centers of official party members.[63]

Yet if the Nazis' success was not complete, it was enough. On March 9, 1933, the day Bavaria was assigned its first Nazi *Reichskommissar*, Streicher staged one final parade to the city hall. As the swastika flag went up over police headquarters, he declared that he was living the proudest day of his life. While storm troopers fanned out through Nürnberg, paying off old scores or simply enjoying themselves by breaking heads, Streicher led a chosen band to occupy the offices of the *Fränkische Tagespost*, his longtime journalistic adversary and the symbol of Social Democracy. In his own mind, Streicher probably reached the peak of his career as he brandished his pistol in the *Tagespost*'s offices and claimed the property for the new Germany.[64] The marginal men had become the establishment.

3 | The Paper

In an era of cliometrics and psychohistory, the use of newspapers as historical sources has a faint odor of mothballs, an aura of doctoral dissertations written in the 1950s. Nevertheless, newspapers remain worthwhile, particularly for determining moods and establishing atmospheres. Lead articles, local news, advertisements, even poetry and fiction, can contribute to understanding the tone of everyday life.[1] For this purpose local and party papers are frequently more useful than sheets with national circulations and national reputations. Even when edited more with shears than ink, local papers appeal to a specific place or a specific audience. Their value is enhanced by the same specificity that makes them such dull work for the scholar. Such papers know their markets and their readers, actual and potential. They can be precisely structured to appeal to a limited area, a limited ideology, or both. *Der Stürmer* during the Nazi struggle for power was just such a paper. It was also a reflection of several general trends in the history of the German press in the modern era.

1

The nineteenth century, with its combination of expanded literacy and improved communications, made the German press an increasingly significant cultural and political factor. With the founding of the Second Empire, Germany's newspaper industry began changing geographically and structurally. Berlin became the journalistic center of the new state; even such well-established papers as the *Frankfurter Allgemeine* took much of their news and many of their cues from their Berlin bureaus. Simultaneously, however, local and regional sheets acquired new importance. Increased disposable income and universal education combined to make publication of local newspaper potentially both profitable and satisfying. Such papers were generally contemptuously dismissed by their national counterparts as *Käseblätter*, fit only for wrapping groceries. But a combination of a careful eye for local and regional news, careful use of wire-service items and filler material, and a personal editorial touch with a bit of flair, produced sheets economically successful and aesthetically acceptable.

This process was closely linked with the altered structure of the German newspaper industry. Between 1871 and 1914 a party press emerged, a press self-described as concerned with loftier problems than the price of cattle or the vagaries of the stock market. No German newspaper in any era had been entirely free of political influence. But where once these papers had been part of the domestic machinery of the state, in the nineteenth century an increasing number of papers were founded by or affiliated with specific political parties, from the Conservatives' *Kreuzzeitung* to the Social Democrats' *Vorwärts*.

This process was a logical result of class and interest-group rivalries in a society where newspapers were the only quick, certain, and respectable means of reaching a large audience. As party rivalries deepened in the course of the century, a number of local and regional papers abandoned their initial above-the-battle position and committed themselves either to a party or to a party line. This increasing commitment to partisan politics reflected economic as well as ideological considerations. As production costs and competition increased, direct subsidies from a political party or advertising from its members could help balance accounts.

As the party press flourished, an increasing number of businessmen founded or purchased newspapers, not for the purpose of expressing ideas, but to make money. Such sheets were frequently called *Generalanzeiger*, a name connoting broad appeal.

These papers avoided overt political commitment whenever possible. When they had to take a stand, they supported what their editors considered to be the mainstream views of the largest possible number of readers and said the best things very conservatively. For this reason the *Generalanzeiger* were the targets of constant criticism by activists and intellectuals alike, dismissed as sources of public corruption for using news only as a means of selling advertising and focusing on scandal and sensation to attract readers.

Respectable or not, the *Generalanzeiger* were successful. In the two decades before World War I, their overall circulation doubled and tripled, primarily at the expense of their more staid competitors. By 1918, almost two hundred German papers carried the word *Anzeiger* somewhere in their titles, and their denigrators were frequently paying them the compliment of imitation. The *Fränkische Tagespost*, for example, published in Nürnberg, established its reputation as the most-read Socialist paper in south Germany by downplaying Marxist rhetoric in favor of local news, and offering entertainment instead of the weighty articles on the nature of the dialectic so popular in other Socialist journals.

By 1894 the German journalists were able to find enough in common to form the *Verein Deutscher Zeitungsverleger*. Like most similar organizations, many of its concerns were technical: wage scales, unionization, and the price of newsprint. But the *Verein* was also concerned with sustaining and extending freedom of the press. Two issues in particular, fought to a victorious conclusion by the *Verein* under the Empire, established precedents which would prove useful to *Der Stürmer* and its editor under the Weimar Republic. One involved denial of the right to hold the responsible editor of a paper legally liable for its contents anywhere even a single copy of the sheet might be read. The *Verein* argued successfully that at best this practice reflected ignorance of how modern newspapers functioned. A journal with a national circulation could not operate under the threat of legal action initiated by offended readers in remote provincial villages. Universal accountability could also be viewed in a more sinister light, an effort to limit press freedom by a form of cat-and-mouse harrassment, exhausting a journal's funds in successive trials of the same case. A second related issue involved the use of malicious mischief paragraphs of the penal code. *Grober Unfug*, argued the *Verein*'s attorneys, was a vague charge, the kind of catchall used by careless or incompetent prosecutors who could not make a solid case against particular sections or issues of a journal, but who nevertheless wished to present a case in court. In 1902 the German supreme court responded with a decision sharply restricting the use of this charge in cases involving newspapers. It was to prove essential to Julius Streicher's journalistic career.

The *Verein Deutscher Zeitungsverleger* was hardly an organization primarily devoted to protecting the feedom of the gutter press. Particularly after 1918, the *Verein* recognized the problem of what it called "driftwood"—the increasing number of papers that stood apart from the essential goals of the *Verein* and, perhaps more importantly, drew readers from the more respectable sheets by an emphasis on sex and scandal. Protests against such papers, however, tended to remain more formal than concrete. Thus a century-long battle for the rights of the press created an environment where *Der Stürmer* could take advantage not only of legal rights, but of a prevailing attitude that an injury to one paper was an injury to all.

This attitude was intensified by the German newspaper industry's experiences with government regulations between 1914 and 1918. The patriotism, not to say the jingoism of Germany's wartime newspapers requires no documentation. Less well-known is the constant battle waged by the *Verein Deutscher Zeitungsverleger* against what it considered unreasonable censorship —the kind of unimaginative regulations that seemed to assume local papers were the primary source of allied intelligence information. By war's end, even conservative journalists were arguing that only a free press could develop and deserve the confidence of its readers.

In theory at least, the Weimar Republic and its journalists were in full agreement. In practice the state frequently initiated administrative or legal action, particularly against the party newspapers that flourished in the atmosphere of permissiveness and controversy characteristic of Weimar in its early years. *Völkisch* and veterans' groups, radical factions of every kind, advocates of political reform through such social changes as free love and nudism—all had their own tabloid mouthpieces. And newspapers were obvious targets for a government seeking to establish stability and legitimacy simultaneously. Unlike political organizations that rapidly learned the trick of assembling the same people under a new name and a slightly altered program, a paper could be banned for a given period and its presses shut down. Any new sheet appearing from the same editorial offices was an easy target for charges of attempting to evade the law. Economic considerations also discouraged publishers of a temporarily suspended paper from attempting to fill the gap with an entirely new sheet. Neither reader loyalties nor advertising revenues could be transferred as easily as party affiliations. It was considered better business to ride out the ban, then resume publication with a clarion call for increased freedom of the press.

The result was a cat and mouse game between the party press and the government. Both radical right and radical left were heavily involved. In the last three months of 1922 alone, fifty-two orders suspending publication were issued. Between 1923 and 1925 the annual average was between thirty and forty. In 1927, however, only four newspapers were suspended. The election year of 1928 was marked by only seven bannings. This decline has been described as proof of the growing consolidation and stabilization of the republic. It also reflects certain less favorable facts. On one hand, the affected journals were hardly inclined to modify their editorial policies in the face of a few days' or even weeks' suspension; on the contrary, they tended to use the fact of being banned as proof of their role in the front lines of the struggle against the Weimar system. On the other, the issues of press freedom and regional autonomy were as important in 1927 as in 1917. Prosecutors and judges were reluctant to risk being pilloried by prestigious and respectable papers as would-be tyrants and enemies of Germany's intellectual freedom merely to secure meaningless judgments against fringe journals.[2] Under such conditions any laws under which political newspapers could be regulated were well on their way to becoming dead letters by the outbreak of the multiple crises of 1929/30.

The evolution of the National Socialist party press cannot by understood entirely in the general framework of Germany's newspaper industry. In one sense a National Socialist press was something of a contradiction in terms. Unlike other elements of the *völkisch* movement, the Nazis from the beginning deemphasized the role of printed propaganda in forming public opinion. Hitler himself made his early reputation as a speaker. The movement's initial adherents included few men with the journalistic ability of their Socialist or Communist rivals. Finally, the Law for the Protection of the Republic bore heavily on journalists of the radical right even in Bavaria. However, these factors did not lead to a complete neglect of the printed word. By the end of 1920, the party had purchased the *Völkischer Beobachter*, a paper with three decades of connection with the *völkisch* movement and debts of a quarter-million marks. Initially it appeared twice a week. By April, 1922, it had only seven thousand subscribers. Yet Hitler insisted that if the movement were to spread among the broad masses of Germany, verbal propaganda alone was not enough. What was needed were newspapers—newspapers of a special kind. Hitler wanted a press that would expose local and national dangers day after day, week after week, year after year; a press heedless of consequences and tireless in its efforts; a press that would be Germany's alarm clock. Stripped of its rhetoric, Hitler's vision involved a "spoken press," written by agitators who would also function as orators. Such a press would not in itself be a primary means of conversion. It would function rather as a means for continuing political education begun elsewhere, in the mass meetings or on the street corners. And this in turn involved decentralization.[3]

Before the Beer Hall Putsch, during Hitler's imprisonment, and after the party once again became legal in 1925, local ties, local loyalties, and local personalities were significant in the evolution of the NSDAP. The *Völkischer Beobachter* at its best could hardly be expected to exercise a uniform appeal in north and south, city and village, suburb and farmstead. Moreover, the more papers in existence, the greater was the difficulty of banning a significant number simultaneously. Particularly after 1925, the NSDAP intensified the process of creating a local press to accompany its national organs. The failure rate of these papers was high. Their editors were chosen more for loyalty to Hitler and his ideology than journalistic competence. Their financing was shaky; prosperous sympathizers and a printer willing to extend credit were often central factors in their survival. Rivalries among Nazis ambitious to secure party recognition for their sheets—the right to display the Nazi eagle and swastika and the corresponding hope of attracting party advertising and subscribers—further weakened the local party press in several regions. It can reasonably be argued that the general press climate in the Weimar Republic was more favorable for any given Nazi newspaper than were the circumstances within the party itself. Even if a journal could overcome the internal obstacles mentioned above, it might not flourish. It could, however, survive or fail on its merits, such as they might be, without worrying too much about government harrassment.[4]

2

Der Stürmer had a more specific famework than the German press and the Nazi party. A major part of Streicher's initial position in the *völkisch* movement of Franconia was his editorship of the *Deutscher Sozialist*. This role proved a hard apprenticeship. Streicher spent most of his time trying to meet the paper's bills. Correspondence files for this period are a mixture of crank letters, requests from authors for honoraria for their essays, and communications from unpaid printers threatening lawsuits. Not until December, 1921, did a print shop agree to print four thousand copies of the paper at 523 marks per thousand, reducing the rates for larger runs. Given the limited circulation of the *Sozialist*, even such favorable terms were impossible to meet. By the time Streicher left the DSP for the DWG and the *Sozialist* evolved into the *Deutscher Volkswille*, printing was done by another company, which informed Streicher in August, 1922, that he had run up a debt of thirty-five thousand marks. The firm gave him six weeks to pay and announced that in the future it would print the *Volkswille* only if paid in advance. In spite of all difficulties Streicher managed to keep the paper afloat and place it at Hitler's service when he founded the Nürnberg group of the NSDAP.[5]

Briefly before the Beer Hall Putsch, the *DV* provided Franconia with a local Nazi paper. Difficulties remained. The *DV* tended to focus on Nürnberg politics, virtually excluding issues of national concern to the NSDAP. From Streicher's personal viewpoint, the paper was still not fully under his control. Its tone and approach were still not popular enough to suit him. In 1923 he introduced a paper that met his criteria.

Der Stürmer has been more attacked than analyzed. Its stomach-turning contents have been too much for even the dedicated scholar. The common contemporary impression of its tone is presented in a clever undated essay "From the Editorial Meeting of a Familiar Weekly Paper." The editor, "Herr Zieher," asks what can be done to make money this week? One of his staff answers that a corpse had been discovered in Deixelfurt. "Zieher" writes a story about a Jew murderer, with appropriate quotations produced by his "Talmud manufacturers." Then someone else describes a tramp named Kalb who took a sausage from an old woman. "Zieher" immediately states that the tramp should be made a Jew, his name changed to Cohen, and his theft changed to rape. The juicier and more ridiculous the story, the more readily it will be believed. And above all, he declares, a picture of a "big naked broad" must accompany the article. Without nudes, the paper will not sell—especially to the schoolboys who are among its best customers. The satire ends whan another staffer declares that the Deixelfurt "corpse" turned out to be only dead drunk. After a moment's reflection, "Zieher" says that the original story should stand—after all, if we pay too close attention to the truth, what will become of the *Volk*?[6]

But *Der Stürmer* was something more than a scandal sheet specializing in invention. From its first issue it was presented as a fighting newspaper, a paper proposing to "fling the truth in the faces of bastards in Bavarian-German style." At one level, this "truth" frequently involved two elements of anti-Semitic writing with roots in the eighteenth century. One, the theoretical, followed patterns established in Eisenmenger's *Entdecktes Judentum* (1700), whose two thousand pages combined extensive and generally accurate quotations of Jewish sources with interpretations distorting those sources by inverting their meaning. The other, the anthropological, traced its heritage to Johann Jacob Schudt's four-volume *Jüdische Merkwürdigkeiten* (1714-1718).

This compendium of real and alleged Jewish folkways, though not intentionally anti-Semitic, spawned numerous successors and offered a wealth of citable examples of differences between Jew and Gentile. *Der Stürmer*'s contents and cartoons also closely resemble those of such contemporary *völkisch* periodicals as Dietrich Eckart's *Auf Gut Deutsch.*[7] From its inception, however, *Der Stürmer* was one of a kind.

The paper's character in part reflected Streicher's experiences as editor of the *Sozialist* and the *Volkswille*. He was convinced that the *völkisch* press as a whole was too conservative, too timid, too intellectual, to attract the attention of the masses. Particularly in Nürnberg, where the *Tagespost* combined the functions of a party sheet and *Anzeiger* not only for committed Social Democrats but for thousands of casual readers, something much stronger was needed. A major element of this strength, in Streicher's opinion, must be simplicity. His long experience as a primary school teacher had demonstrated to him the wide gap existing between the educated classes and the mass of Germans who were more than functionally literate but whose reading skills, available time, and intellectual energy were limited. To descriptions of his journalistic technique as simple-minded invective expressed in childish language, Streicher replied that he wrote for an audience demanding "that sort of thing." A man returning from a day's work, Streicher declared, had neither the will nor the energy for heavy reading, and in this sense, *Der Stürmer* acknowledged a debt to the *Generalanzeiger* format as well as to the party press.[8]

Der Stürmer might aim at the ductless glands, but its style was more sophisticated than its critics are willing to concede. Its tone may be aggressive, loud, crude, and banal—but it is above all comprehensible. The extensive use of superlatives, bold-faced type, and interlining made the lines of argument easy to follow for the hasty reader as well as the unsophisticated one. Streicher was reluctant to use even the specialized jargon of the National Socialist movement. A careful reading of *Der Stürmer* reveals only a few of the stock words and phrases of the Nazi language. None was complex or double-meaning; none had meaning only to *völkisch* initiates. *Alljuda*, for example, was one of Streicher's favorite terms, but it had been common currency long before the

1920s among anti-Semites as a shorthand term for the international Jewish conspiracy. *Asphalt* as a negative adjective describing the effect of ubanization on people and institutions was similarly familiar. *Verjudung*, the intrusion of Jewish influences and attitudes on German institutions, dated to at least the 1880s. The constanly reiterated phrase, "Judentum ist Verbrechertum," was universally employed by *völkisch* papers and speakers; and Heinrich von Treitschke gave the paper its masthead slogan: "Die Juden sind unser Unglück."[9]

Streicher, in short, deliberately intended to produce the kind of paper that anyone and everyman might purchase to read on a streetcar, or peruse in a *Gasthaus* or barbershop—perhaps with the front page turned back if one had any pretense to culture or education. Contemporary parallels might well be Axel Springer's *Bild-Zeitung* and its local equivalents. Few Germans will admit reading these papers, but virtually everyone in the Federal Republic seems more or less familiar with their contents.

These parallels can be legitimately drawn only in the sense of language and style. The purposes of *Der Stürmer* bore little or no resemblance to those of the contemporary *Boulevardblätter* of the Federal Republic. Education, amusement, even advertising, took second place to the struggle against world Jewry and its creation, the Weimar system. Once attracted, the readers were subjected to a well-integrated propaganda offensive. Manfred Rühl divides the paper's approach into five categories. The most important was hate propaganda, focusing on the Jew as not only a priori inferior, but as the concrete embodiment of every negative image Streicher could conceive of or absorb from public opinion. Second, *Der Stürmer* made extensive use of fear propaganda, again focusing on the Jew as a concrete object of whatever diffuse anxieties might be current in Nürnberg and Germany. Third, *Der Stürmer* gave free expression to envy propaganda. Few issues did not include an article or two describing the freedom of Jews, foreigners, or freemasons to do what they wished in the Weimar Republic—naturally, at the expense of honest Germans. The fourth element of *Der Stürmer*'s propaganda offensive involved arousal of sympathy for one's own kind, with corresponding hostility towards outsiders and "others." For Streicher, this sympathy involved rigid racial lines, with no room for the "upright Jew" whose existence was the bane of so many Nazi ideologues. Even when "the Jew" as an abstraction could be offered as totally alien, totally evil, a symbol of everything un-German, there remained the Jewish storekeeper, the Jewish cattle-dealer, the Jewish colleague—people one *knew*. Much of *Der Stürmer* was devoted to exposing these men and women for the vermin they were, stripping away the masks they adopted for purposes of deception. And this process in turn led to the fifth weapon in *Der Stürmer*'s propaganda arsenal: a constant appeal to the German as victim, as underdog. Throughout the *Kampfzeit* Streicher's paper presented the Nazis as a group of people banded together to help their community in every way possible, both passively and actively, against an overwhelmingly powerful, supremely cunning enemy whose final triumph was fast approaching. For *Der Stürmer*, Germany's clock always stood at two minutes to midnight.[10]

3

Certainly the most familiar characteristic of *Der Stürmer* is its anti-Semitic cartoons. Yet this feature of the paper was slow to develop.

Not until April, 1924, did *Der Stürmer* feature its first direct cartoon attack on the Jews—a sketch of a hook-nosed profiteer with a caption in "Yiddish German" asserting that business was excellent and that if only he could buy a new face he would be a real German.[11] Anti-Semitism remained the primary theme of *Der Stürmer*'s cartoon repertoire, but the few cartoons the paper published were undistinguished. The drawings were stiff: bodies without life, faces without expression. The captions were wordy. This changed in December, 1925, when Philip Ruprecht first appeared on *Der Stürmer*'s front page. "Fips" was born in 1901 in Nürnberg, served in the navy during World War I, then drifted to Argentina. In 1925, he emigrated to Germany after failing to make his way as an artist and cartoonist in South America. With a wife and two children to support, he soon turned instead to caricature.

Ruprecht's commitment to *Der Stürmer*, initially at least,

was as much financial as ideological. He did some free-lance work for the *Fränkische Tagespost* before showing samples of his cartoons to Streicher. Streicher liked them well enough to offer Ruprecht twenty-five marks per cartoon. If they were well received, he promised more. Ruprecht's problem lay in collecting. Between December 5, 1925 and February 20, 1926, he received a total of 410 marks, including payment of 50 marks for one cartoon, and only 10 for another. But shortly thereafter payments bacame so irregular that Ruprecht threatened to bring charges. He was dissuaded only by his own lack of funds to pay an attorney. And by that time he had become sufficiently famous —or notorious—as a *völkisch* cartoonist that he could not find enough work elsewhere to support his family. Streicher then informed Ruprecht that he could work regularly for *Der Stürmer* —*if* he abandoned any notion of pressing charges against the paper. Ruprecht seems to have bound himself to *Der Stürmer* even more firmly by periodically borrowing money from it. Whether through improvidence or impecunity, as late as 1928, he was complaining that he was still dodging his creditors. Signed promissory notes guaranteed that he could not dodge his employers.[12]

It must have been increasingly difficult for Philip Ruprecht to avoid anyone in Franconia. In little over a year his work had become such a feature of the paper that its occasional absence brought sharp protests from salesmen who regarded "Fips's" cartoons as a major attraction for prospective customers.[13] His talent, as opposed to his notoriety, remains a subject for debate. Manfred Rühl argues that "Fips" was only interested in raising emotional hatred against the Jews, that he lacked the desire to become a true caricaturist.[14] Contemporaries were of at least two minds. One of the numerous trials in which *Der Stürmer* was involved featured a discussion of the nature of certain drawings in the newspaper—sketches of the heads of the plaintiff in another case and his attorney. Erich Wilke, a Berlin artist summoned as an expert witness, said that the sketches were done by a good artist, but did not resemble photos of the men in question. Professor Max Körner of the Nürnberg *Kunstschule* declared that he knew Ruprecht personally and regarded his gifts for both portrait and caricature as proven. The sketches in question, however, were not caricatures at all. Körner, after a learned digression on the history and nature of caricature, pronounced the drawings to be simply poorly executed portraits. Ruprecht, he declared, could do far better if he wished.[15]

Perhaps the best method of settling the argument is to put Fips's work into the context of caricature in general, and German anti-Semitic caricature in particular.[16] Like any artist, the caricaturist seeks to capture the essence of his subject, to reveal what is hidden behind public masks—but he has a special purpose. Caricature is, at least in theory, a sophisticated attempt to make its victims contemptible through ridicule. It can only exist in a sophisticated society, one where the audience and the victims alike are sensitive to this particular type of visual attack, and where the art of portraiture has evolved sufficiently to develop variant forms. Certainly the Jews had been the subjects of contemptuous drawings and sculpture in Germany since the Middle Ages. But the "Jewish type" used with such devastating effect by Ruprecht only emerged during the seventeenth century. Before this time Jews were identified symbolically rather than physically: by tall hats, money bags, and similar items. The creation of physical forms of caricature began with giving all male Jews beards—a pattern reflecting accurate observation as much as anti-Semitism. The process of distortion bagan with the nose. Since this contributes much to the character of a face, even a small exaggeration of it can suggest greed, lust, and similar undesirable qualities. The hooked nose with its flaring nostrils rapidly became a staple of Jewish caricature. By the turn of the eighteenth century two other stock features had been added: flat feet and crooked legs.

The roles assigned to these physical stereotypes reflected perceived social problems. The Revolution of 1848 deepened existing class antagonisms. The rise of industrialization offered new images of the Jew as capitalist, exploiting the toiling masses, and the Jew as banker, ruining farmers and small businessmen. This climate fostered the development of the political press, discussed earlier in the chapter. It also promoted a humorous literature—specifically, an anti-Semitic joke press. In the 1830s the *Goedtsche Verlag* of Meissen issued numerous satirical pamphlets written in a caricatured Yiddish-German. Cartoons were correspondingly popular. Initially some of them embodied more German humor than anti-Semitism. "Little Israel Has Swallowed a Ducat" featured a child perched on a chamber pot, with a gaggle of anxious relatives encouraging the reappearance of the coin with appropriate purgatives. The lack of taste this suggests to an American reader should not obscure the fact that toilet jokes have been and remain a major staple of German low comedy. The cartoons, however, rapidly became cruder and uglier.

By the end of the century such anti-Semitic papers as the Vienna *Kikeriki* and the Dresden *Antisemitischen Bilderbogen* had discovered the profits of sex. Their cartoonists ascribed to Jews a strong sex drive combined with a complete lack of scruple in gratifying it, a taste for Gentile women, and a tendency to reduce the victims of their pleasure to streetwalkers before abandoning them. In particular, the Jewish theater director emerged as a negative stereotype, more concerned with garters and corsets than acting talent, preferring to negotiate contracts on a chaise lounge.

It seems legitimate to suggest that this approach reflected public tastes in soft-core pornography projected onto a section of the community with which such liberties could be taken. It also incorporated a new and dangerous twist. From featuring amusing or unpleasant things done by Jews, anti-Semitic caricature increasingly attacked Jews as Jews. Such papers as the Dresden sheet, *The Devil in Germany*, specialized in blunt hate-mongering. "Jews and Students" showed a Jew whose usury had driven an undergraduate to suicide presenting a bill to the grieving parents. In "Jews and Patients" a weeping German woman was shown leaving the office of a Jewish gynecologist. The precise reason for her tears was left to the readers' imagination—an effective device in context.

World War I and its civil truce brought these expressions of anti-Semitism to a temporary end. Even "harmless" jokes about Jews as profiteers or coupon clippers disappeared from such papers as the *Fliegende Blätter*. But by 1918 the traditional stereotypes had reemerged in full flower. Ruprecht was hardly working in a vacuum when he presented the *Stürmer* Jew, with his swollen body, long, hairy arms and hands, big ears, huge, hooked nose, bulging eyes, swollen lips, and short, crooked legs.

"Fips" did not confine himself entirely to anti-Semitism. He could sketch the "Slave Yoke" of the Dawes Plan, or present Mayor Hermann Luppe as "the pillar of republicanism in Bavaria"—the reality being a crumbling monument propped by radical newspapers.[17] But his most effective cartoon figure remained the Jew, whom he cast in a never-ending variety of roles.

The Jew could stand for the postwar system. In 1928 Fips faced charges of libeling the republic for an election poster featuring a fat Jew in a black-red-yellow striped bathing suit as a symbol for Weimar. The charges were dismissed. The Jew could be a parasite. "The Flea," crushed by a Jew, lamented the survival of the *real* bloodsucker. He could be a criminal. One sketch showed Jewish speculators comforting themselves at the arrest of one of their number with the thought that "nothing will happen . . . at worst (he) pays a few thousands' fine, and has made millions." Three Jewish patients in "Dr. Fips's Sanatorium" told each other that if the Nazi advance continued "our sort" would be receiving prison sentences instead of taking cures.[18]

Fips's Jews were always alien. "In the Summertime" showed a Jewish couple, conspicuous in department-store versions of Bavarian *tracht*, bewailing the fact that no matter how "native" they went, their Jewishness remained plain. This carom shot off countrymen's assumed dislike for tourists was matched by "Jewish Culture," juxtaposing youthful Aryans enjoying a day in the country with Jews leering at a performance of "Sweet Sin," the newest hit film directed by Ernst Ludwig Spittoon, text by Siegfried Flatfoot, and photography by Moritz Toiletpaper.[19]

Ruprecht could draw contrasts between Jew and German even more sharply. "For Whom the Sacrifice?" featured a one-legged Aryan veteran vainly holding out a beggar's hat to prosperous and ugly Jews. Another sketch presented a Jew too busy to reach into his pocket to give five pfennigs to a war cripple, but with ample energy to climb into his big car. Automobiles were a favorite Fips symbol. "In Little Things as in Big Ones" featured a Jewish-driven luxury auto splashing mud on a respectably-dressed Aryan, who was informed, "That's what happens when you don't get out of our way, goy." In a somewhat lighter tone, "Two Kinds of People" had motorized and scrawny Jews saying of Aryan hikers obviously glowing with health, "How many kilometers can they make afoot?"[20]

To anyone familiar with contemporary German driving habits, these particular drawings have a certain inverted humor. But they also are excellent illustrations of *Der Stürmer's* appeal to the German as underdog. Fips labored mightily to reinforce the dream of a day when Germans would take universal revenge for general wrongs. "The Struggle Continues," with its giant fist, broken fetters on the wrist, thrashing tiny, cringing Jews, must have struck many a responsive chord among *Der Stürmer's* readers.[21]

Ruprecht's cartoons will be presented in many contexts in this work; the above paragraphs merely serve to introduce his style and approach. But one more significant point deserves mention. Fips was a master at sketching sensuous female figures. Erotic, as opposed to merely pornographic, cartoons are not easy to draw. Ruprecht seemed able to produce them almost automatically. His scantily-draped maidens are often worth a second glance even in the era of *Penthouse* and *Hustler*. Sometimes they were gratuitously included—a chemise-clad chorine, legs and pubic area skillfully outlined, being ogled by two Jewish theater directors. More often they were drawn to make a point. A nude woman, her hands chained over her head, bare breasts highlighted, lies helpless before the attack of serpents crawling from a Talmud. Truth, bound to a cross by lawyers and judges, is a long-legged, full-breasted blonde wearing only a strip of cloth at her hips. Readers could shake their heads while smacking their lips.[22]

Any evaluation of Philip Ruprecht's talent must inevitably be subjective. But without denying the repulsive nature of his theme, a comparison of his work with the huge collection of anti-Semitic caricatures available in the *Stürmer-Archiv* in Nürnberg suggests a significant superiority over predecessors and contemporaries alike.[23] Fips introduced no new types, no new approaches. It was his genius in handling the conventional and the familiar that gave his cartoons their force and contributed significantly to *Der Stürmer's* audience appeal.

The names on the snakes include those of alleged Jewish sex criminals, and of the sex researcher Magnus Hirschfield.

Der Floh

Sch werd kaputt gemacht und der darf leben, der Jud, obwohl er von uns be
der größere Blutsauger ist

THE FLEA. "I'm finished off and he's allowed to live, the Jew, even though
he's the bigger leech of us two."

JEWISH CULTURE. "From nature to the unnatural."

In Little Things as in Big Ones. "That's what happens when you don't get out of our way, goy."

4

If Fips's cartoons were the highlight of the paper, they were nevertheless only one element of it. And when the satirists had "Herr Zieher" asking what could be done to make money today, they scored a definite point. Unlike many political sheets, *Der Stürmer* was Streicher's private property. When he signed the original publishing contract with printer Maximilian Hardel, the two men agreed to divide all profits evenly, but Streicher was the sole owner. Hardel only retained publishing rights.[24] Streicher's teacher's pension was hardly sufficient to support his family in penury, to say nothing of sustaining that taste for the good life mentioned earlier. His earlier experiences as an editor of *völkisch* papers had convinced him his cause and his bank account alike were best served if he could provide a readable work at the lowest possible price. And one sure way to do this was to cut corners in the editorial office.

After some initial experiments, Streicher settled on the "Berlin Format" as the best balance between cost and readability. By its second issue of 1924, *Der Stürmer* was printed in three-column octavo. Page one featured a headline introducing the lead article for the week. This increasingly appeared inside the paper, as a means of encouraging prospective readers to buy the sheet instead of reading the headline story from newsstand display copies. The first page also usually featured a cartoon, sometimes related to one of the articles, sometimes independent. The page was closed at the bottom by *Der Stürmer*'s motto, simultaneously famous and notorious: *Die Juden sind unser Unglück!*

The typography was amateurish. The titles and introductory phrases of the articles often bore little or no relationship to the contents. Short articles might be printed in two sizes of type, while longer ones were run in the same size—a fact likely to discourage Streicher's prospective audience from reading them. Italics and interlining were similarly designed to catch the eye rather than involve the intellect. But cheap printing kept costs down.[25]

A second major source of economy, particularly in *Der Stürmer*'s early years, was Streicher's insistence on keeping his overhead to a minimum. Apart from Nazi party bulletins, his primary sources of information were his readers. The material in Streicher's files indicates that few if any contributors expected much in the way of cash payment. They offered their material to air a grievance, or as a service to the movement. At most they asked for a few reprints or some free advertising. Occasionally a professional or semiprofessional journalist would contact Streicher—men like the publisher of the *Hakenkreuzler*, who in December, 1925, informed his colleague that his own paper had been banned and asked if he could write a bit for *Der Stürmer* to make extra money.[26] But Streicher had little need for paid contributors while he could count on zealots. Frequently their letters or essays would be printed with little or no alteration. A few italics, a title clipped to the sheet, headings and signatures cut off or crossed out, and *Der Stürmer* had another column.[27]

Anonymity was a common feature of *Der Stürmer*. Unless lead articles are signed, it is extremely difficult to distinguish individual styles among the paper's staff. Most of the important pieces seem to have been written by Streicher himself. Karl Holz's first article appeared in 1924; for the rest of the decade he was one of the major contributors. Fritz Hülf, a medical student at Erlangen, did some staff work before his graduation. By the 1930s, Ernst Hiemer and Franz Fink had been added to *Der Stürmer*'s list of writers. But none of them developed a distinctive approach, or even a specialization. Through admiration and intimidation, they followed the pattern established by Streicher—a task not particularly difficult for anyone with a bit of education and a little practice.[28]

Der Stürmer was not unique in this editorial pattern. Nineteenth-century dime novels, twentieth-century western and adventure series featuring the same central characters, hard-core pornography—all these genres have been produced by several writers working under a common pseudonym. When style and structure can be readily imitated, why confuse prospective readers with a long list of authors? However, in the context of the German newspaper profession, with its well-developed traditions of individuality, Streicher's approach seemed just one more proof of his determination to produce a paper so uniform in style, theme, and content that no reader could possibly be confused by the unusual.

Given *Der Stürmer's* well-established, well-deserved reputation for mendacity, it is necessary to note that Streicher was not completely indifferent to accurate reporting. It was his boast that he printed only the truth—and if this was a gross exaggeration, *Der Stürmer* at least preferred to have a defensible court case. Streicher's attitude is clearly illustrated by a letter of August 8, 1930, responding to an essay describing in revolting detail the repeated appearance of dead rats in beer kegs furnished to taverns by a named brewery. It was the kind of story tailor-made for headlines, a cartoon or two, and editorial attacks on Jewish pollution of the German national beverage. It would almost certainly have generated some strong public responses. Yet Streicher informed the author that unless he could provide witnesses, the paper could not use his well-composed report. Unsubstantiated allegations of this kind could only damage the cause of anti-Semitism, National Socialism, and the *völkisch* movement generally.[29]

If imitation is truly the sincerest form of flattery, then Julius Streicher was one of the most flattered editors in Germany. In town after town imitation *Stürmers* appeared—*Der Streiter* in Forchheim, *Sturmfahne* in Würzburg, *Die Kanone* in Nürnberg itself. Most of them were short-lived; *Die Kanone* got as far as four issues. They were also handicapped by their exclusive concentration on local affairs. The *Kampf*, for example, was marketed intensely in Bayreuth during 1931, and was apparently welcome in *völkisch* circles of that city. But outside of Bayreuth it seems to have attracted almost no readers. Other anti-Semitic scandal sheets started and stopped, merged and disappeared, with bewildering regularity. *Der Stürmer* went on and on—a journalistic phenomenon that baffled the Bavarian authorities, who considered the newspaper to be one of the major reasons for the growth both of National Socialism and of Streicher's power within the movement.

Part of the paper's success depended on marketing. From *Der Stürmer's* inception Streicher proved himself skilled at promoting his product. There was nothing unusual about the outlets Streicher found for the paper. Initially he depended on street vendors and small newsdealers. Some of these men and women were committeds adherents of the *völkisch* movement, like Paul

Klury of Eichstätt, who sold the paper from its earliest months of publication.[31] Others seem to have been victims of the hard times of the 1920s—people who were willing to sell anything to make a few additional cents. Periodically these individuals ran into difficulty with local authorities for peddling without a license, working after legal hours, and similar behavior patterns characteristic of men trying to make a living the hard way. In 1931, for example, a citizen of Leutershausen filed a complaint against Johann Schuh for selling an issue of *Der Stürmer* which had been banned by the Nürnberg police. Schuh informed the authorities that he had sold around sixty copies of the forbidden sheet without anyone informing him that he was doing anything illegal. He sold the paper, he declared, only as a means of keeping his six-person household off relief rolls. Schuh was not one of Leutershausen's foremost citizens; he had previous convictions for petty theft, begging, stealing wood, and similar minor offenses. But he was also seemingly considered a poor man driven to petty crime by hard times. At least neither the original complainant nor the gendarmerie pressed charges.[32]

Streicher encouraged his followers to avoid patronizing newsdealers who did not sell Nazi papers, and to urge barbers, restaurant owners, and tavernkeepers to subscribe to *Der Stürmer*. Sometimes their efforts went to extremes. As late as February, 1933, the proprietor of a *Gasthaus* complained that an overaggressive *Stürmer* salesman threatened him with violence if he did not allow him to sell Streicher's paper from table to table daily. Since the tavernkeeper was thirty-five years old and wore glasses, he appealed to the Nazi Party for assistance. But the real significance of the complaint was in its conclusion. The petitioner declared that he only refused permission because of previous contractual commitments. He was quite ready to have the salesman come by occasionally, and to show good will he was subscribing to both *Der Stürmer* and the *Völkischer Beobachter*, which would henceforth be available to his customers.[33]

Given the date of his complaint, this particular businessman might simply be described as able to read the handwriting on the wall. But when the Nazi movement was at its nadir, in 1927, the police of Bayreuth described *Der Stürmer* as being sold "in significant numbers" in taverns and on the street. Even the newsstand in the railroad station sold it under the counter. The firm owning the concession might call *Der Stürmer* a mixture of lies and pornogaphy, but their local representative was still willing to risk the loss of his franchise rather than alienate his steady customers.[34]

This seems to have been the central idea inspiring many of *Der Stürmer*'s vendors. Few of them carried large numbers of the paper relative to the total size of their stock. But a few dozen copies were often good business. *Der Stürmer*'s readership was consistent and enthusiastic. The kind of man who would write to Streicher declaring *Der Stürmer* was in a class by itself, a first-class literary chocolate bar, superior to the best novels, might mix his metaphors a bit, but also would not be likely to accept journalistic substitutes.[35] As early as 1925 a Berlin newsdealer operating six stands was offering to sell *Der Stürmer* on commission.[36] A cursory examination of the reports from various police stations on the confiscation of banned issues indicates the way *Der Stürmer* spread. Initially, virtually all of the reports came from towns in Bavaria or close to the border. By 1932, *Der Stürmer* was a problem for police as far afield as Hamburg, Wilhelms-haven, and Königsberg.[37]

Law as well as economics was on Streicher's side. In May, 1924, the *Bahndirektion Nürnberg* refused to allow the sale of *Der Stürmer* in the railway station. Three years later, after a series of appeals the *Deutsche Reichsbahn Gesellschaft* reversed the Nürnberg decision and allowed *Der Stürmer* to take its place with the other literature available to travelers.[38] The same year, three Nazis made a test case of being arrested for distributing free of charge back numbers of *Der Stürmer* in the Gunzenhausen cattle market. The charge, malicious mischief for peddling without a license, did not stand in court. The decision in favor of the defendants stated that they had offered no direct provocation to anyone, even the many Jews attending the market. Numerous witnesses agreed that the "Christians" to whom the paper was offered accepted it willingly. The Gunzenhausen *Amtsgericht* accepted *Der Stürmer*'s right to advertise itself by distributing free copies of the paper. The significance of this case is reflected in a memorandum of the Nürnberg-Fürth police. Written two months after the final decision, it recognized the many legal ac-

cusations proved against the sheet, but also informed the Rothenburg *Bezirksamt* that a precedent now existed allowing distribution of the paper for advertising purposes.[39]

This did not mean that salesmen could peddle their papers
for profit without police permission. Enforcing this regulation,
however, could pose more problems than it solved. Images of the
forces of law and order harrassing a street vendor were not calculated to increase police popularity, even among non-Nazis. The
National Socialists themselves grew increasingly expert at more
subtle forms of evading or mocking the law. In March, 1932, a
police report described a meeting at Rothenburg at which National Socialist literature was being sold without permission.
When the salesman was requested to cease and desist, Karl Holz
addressed the audience: "your famous police force forbids us to
sell literature. So come to the table, lay down ten pfennings, and
pick up your pamphlets. The table will be selling it, and they can
arrest the table!" The Rothenburg police conceded that Holz had
made them look ridiculous, particularly since the meeting ended
before the officers on the scene could decide what to do next.
When they decided to file charges, Holz's immunity as a member
of the Bavarian Landtag proved all the protection he needed. For
such a petty offense it was so unlikely that the Landtag would lift
his immunity that the police were dissuaded by higher authority
from pressing the matter.[40]

One final means of advertising *Der Stürmer* existed:
showcases. As the paper prospered, Streicher encouraged local
party groups to set up these displays, change issues weekly, and
protect them against vandals. The local Nazis were rewarded by
seeing their names in print as "Stürmer Guards." Since *Der
Stürmer* was the kind of paper which could easily be skimmed by
someone standing in front of such a case, its casual readership
probably increased to some extent. Streicher benefited from his
display cases in still another way. It was impossible to protect
them day and night. Periodically one would be damaged or
demolished, whether by political rivals or mischievous schoolboys. Each incident gave Streicher, directly or through his local
correspondents, and opportunity to take the high ground against
stealthy foes of free expression who could only be inspired by
Jewish money.[41]

Like the rest of the newspaper, *Der Stürmer*'s advertising was unusual. Normally advertising is a major economic basis of a paper, but *Der Stürmer* was likely to be attractive only to a specialized clientele. Not until the second issue of 1924 did *Der Stürmer* feature its first ads. The half-page of small and middle-sized notices established a pattern which was to remain virtually unchanged for a decade. Dr. Hanns Krafft, Streicher's lawyer, submitted a discreet advertisement. Conrad Raschbacher offered his services as a *Rechtsagent*, a kind of ombudsman specializing in complaints against the city and questions of rent and housing. More orthodox business included a clothing store, a watchmaker, a "shoe clinic," two or three taverns, a small factory specializing in baby carriages.[42]

Streicher deliberately kept the cost of a *Stürmer* ad low as a means of attracting the little men of Nürnberg's business community. Throughout the *Kampfzeit* the number of advertisers and the size of their ads tended to reflect a combination of Nürnberg's economic conditions and the status of the Nazi movement. The most faithful as well as the largest advertiser was the clothing store Josef Heinrich, which ran ads regularly from early 1924. Streicher also accepted inserts from lingerie shops, with accompanying Sears-Roebuck style drawings of models dressed, or undressed, in the firms' products.[43] In peak seasons, particularly around Christmas, a given issue could have as many as three pages of ads, mostly small and middle-sized notices. In slack times, or when the paper's notoriety might be greater than usual, the number of ads would sink until they filled only a single page. Party notices appeared occasionally. Such special events as the Nürnberg *Volksfest*, held in August and September, 1927, would run large advertisements in the implied hope of attracting swastikaed spectators.[44]

Potential advertisers were encouraged by periodic notices and circulars requesting *Der Stürmer*'s readers to read the paper's ads. A more elaborate scheme involved preparing a list of "German businessmen" in Nürnberg, then requesting all party comrades to save the receipts whenever they made a purchase at one of these firms. The receipts would be turned over to *Der Stürmer*, which would in turn show them to the firms concerned, thereby proving concretely that it paid to advertise.[45]

Der Stürmer offered a limited but useful forum for certain specialized goods. One SA man began producing a line of cheap cigarettes with such labels as "Alarm," "Storm," and "New Front," each package offering a free card picturing an eighteenth-century military uniform. While support for his product never became official in Streicher's *Gau*, *Der Stürmer* was ready enough to sell him advertising space.[46] For the Christmas season of 1929, readers could buy their children windup models of Hitler and his storm troopers.[47] Similarly the *Gasthaus Zum Stürmer* made periodic appeal for storm troopers' custom in 1924 and 1925.

Der Stürmer's advertising had its personal side. An increasing number of men and women sought jobs through the paper, frequently expressing a preference for *völkisch* employers, or describing themselves as rendered jobless through their party acitivity.[48] *Völkisch* choruses advertised for members.[49] An occasional notice requested "friendship," with full discretion guaranteed any replies.[50] One optimistic party comrade, needing a thousand marks to build up his shoe store, requested aid from fellow Nazis.[51] And pet lovers could take heart from an ad in *DS* 30, 1927, offering for sale one Angora kitten.[52]

However important direct advertising might have been, Streicher accepted other means of support as well. Nürnberg gossip periodically hinted of donations made by East Elbian Junkers, or by Bavarian or Silesian industrialists. No reliable proof of such support, however, has ever appeared. And given the limited extent of capitalist financial support for National Socialism before 1933, it seems safe to suggest that a millionaire secretly interested in aiding the *völkisch* movement, the Nazi Party, or the cause of anti-Semitism, could have found more congenial outlets for his money than Streicher's scandal sheet. If nothing else dissuaded him, the risks of exposure in one of the paper's numerous court appearances might well act as a deterrent. On the local scene, however, Streicher was apparently not above two forms of discreet blackmail. He or his associates would suggest politely to certain citizens that an advertisement or a generous contribution might help *Der Stürmer* overlook behavior which could prove embarrassing if brought before the public. Streicher also discovered that some people were willing to buy large numbers of an issue attacking them. As a result he boasted of making the paper even cruder and coarser, keeping it alive by embarrassing rich businessmen. These allegations are difficult to prove. Streicher was far too clever to put anything in writing, and the overall tone of the paper was so low at best that it is impossible for the modern researcher to unearth internal evidence of attacks made solely for economic reasons. The stories, however, remain alive in Nürnberg, and have a ring of plausibility.[53] What is certain is that *Der Stürmer* made money. What remains questionable is how much.

5

Der Stürmer sold cheaply. During the inflation of 1923 its price briefly climbed as high as a million and a half marks. When it resumed publication in 1924, however, *Der Stürmer* sold for twenty pfennigs and kept this price for its regular issues throughout the Weimar years. Subscribers could save a bit: by the month the paper cost at first eighty pfennigs, then ninety, then sank to eighty-four. The marginal difference between subscriptions and newsstand costs reflected the fact that Streicher expected to make most of his sales on the street. Perhaps too it might have reflected a certain reluctance on the part of even loyal Nazis to have such a paper delivered to their homes. One could easily purchase it at a newsstand, then conceal it in briefcase or pocket until it could be enjoyed in private, with limited risk of political or personal reprisals.

Given the limited number of subscriptions, circulation figures are difficult to determine. During his trial in 1945, Streicher's attorney did his best to minimize them, declaring that before 1933 the average circulation of *Der Stürmer* was only around six thousand. Only after the seizure of power, with the full and open support of Adolf Hitler, could Streicher count on six-figure sales.[54] This argument for limited circulation before the *Machtergreifung* has been generally accepted by historians, and even described as remarkable for a financially unsupported sheet which had to compete with other Nazi papers. But solid evidence indicates that production and circulation figures of *Der*

Stürmer were a good deal larger than commonly reported. The source of the material is an investigation of Streicher's finances made in December, 1927, by the Nürnberg police at the request of the prosecutors' office. Streicher was paying taxes only on his salary as a suspended teacher. Moreover, the amount of his income would be a major factor in determining the judgments to be assessed against him in fines and penalties. The police dug into their task with enthusiasm. Their final report stated that the number of *Stürmers* printed weekly varied between seventeen and twenty thousand, with the larger figure usually meaning some particularly juicy scandal. The number of subscribers was "very small." Most of the papers were distributed directly from the publishers' offices to newsstands, though Streicher had acquired one middleman who took three thousand copies weekly at twelve pfennigs, then resold them to retailers at a two-pfennig markup. The police declared that exact sale figures were impossible to determine. Those who were in a position to know were not particularly communicative. However, observation over a period of time suggested that approximately four thousand copies of each issue remained unsold.

Accepting an average sale of thirteen thousand copies weekly, *Der Stürmer's* income from sales would total 1,560 marks. To this must be added revenue from the ads. At twenty pfennigs per line, with a one-third rebate to steady customers, this averaged three hundred marks. This gave a total of 1,860 marks, while the police calculated *Der Stürmer's* expenses in marks as follows:

Wages for typesetters	40	
Paper costs	168	
Printing (for a run of 17,000 copies)	348	
Editor's salary	115	(prorated from 500 marks a month)
Publisher's salary	140	(prorated from 600 marks a month)

Delivery costs	46	(prorated from 200 marks a month)
Advertising manager's salary	35	(prorated from 140 marks a month)
Artists' salaries	50	
Postage costs	100	
	1042	marks in weekly expenses

Simple subtraction gave the paper an average profit of 818 marks weekly. This included honoraria to writers and subsidies to people who might sell the paper outside of Nürnberg. But neither of these expenses was very large, the police declared—particularly since they had deliberately set income figures low and calculated expenses at the maximum.

In addition to his income from the paper, Streicher received a hundred marks a month as an expense account from an un-named source, two hundred-fifty marks monthly as a suspended teacher and four hundred-fifty marks monthly as a Landtag deputy. Deduct ten percent of his Landtag salary as a required donation to the Nazi party, add fifteen marks for each Landtag committee meeting he attended, make similar minor adjust-ments, and Streicher could rely on an income of over four thou-sand marks monthly. In Nürnberg in the 1920s, this was more than adequate to support his flamboyant life style, and removed any justification for accepting pleas of poverty and reducing his fines.

The figures in various versions of the report show some minor inconsistencies. The overall image they convey is of a pros-perous small business, depending heavily on a combination of staff and reader loyalty—as indicated by the low salaries of the employees and the heavy dependence on unpaid contributions—with low-priced, high-volume turnover. The Nürnberg police, in short, provide strong statistical foundations for the description of the paper offered in this chapter.[55]

Der Stürmer 's documented profit potential was not a mat-ter of public knowledge, but rumor generally credited Streicher with profiting more than a good Nazi should from work supposed to aid the movement. The *völkisch* correspondent who declared that the swinish articles in *Der Stürmer* made him ill and told Streicher that he was nothing but a Jew who saw everything in terms of money may have been a bit extreme.[56] But the party itself was apparently concerned with Streicher's interest in personal gain. In 1925, responding to an increase in local papers claiming some connection with the National Socialist movement, party headquarters issued a circular on the subject to all gauleiters. This document proclaimed the *Völkischer Beobachter* as the official newspaper of the party, required reading for National Socialists. But it also mentioned *Der Stürmer* by name as a "recognized" party organ, and declared that others could achieve the same status by applying through the local gauleiter. Seven years later, Hitler listed those journals whose editors belonged to the party and were therefore entitled to use the movement's eagle-and-swastika insignia on their mastheads. *Der Stürmer* was thirteenth on the list. But the same circular declared that while the struggle for existence was an essential element of history in general and National Socialism in particular, it must be conducted honestly. Hitler therefore forbade any official to use his party post either to forbid or to encourage a particular paper.[57]

Like all other Nazi papers, *Der Stürmer* was periodically warned about the use of party names and symbols for advertising purposes. Ads were always welcome, but not when they included swastikas. Gauleiters were also cautioned against making party membership lists or subscribers' lists available to other businessmen, even if they paid for the privilege. National Socialism did not exist to provide customers for middle-class merchants.[58] On occasion Streicher's wrist was slapped directly. Thus in June, 1928, Hitler warned all Nazi editors against publishing essays or report which might incite to violence. His declaration of intent to assume power peacefully remained valid, and Streicher was reminded of it sixteen months later when *DS* 41, 1929, published an article in praise of paramilitary exercises. Almost immediately he received a letter stating that though the article itself was inoffensive, it gave a toehold to potential critics of National Socialism as militaristic. He was warned not to repeat his error—and by this time, Streicher listened to warnings from Hitler.[59]

These and similar difficulties were minor, however, compared to the conflict between *Der Stürmer* and *Die Flamme*. On the surface, *Die Flamme*, which began publishing in Bamberg in 1926, was merely another imitation *Stürmer*. Its style and format were alike unremarkable. But this paper was published by Gottfried Feder, another of Hitler's early comrades and at least a potential rival to Streicher's position as the party's chief anti-Semite. Feder not only proposed to sell the paper in Nürnberg; he announced his intention of transferring his publishing operations to that city as soon as possible. Feder seems to have been ambitious enough to dream of absorbing several of the other imitation *Stürmers*, then using his status in the party and his parliamentary immunity as a *Reichstag* deputy to imitate and outdo Streicher in a contest for control of the Nazi press in Franconia.[60]

The struggle began on an innocuous note on June 18, 1927, when Streicher sent a letter to *Die Flamme* criticizing its accepting advertising for a "well-known Jewish film," Serge Eisenstein's *Potemkin*. When a paper bearing party insignia propagandized for this "filthy film," then business had indeed conquered ideology. Should this happen again, Streicher declared, he planned to complain directly to party headquarters. Feder's answer was conciliatory. It stated that the *Völkischer Beobachter* itself had featured several half-page ads for *Ben Hur*, a film far more open in its portrayal of Jewish virtues than *Potemkin*. In the final analysis, however, *Die Flamme* recognized the validity of Streicher's position and agreed to deal appropriately with similar ads.[61]

For Streicher this was not enough. He continued protesting against what he considered Feder's infringement on his territory despite repeated warnings from Hitler that the task of the party press was to fight external enemies, not party comrades, and threatening with expulsion any editor whose paper contained attacks in any form on fellow Nazis. Streicher accused Feder of deceiving him by circulating *Die Flamme* clandestinely in Nürnberg, of abusing the party insignia, and of overcharging for lectures. More to the point, he used his carefully nurtured influence with wholesalers, newsdealers, and street vendors who handled *völkisch* literature to keep them from selling *Die Flamme* and any other literature produced by Feder.[62]

The political infighting is less important for present purposes than the complete victory of Streicher and *Der Stürmer* on the newsstands. Streicher not only succeeded in forcing Feder from Nürnberg; he drove him out of Franconia entirely. The *Fränkische Verlag*, Feder's publishing house, moved its operations to Darmstadt. Feder himself tried to publish *Die Flamme* in Berlin; then in 1932 sold the publishing house in Darmstadt outright. *Der Stürmer* still held the field in Franconia as the Nazis neared the levers of power.

II

Der Stürmer
AND THE JEW NEXT DOOR

A major challenge of political anti-Semitism involves over-coming the images of the "Jew next door"—the living, breathing acquaintance or associate whose simple existence appears to deny the validity of that negative stereotype, the "mythological Jew." Jonathan Sarna quotes Freud to the effect that delusions remaining intact in the face of reality probably do not spring from reality.[1] Yet a good part of every issue of *Der Stürmer* was devoted to establishing as a reality the fact that the "Jew next door" was merely a Jew as yet unexposed. During World War II the Nazi Propaganda Ministry produced an effective, if infamous, newsreel showing "typical" ghetto Jews, then showing the same men and women dressed and coiffed in current German styles. The purpose, to arouse anxieties by showing how difficult it could be for even a trained eye to spot a properly camouflaged Jew, was not original. Fifteen years earlier, *Der Stürmer* was running feature stories on how to discern such physical characteristics as small stature, flat feet, and a roll of fat at the neck, how to pick up the singsong cadences of German as spoken by a "racial" Jew, and how to train the olfactory nerves to discern the "sharp, sour-sweet odor" the Jew bore as an inescapable identifying mark![2]

Such physical characteristics were less important than Jewish behavior. The direct anti-Semitism of *Der Stürmer* is most often described in terms of undifferentiated pathology. Its themes are in fact simple—so simple that on first reading they appear like an endless written version of "Chopsticks": the same notes struck over and over in varying combinations with manic intensity. A closer examination, however, shows that Streicher's attacks on Jewish behavior can be presented in three categories. His first and favorite theme was the Jew as sex offender: seducer and rapist, exploiter of teenaged employees, and accoster of respectable women. His second concentration was on the Jew as businessman, which meant cheat, liar, and thief. Finally, Streicher delighted in presenting the Jew as bad neighbor, prevented by his very blood from behaving in a civilized, humane fashion. Each campaign will be discussed in a separate chapter.

4 | The Jew as Sex Offender

Among the most common impressions of *Der Stürmer* is that the paper specialized in sex stories involving Jewish men and German women. Most of them are considered either the products of Streicher's diseased imagination or, when some facts supported the allegations, are discounted by the explanation that every ethnic and religious community has its small share of undesirables.[1] Both generalizations are accurate. Nevertheless a systematic discussion of *Der Stürmer*'s assorted descriptions of the Jew as sex offender can provide insight into more than the workings of Streicher's mind. *Der Stürmer* reported, however unsystematically, the kinds of sexual anxieties that affected its readers—or which Streicher believed might influence them. This campaign against the Jew as sex criminal involved three distinguishable approaches. Jews could be featured in Streicher's pages as violators of the innocent, as perpetrators of bizarre sex crimes, and finally, as ritual murderers—an offense whose sexual overtones, at least in *Der Stürmer*'s pages, far outweighed any other possible violations of the Weimar criminal code.

1

Streicher's own views on the subject of Jews and sex require little elaboration. As early as March, 1924, a police report quoted him as declaring that a German woman engaging in sex relations with a Jew should have her head shaved; a German man crossing the sexual line should have his penis cut off. When the police forbade the Nazis to hold special meetings for women in order to explain in detail how "Jewish seducers" operate on the grounds that such meetings offended public morals, *Der Stürmer* performed this necessary task in print. Streicher made full use of the jargon of "race pollution," deploring in issue after issue the repeal of the medieval laws forbidding under pain of death or mutilation sexual relations between Christians and Jews. Adulteration of food was legally punishable, Streicher argued. Why should not a similar law protect German blood from adulteration by its unwelcome racial guests?[2]

Even a scandal sheet is helped if it can find some basis for its allegations. One useful technique involved stressing generalized Jewish sexuality. This point required little originality. In the popular culture and pornography of Germany, and central Europe generally, the Jew often played a sexual role similar to that assigned the black male in the United States. He was presented as combining oversized genitals, insatiable appetites, and an irresistible approach. One of the funnier manifestations of this stereotype came from the Coburg *Volksblatt*, a left-wing paper which in 1926 published a set of verses signed by "Bobby" and entitled "Love and Swastika." In them a Nazi, caricatured as a poverty-stricken, pseudo-aristocratic type, lost his girl friend to a Jew who "broke her maiden's heart"—and by obvious implication, her maidenhead—that same night. Where, Streicher asked in wrath, were the public prosecutors supposed to prevent the publication of such filth? More importantly, where were the German men who would whip the ass of "Bobby" of the Coburg *Volksblatt* until he lost his taste for poetry?[3] For *Der Stürmer*, the Fips cartoon, "Decide,"featuring a German girl considering two swains, one a blond and muscular Aryan, the other a *Stürmer* Jew, established the real dichotomy.[4] The challenge lay in exposing the Jew for what he was.

Jewish males in Streicher's world matured early and remained active at advanced ages. A nine-year-old schoolboy was described as having consummated the rape of an innocent working girl. A seventy-year-old man was fined for accosting a woman in public.[5] The objects of this lust were inevitably Gentile. Streicher described the reaction of a Jewish father to his daughter's seduction in a tourist village by another Jew: "Why one of our people? You could have taken a goy!" The statement, apparently made before a number of local witnesses, is at least plausible. It took a Streicher, however, to make paternal rage the expression of a universal plot. *Der Stürmer* periodically featured stories of rabbis who mourned their daughters as dead for even wishing to marry a Gentile, or accounts of rabbinic courts which argued Gentile women into divorcing their Jewish spouses after years of serving their lusts and bearing their bastards.[6]

The reluctance of the German Jewish community to assimilate through intermarriage is well-documented, as is the extreme hostility of the Orthodox Jews of eastern Europe to a process which historically required both religious conversion and severing any association with the Jewish community. In *Der Stürmer*'s columns, however, this indicated recognition of something the Germans seemed to have long forgotten: the need for maintaining purity of blood, whatever the personal costs might be.

A German girl who had sexual relations of any kind with a Jew was dead to her people, and the Jews well knew it. Once his purposes were accomplished, the Jew quickly revealed his true nature. Among *Der Stürmer*'s earliest exposés was an alleged excerpt from a Jewish doctor's correspondence to "an Aryan woman" who had served as the object of his vile lust. What did a man deserve who could tell a former lover that she could "kiss my ass, but only figuratively, since even this part of my body is too good for direct contact with you"? What was required to demonstrate to German women that Jews were different in essence from the race on which they preyed? Constant corroboration was provided by correspondents like the one who signed himself "Heimdal" after the herald of Norse mythology. This individual seemed to have little more to do with his time than prowl Nürnberg seeking sin. One spring day he ate at an expensive restaurant, "full of Jews," including two seated at his table as the crowd increased. First they talked business. Then one asked his friend in a "Yiddish" accent: "How's it coming with the blonde Margaret? Get her yet?" The reply was "Yeah, I took care of her yesterday." The two went on to discuss details. The girl refused to come to her lover's apartment for fear of scandal, so the affair

Der Talmudjünger

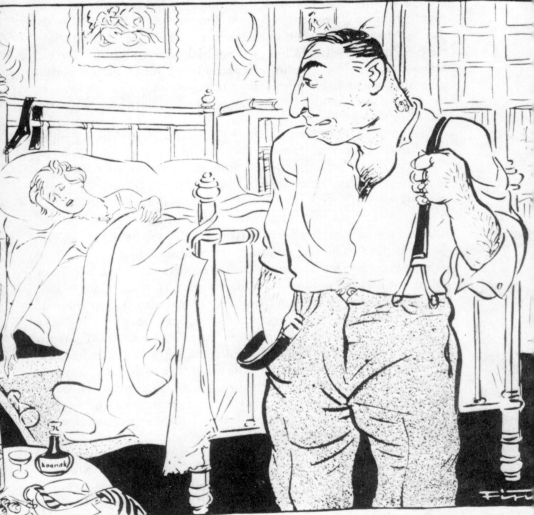

as dem Goi ein Tempel, ist unsereinem Bedürfnisanstal

The Talmudist. "The goy's temple is our toilet."

was consummated in a hotel. When taunted by his friend for going to so much trouble, the seducer replied that the girl could walk the streets to repay him.[7]

When his victim became pregnant, the Jewish seducer's normal technique was to begin by denying paternity, then to offer to pay for an abortion, then to haggle over every mark of child support. When all else failed, he could emigrate to the United States, like the Jew who impregnated two women almost simultaneously and left his home town one step ahead of the law. In the face of such evidence, Streicher asked, what idiot dared say Jews are human beings like us?[8]

Cynics or feminists might suggest that such incidents proved that Jews were in fact *exactly* like everyone else. To convince any doubters, Streicher proposed to show that the price for violating the law of blood could be even higher. *Der Stürmer*, for example, occasionally defended a woman who murdered her illegitimate child in a fit of desperation at bringing a Jewish bastard into the world.[9] After all, what recourse did she have? However, the facts in cases of alleged abortion or infanticide often differed so widely from *Der Stürmer*'s initial reports that even Streicher could not hope to pursue them effectively. The claim, for example, that a Regensburg girl died of an illegal abortion in August, 1927, provided a story or two as an opening ploy. But the Regensburg prosecutor's office promptly sent NSDAP headquarters a full report. None of the attending physicians witnessed any signs of an abortion or its aftermath; the cause of death was blood poisoning. While the prosecutor's office made no overt threats, it strongly implied that further pursuit of the matter would leave both the party and *Der Stürmer* open to a wide variety of legal measures.[10]

Abortion was the kind of criminal activity having too much evidence and too many legal documents to be good *Stürmer* material. Generalized warnings against the perils of taking a Jewish lover were considered more effective. A dramatic Fips cartoon showed a German girl leaving the office of "Doctor Cruel," tears in her eyes and syphillis sores on her face. The caption quoted the doctor, "What do you mean, too bad; nothing can be too bad for a *goya*."[11] In 1929 *Der Stürmer* ran a lengthy feature story about a "good old mother" whose daughter moved to Nürnberg, bore an illegitimate child to a Jew, then continued to associate with Jews. The old lady threatened to disinherit her. The daughter responded by having her mother declared incompetent. The distraught woman then turned to Streicher for assistance, declaring that she was seventy-four, had worked hard her whole life, and could not see what she had done wrong! Similar pathetic tales of women abandoned to raise illegitimate children, or women persecuted by Jewish husbands wanting a divorce, fit the format of a confession magazine as well as that of an anti-Semitic fighting newspaper.[12]

The stories could keep readers aroused in several ways. *Der Stürmer* never lacked information on intimate relationships between Gentiles and Jews. This could be two names on an undated slip of paper torn from a notebook, with the accompanying statement that the couple was "not engaged, but had carried on an open affair for years."[13] It could be an hysterical note written in 1924 by a committed Nazi zealot, beginning by describing the "ever more shameless" behavior of a Gentile woman with her Jewish lover, then sliding into an attack on the conspiracy of "Jews, Jesuits, and German Nationalists," and concluding with a prayer of longing for Hitler's release from Landsberg.[14] It could be a report from a farmer who saw a car driving into his woodlot, followed it, and observed events from the underbrush for an hour, until the lovers in the auto saw him. This rural peeping tom capped his behavior by taking the car's license number, discovering that it belonged to a Jew, and phoning his news item to *Der Stürmer*.[15]

Streicher's major problem lay in sorting the gossip and deciding which items made the best reading. Periodically he could threaten women who kept company with Jews. By providing the name of a town and a warning that if the guilty parties did not cease "acting like whores" they would find their names in *Der Stürmer*, Streicher could easily generate a shotgun effect.[16] He could feature stories of Jewish officials forced to resign their posts for seducing their colleagues' wives.[17] As *Der Stürmer's* printing techniques improved, he could branch into photo journalism, running a series of candid shots allegedly showing a German girl allowing herself to be picked up by a Jew in a specific Nürnberg street.[18]

All of these reports had a basic drawback as fear propaganda. They involved cooperation. Even a *Stürmer* reader who took them at face value could be comforted by reasoning that one could avoid such fates simply by avoiding Jews. The Jewish rapist, however, made no pretense of seeking acquiescence.

Rape cases were a *Stürmer* specialty. Sometimes the alleged victim was lame. Sometimes she was feebleminded. Sometimes she was underage—thirteen-year-olds were favorite targets. She might be the daughter of a German hero who died in the trenches and left his family unprotected. Or she might be the wife of a man forced out of a job by the depression, like the mother of three children who twice managed to fend off the advances of a rabbinic student.[19]

As a spinoff, Streicher frequently reported attempts at child molesting. When a teenaged girl entered a small-town dentist's office she hardly expected to find a Jewish patient who flattered her, "fondled" her, then invited her to a movie. This individual was sentenced to eight months as a first offender—perhaps he had only intended to take his mind off the coming session with forceps and drill. In another small town, a storekeeper with a reputation for being fond of young girls found himself facing charges when a thirteen-year-old told her father of his "funny behavior." The seven-month sentence given him by the court hardly satisfied *Der Stürmer*, which declared that in a Nazi state such a monster would never leave the hall of justice alive.

Perhaps the most graphic of these tales concerned a German woman who turned away an eighteen-year-old Jewish traveling salesman, then heard her daughter scream that the youth had "done bad things to her" with his hand. A medical examination confirmed that the child's genitals had been disturbed by force with a finger. Brought to trial, the accused defended himself with a combination of previous good character and a history of epilepsy in the family. The prosecutor did not press for a conviction, but left the verdict to the discretion of the court. As a result, the child molester was acquitted—and then offered his victim's family money not to talk to reporters![20]

In order to convince those still willing to believe that even such situations could be averted by never talking to strangers, Streicher required incidents that literally might happen to anyone—insinuations, passes, and outright attacks on all classes and backgrounds. Weimar Germany offered a major source of such incidents: the railroad. It was a place where observation and eavesdropping could be done easily and unobtrusively. In the station itself a man might be seen taking a woman not his wife to lunch in the restaurant. And if that man was a prominent Jewish lawyer, he might find himself in *Der Stürmer*'s pages, facing a situation where public denial would almost certainly deepen the scandal.[21] A person using the station toilet might see a man exposing himself and requesting two children "to do things which cannot be represented." Flashers of all heritages tend to favor such places. All that *Der Stürmer* needed was to wait for charges to be made against a Jew. And if he had a long record of similar offenses, so much the better.[22]

Once on board the train, the opportunities for sin, scandal, and misunderstanding increased geometrically. The process began with the construction of German railway coaches. Divided into compartments holding up to eight or ten people, more or less cut off from the outside world, they fostered interaction of all sorts in a way impossible in coaches or buses whose seats faced in the same direction. Given the variety of passengers riding any given train on any given day—tourists, traveling salesmen, commuters, and young girls visiting distant relatives—anything might happen. An outraged correspondent reported his experiences in the Ulm-Munich *D-Zug*. A jovial-looking "Jew" sitting next to a young girl began peeling a banana, commenting all the while on how easily the skin could be pulled back—just like the skin on something else resembling a banana. He continued by saying that when the train reached Munich they would go dining, then she would accompany him home to make the acquaintance of that banana. By this time, the letter-writer was so angry and embarrassed that he told the man to make himself scarce or get his face broken. The would-be seducer promptly sought another compartment.

Though there is no evidence beyond the letter-writer's opinion that the man involved was Jewish, the incident probably happened, and in roughly the way it was reported. The attempted pass was crude, but not implausible. The letter has none of the hysterical undertones common when Streicher's correspondents discussed sexual matters. It includes the name and address of the girl as proof of the rescuer's story. If it was a hoax or a fantasy, it is a reasonably convincing one.[23] A letter similar in tone, and this time published, told of a German girl who sat across from a "Jew" between stops, then left her compartment blushing. When the correspondent asked her what the "dirty Jew" wanted, the girl was too ashamed to say, only asking that he watch her luggage while she found another compartment. The correspondent ended his letter by asking what was happening. Was there a deliberate plot to corrupt German girls; was a white slave ring operating in south Germany; or was he simply a witness to an isolated event?[24]

Der Stürmer's answer was obvious: no Jew ever behaved innocently, even in public. When one of them paid a fine of fifty marks for kissing a girl in a train against her will, those Nürnberg papers which bothered to report the incident treated it as a joke —an expensive misunderstanding. Streicher instead asked why no one but *Der Stürmer* published the offender's name and race. When a Jew attempted to pick up a "blonde girl" only to find himself literally in the hands of her angry brother-in-law, he behaved in a reasonably typical fashion for one caught in such a situation. He tried to talk his way out of trouble to the extent of giving a false name. Taking the man to the police and attempting to press charges seemed like an overreaction even to the officers, who simply told him to go home. But Streicher made sure that his readers were made aware of the latest scandal.[25]

If being accosted in a train or approached in a theater could happen to any female *Stürmer* reader, and if rape was always presented as a possible outcome of these apparently innocent events, one major element of fear still remained missing. The theme of helplessness before powerful authority figures, treated as a major element of German film in Siegfried Kracauer's classic *From Caligiari to Hitler*, was and remains also a staple of German women's fiction.[26] Descendants of Faust's Gretchen, the eternal victim redeeming her betrayer by sheer nobility, can be found in magazines and *feullitons* from Bremerhaven to Berchtesgaden.

In the years before World War II, a favorite literary way of establishing this helplessness was to place the woman in a clearly subordinate position in the household: a governess or a servant. Images of the servant girl as a symbol of threatened virtue were reinforced by the social realities of the single-servant households increasingly common among Weimar bourgeoisie in reduced circumstances. The "maid of all work" was in constant contact with the household's males, without even the protection of servants' hall gossip.

In this context, the surprising element in *Der Stürmer*'s accounts of servant girls molested by Jewish employers is that they are so few and so innocuous relative to the paper's other scandals. Typical is the breathless report of a man of sixty-four who first offered his servant a five-mark raise, then tried to "attack" her. The seriousness of his intentions can be judged by the fact that his proposed victim resigned to protect her stomach rather than her virtue. Who could work, she asked, on a single piece of bread and half a knackwurst per day?[27]

When *Der Stürmer* did find something more in the master-servant relationship than pats and pinches, it made everything possible of the opportunity. A featured item from Salzburg involved a country girl new to life in the big city. She awoke one night to find her employer standing by her bed, whereupon he forced her "to do things with her hand which are described in the police records!"[28] Closer to home, a servant in a Jewish household in Ottensoos vanished in February, 1927. In mid-March, *Der Stürmer* began printing rumors that she had thrown herself into the river for shame. It described her working life in terms from a Dickens novel. For fifteen marks a month she spent day after day washing clothes over a freezing tub. Finally she caught cold herself, and as a result wet her bed. Her employers made her hang out the linen "to show what a sow she was." Shortly thereafter she disappeared. When her body was in fact found in the river, *Der Stürmer* wondered in print if she had been "disgraced" and made away with.[29]

Autopsy results showed the girl was still a virgin. After careful investigation, the police documented the case as simple suicide.[30] Such stories, however, almost certainly had some effect. How many girls kept their doors double-locked and walked in fear of their employers, ready to misinterpret even a normally friendly gesture? How many wept over the overtly fictional story of "Rosele," the beautiful farm girl who went to work for a Jewish family, then was raped by the son of the house. Her first thought was of home, but as she gazed through the window at the peaceful family scene, she knew she could never again be part of that community. Her frozen body was discovered the next morning—a warning to all young women attempting to help their families or support themselves by entering service in a Jewish household.[31]

A related theme of Jewish sexual exploitation featured in *Der Stürmer* involved the employer who took advantage of his working girls. This was a significant element in German popular literature since before the turn of the century, a story line acceptable to practicing Socialists, anti-urbanists, and romantics alike. *Der Stürmer* found most of this material in reports from offices, stores, and small factories in Nürnberg and surrounding communities—businesses small enough for employers and workers to have direct contact.

Objectively, apart from the ever-present possibility of mutual attraction, women attempting to keep "respectable" jobs in Weimar's fluctuating economic climate faced unenviable circumstances. Both business offices and retail firms were likely to cut costs by reducing wages, lengthening hours, and putting on more and more pressure to increase production or sales during the working day. In this environment some employers and supervisors took advantage of the situation. Some women were ready to go to any lengths to remain employed. Streicher could draw his stories from a steamy combination of office gossip, broken love affairs that ended in court, and letters from outraged parents or co-workers. Accusations against Jewish superiors ranged from attempting to get an employee to read passages from an erotic book, through letting employees run into debt and work it off in bed, to making prospective employees, especially in clothing stores, show themselves in chemises or less. Sometimes even clerical errors could be atoned for with sexual favors.[32]

The modern researcher has the same problem as the casual reader of a half-century earlier: just how seriously does one take the assorted accusations and allegations printed in *Der Stürmer*? In 1925, the paper published a lead article written like a bad novel. Its theme was the marriage of a peasant youth to a Nürn-

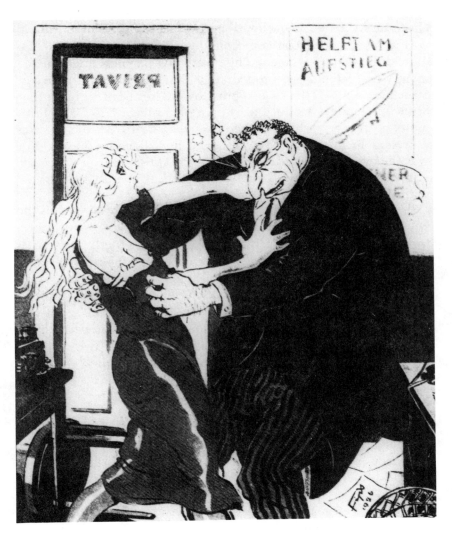

A typical Stürmer image of the Jew as employer.

berg girl forced by poverty to go to work as a bookkeeper, then forced by her Jewish employers to labor nights and Sundays as well. But this was only the beginning. As her salary rose from 80 to 140 marks monthly, her superiors simultaneously "awakened the animal in her" and "poisoned her soul," demanding unspecified sexual services in return for higher pay.

The story sounds at best like something repeated in a *Gasthaus* by an angry husband, and in fact the woman's husband was a Nazi and estranged from his wife. But Streicher also named the males involved. They were law partners and married men, who filed charges immediately. That particular article cost Streicher two months in jail, plus costs. The court declared that Streicher made no effort to support his allegations. The testimony of the purportedly ruined bookkeeper proved that she was very seldom in the office of either of her alleged seducers. Nor was she ever threatened with dismissal. Anti-Semitism was not a crime in Germany, the court declared, but it must be pursued within the limits of the law.[33]

At the other end of the reality spectrum in this area was the Nürnberg merchant with a legally proven weakness for secretaries and bookkeepers. His defense was that elderly men often make jokes and pinch young girls and that no one really expects such behavior to be taken seriously. When arguments were presented that the defendant's behavior had gone beyond a pinch or two, his attorney declared that the "old fool's" only guilt was that he could not resist the temptations offered by modern young women and their seductive fashions. The court was not impressed, and imposed a fourteen-month jail sentence. Yet even this man was able to collect four hundred marks damages because of the lurid and libelous nature of *Der Stürmer's* feature articles on the case.[34]

When accusations of sexual exploitation came to trial, the lines of argument were usually of the "you're another" variety. The accused, many of them married, all with positions to protect, did their best to damage the character or credibility of the women, and frequently succeeded—giving *Der Stürmer* an opportunity to attack high-priced Jewish lawyers. In the absence of clear evidence of direct force, when pregnancy was not involved, sentences tended to be minimal, in the neighborhood of six months, and then often commuted. But whether the situations involved seduction, mutual agreement, or submission under the threat of dismissal, *Der Stürmer*'s message was the same. Once again, it was Fips who put it in capsule form in two effective cartoons. One showed a Jewish boss telling an office worker: "Miss, you are discharged as of tomorrow, or if you wish to remain, you can discuss it in my apartment this evening." The other featured a dialogue: Jew: "Go on, you sheep, you don't know what you lose when you go." Salesgirl: "But I know what I'll preserve!"[35]

Another useful item for *Der Stürmer* was the sale of women into foreign brothels. In six months during 1926 alone, Streicher declared, 3,700 German women disappeared into whorehouses. The main focus of this white slave traffic, according to *Der Stürmer*, was Argentina. The brothels of Buenos Aires were run entirely by Jews, who even had their own synagogue with over four hundred members. The price of a blonde, blue-eyed girl was initially around 250 English pounds—a sum reduced as the merchandise grew more shopworn. For Jews it was a business like any other. Some of them traded in cattle, others in human beings. To a true Jew no essential difference existed between a cow and a Gentile woman. The beginning involved dinner dates in a handsome auto; the end meant leaning against a lamppost awaiting chance passers-by; and all of it was for the benefit of Jewish pimps.[36]

A Fips cartoon set *Der Stürmer*'s tone by having a Jewish revue director inform his eager chorines that if they did well for him in Germany, he could guarantee them first-class engagements in South America. Streicher wasted no opportunity to arouse suspicion of white slavers at work. An ad in a rural paper seeking two female farm workers for a "German-speaking" farmer in France seemed innocent enough on the surface. It could even be presented as a praiseworthy attempt to preserve *Kultur* in the temporarily lost provinces of Alsace-Lorraine. But as far as Streicher was concerned, "everyone" knew this ostensibly German farmer was a Jew, and therefore could want the girls for one purpose only—their ruin and eventual sale.[37]

The paper also featured numerous stories of girls who took candy from strange men in train compartments, then dozed off and awoke unharmed. Streicher suggested morphine; experience suggests motion fatigue. Similarly, a car stopped by the police containing two "senseless" narcotized girls might have had no more sinister overtones than a private cocaine party. But *Der Stürmer*, with its own impeccable logic, declared that Jews had to be involved, since "everyone" knew Jews were pimps, and pimps drugged their victims.[38]

Innocent maidens, however, could count on one defense. A correspondent reported that the blonde daughter of a friend was constantly being accosted by Jews—until she began wearing an iron cross around her neck. Streicher might have preferred a swastika, but any nationalist symbol would produce the effect of a magic charm as frightening to Jewish procurers as garlic to a vampire.[39]

Jewish homosexuality played a relatively minor role in *Der Stürmer*'s image of the Jew as sex criminal. A report on a Jew alleged to perform oral sodomy on young boys; an article on the suicide of a "pious Jew" who hanged himself when convicted of child molesting—these were minor items.[40] Arguably, homosexuality was an uncommon characteristic of Jewish males. Arguably too, homosexuals of any background, Jewish or Gentile, preferred to remain carefully closeted even in the relatively permissive atmosphere of Weimar Germany. The best *Der Stürmer* could do was attempt to connect such gay periodicals as *Neue Freundschaft* and such homosexuals as Magnus Hirschfeld with a Jewish conspiracy to destroy marriage and the family.[41] On only one occasion did Streicher find a vulnerable local target. In 1926 *Der Stürmer* ran one of its largest headlines ever: "The Homosexual Rabbi of Ansbach." Written in a sultry, lip-smacking style, the accompanying article described alleged assembly-line seductions of young blond Christians, the Jew "snorting like a hippopotamus" as he flung himself upon his victims. With these major exceptions, *Der Stürmer* preferred to present its Jews as heterosexual dangers to German virtue.[42]

2

Der Stürmer featured five major criminal cases combining Jews and sex. The first was routine. A man shot his pregnant lover, then beat her to death. The killer's trial gave the local Nazis an opportunity "to show the Jews who got rich during the inflation" what the *volk* thought of them. It also gave the town's deputy mayor an opportunity to make a speech declaring that this horrible crime showed the necessity for returning German youth to decency and morality by forcing them to go to church. Unfortunately for Streicher's purposes, the case was too plain to provide good propaganda. Less than nine months after his arrest, the "Gerolshofen Girl-Killer" was tried and executed. All *Der Stürmer* could do was rejoice that he had been unable to buy his way out of the death cell.[43]

The last two issues of *Der Stürmer* for 1925 featured a cartoon of a German girl fighting off a *Stürmer* Jew, accompanied by a lengthy article on Louis Schloss, who "looked more like an ape than a man," had obscene pictures on the walls of his apartment, and had apparently been conducting an affair with his housekeeper. One night she invited a girlfriend for a threesome. When the newcomer resisted, her clothes were torn off; she was beaten with a dog whip, then raped.

Schloss's prompt arrest resulted in a trial which kept Nürnberg buzzing throughout the spring of 1926. "Torture-Jew Schloss," as *Der Stürmer* dubbed him, was apparently a sadist who focused on bondage and discipline. His approach was to invite women to his apartment, "ply them with wine and liquor," then go to work. The prosecutor's office demanded a six-year penitentiary sentence. The defense attorneys argued that Schloss was deranged and belonged under a doctor's care rather than a warden's supervision. For *Der Stürmer*, this showed that Jews knew it was easier to get a dangerous criminal out of an asylum than a prison. Only a Jew, Streicher declared, could argue with a straight face in a German court of law that since prison would not improve a criminal, he should in effect be freed. The argument did not convince the court either, since Schloss received a four-year penitentiary sentence.[44]

Der Stürmer's reports on the Schloss case produced a flood of correspondence that even Streicher regarded as too extreme to publish. One letter, for example, gave a scholarly source for a punishment inflicted in Prague in 1530 on a Jew who had sexual relations with a Gentile woman. His penis was inserted in a cask filled with pitch, which was then ignited. A dull knife was placed beside the Jew and when the pain of having his genitals slowly roasted off grew too great, he castrated himself. Then he was torn to pieces by dogs.[45]

Of such fancies are mental patients and concentration camp guards made. More immediately, appealing to this kind of audience apparently sold papers. With Schloss sentenced and imprisoned, Streicher promptly sought a new sex crime. In the spring of 1926, he discovered a possibility when a respectable Nürnberg citizen, Alfred Guckenheimer, was accused of attacking his children's nursemaid. By *Der Stürmer*'s own account, the girl seems to have been more frightened than injured; initially the public prosecutor could find no grounds for pressing charges. In issue after issue, however, *Der Stürmer* asked why this "prominent Jew" was not facing a court of law. Public pressure increased to the point where the prosecutor did begin collecting evidence in the case.

The results of the trial were as unexpected to the police as they were gratifying to Streicher. Guckenheimer cut a poor figure compared to the girl. She impressed the court as a child of a large and poor family who had entered service with "high ideals," defended her honor as strongly as possible, and was able to produce both medical testimony that she was not hysterical and a large number of character witnesses. The result was a sentence of fourteen months for attempted rape.

This was not enough for Streicher. Almost as soon as the judgment was pronounced, he compared its brevity with the sentence imposed on Gentiles guilty of similar offenses. Is this justice? he asked. Are the courts truly blind? Or is Guckenheimer punished so mildly only because he is a Jew with influence? Compared with Schloss, Guckenheimer was a small fish—but only in terms of his offense. Guckenheimer was a respectable citizen of Nürnberg, as opposed to being a criminal who happened to be Jewish. This was the first really solid opportunity Streicher had had to make a specific case of criminal sexual behavior against a Nürnberg Jew who could reasonably be described as established.[46]

The limits of relying on familiar events to fan sexually based anti-Semitism were also indicated in 1926. Just before Easter, a scandal combining sex and religion in a way Streicher himself could not have better planned erupted in Nürnberg's *Spittlertorgraben*. Otto Mayer aparently specialized in bondage, paying women to come to his rooms and let themselves be tied in various fashions. He also seems to have been more or less obsessed with crosses. At least he built one in his apartment. When a streetwalker refused to let herself be bound on it, he did not insist. Nor was his behavior violent. The Nürnberg prosecutor's office, treating the case as routine, asked for a six-month sentence for procuring; Mayer received five months.

Der Stürmer printed repeated accounts of the "Criminal Den in the Spittlertorgraben." It asked why Mayer was not punished for his shameless misuse of the most sacred of Christian symbols. The sentence was described as an insult to healthy public opinion. Streicher even went so far as to charge the Nürnberg prosecutor's office with deliberate neglect of duty. Somehow, none of this material seemed to generate a public spark. Mayer's bohemian life style may have hindered Streicher's attempts to portray him as a "typical" Jew. What seems more likely is that reader interest in such cases could be sustained only by levels of scandal and salaciousness difficult to develop when the general course of events was public knowledge.[47]

Der Stürmer's last major sex case under the Republic came in 1932. A Gentile servant girl in the north German city of Paderborn was impregnated by the son of her Jewish employer, who bungled a do-it-yourself abortion, then tried to dispose of the corpse by dismembering it and feeding at least part of it to the hogs in which his father dealt. The time and circumstances seemed tailored for a *Stürmer* triumph. Instead the paper consistently slid into discussions of the case as a ritual murder as opposed to a sex crime. It was therefore just as consistently confiscated, and its responsible editor indicted and tried for offenses against religion. In a series of decisions in September and October, 1932, the *Amtsgericht Nürnberg* ruled that *Der Stürmer*'s description of ritual murder and its descriptions of the Jews as ruled by secret laws were punishable under the Weimar Penal Code.[48] The message was clear. Reporting even the most lurid sexual allegations as news could be tolerated. Suggesting that they were part of a religious conspiracy was a criminal act.

Nevertheless Streicher's insistence on the ritual, as opposed to the sexual aspects of the case was no accident. It involved instead the third element of his campaign against the Jew as sex offender: The Jew as ritual murderer.

3

The best-known number of *Der Stürmer* is probably the hideous ritual murder issue of 1934, with its front-page cartoon showing Jews catching in a basin blood from the severed jugulars of blonde women and children, and its accompanying articles written in a similar vein. What is surprising is how little original material that particular issue actually contained. Most of its substantive contents had been presented years earlier in *Der Stürmer*'s pages. Simple, overt accusations that Jews were required to perform human sacrifices as part of their religious ritual were, however, punishable even in the last days of the Weimar Republic, and Streicher had to behave correspondingly circumspectly.[49]

One way around the courts was to report as news items every actual or purported ritual murder trial staged anywhere in central Europe. A story from Poland involving the alleged ritual slaying of a teenaged girl by three Jews offered material for articles and cartoons which might skirt German law, but did not obviously violate it. And when Polish coroners declared that the "murdered" girl met her death falling from a wall, this only offered fresh opportunities to accuse the Jews of buying Polish justice.[50]

Another effective approach was to repeat, sometimes with embellishments, every allegation of ritual murder made against Jews in the Middle Ages. In Germany and Austria, some of these legends had generated local saints' cults combining popular piety with a minor tourist attraction. When other papers criticized the stories as fairy tales, *Der Stürmer* could count on receiving mail from angry rural citizens denouncing city slickers for mocking their faith; letters from tourists who said that they had read all about it in their guidebooks and therefore it had to be true; and offers from old-line anti-Semites to make available source

Bahn frei!

"Make way."

material on medieval Jewish blood rituals collected over years of study.[51] When local history failed, *Der Stürmer* ran attacks on the feast of Purim, which Streicher regarded as not the harmless, carnival-like holiday the contemporary German Jewish community celebrated, but rather a deliberate memorial to the mass murder of seventy-five thousand Aryan Persians.[52]

News stories, local history, and public celebrations with secret meanings were the surface manifestations of *Der Stürmer's* and Streicher's firm belief that ritual murder was an essential part of the Jewish racial and religious heritage. In issue after issue of the paper, in and out of court, Streicher argued that the "blood libel" camouflaged the actual existence of a blood cult. He used quotations from the Talmud, "interpreted" by expert witnesses. He suggested that readers of the Old Testament consult Isaiah 57:5, or count the number of references to sacrificial slaughter in any of the chapters. If this remained unconvincing, one could check the entry *Opferkult* in the *Realenzyclopedie für protestantische Theologie*, or listen to any Holy Week sermon in a "truly Christian" church. If nothing else, Streicher argued, the simple number of trials for ritual murder, the sheer bulk of pamphlets, books, and articles on the subject produced by lawyers and theologians over the years, suggested that there *must* be some fire beneath the smoke.[53]

The shortcomings of these arguments scarcely require consideration. They were, however, valuable as a framework and lead-in to local crimes of violence. Once more, given a normal percentage of criminals and perverts in the Weimar Republic, all that Streicher needed was patience. Some murders were bound to feature young victims with cut throats. Some suicides were bound to involve slashed wrists or severed jugular veins. As for the draining of blood, damp ground, or a body moved after a murder could account for the absence of clots and puddles well enough for *Der Stürmer's* purposes. One of the first uses of "Ritual Murder" as an article heading with a German content came in the summer of 1926 and referred to an incident in Breslau. Two children had been found dead, their blood drained, in what Streicher described as the "classic pattern" of ritual murder. Four months later *Der Stürmer* ran another article with the same title, this time describing the discovery of a

Bavarian village child with a slit throat, but carefully avoiding the issue of whether he had also been bled.[54]

Streicher's first big opportunity to test the issue of ritual murder close to home came in 1928, when the corpse of a twenty-year-old student was found outside the town of Gladbeck. He had been castrated and his throat cut by what the police described as a "professional stroke." *Der Stürmer* made great play with the alleged information that the youth had been killed and "bled" in a room in town, then dressed and dumped in a ditch. Such strange incidents, Streicher declared, accounted for the disappearance of many women and girls, as well as young men.[55] When in the same year, two young women taking a cure in the Black Forest were found stripped and robbed, their throats cut, the local police, under pressure to take some kind of action quickly, followed the time-honored practice of arresting a "foreigner" whose papers "were not in order." Since there was no other evidence against him, the district court in Freiburg ordered his release. But *Der Stürmer* argued that the alien was Jewish, and his quick exoneration was only part of a conspiracy to prevent a full investigation of the possibility of some sort of ritual murder.[56]

Nineteen twenty-nine offered an even juicier case when a small boy was discovered dead on the island of Manau. The police described it as a sex crime, but could discover no clues to the perpetrator's identity. According to *Der Stürmer*, however, the villagers were declaring that it was "too close to Easter" for the official explanation to be correct—especially since the corpse showed several attempts had been made to open the veins, and the throat had been cut by an expert. For Streicher, "the voice of the people [was] the voice of God." He and his followers discussed the question throughout Franconia.

Der Stürmer had an advantage in its ostensible news reporting: murders of this kind can be notoriously difficult to solve as quickly as public opinion demands. When the judge investigating the Manau murder suggested that the fatal wound was not a slash, but looked like something made when the child fell on a pointed stump, or was perhaps attacked by a roebuck, he opened himself to Streicher's ridicule in full force. *Der Stürmer* quoted a forester who declared that the roebuck never attacked human beings, and that its horns were too soft to tear even a child so badly. How, Streicher asked, could even a Weimar judge confuse so harmless an animal with a wolf—or perhaps a Jew?

The Bavarian Rabbinic Conference produced an open letter denouncing the blood libel. They sought support from other political parties, from the Bavarian Ministry of Justice, from the Landtag. Some of Streicher's critics held counter-meetings, only to learn that that particular game could not be played by novices. In Würzburg, for example, a Protestant pastor, a Catholic theologian, and a Jew were the featured speakers at a meeting also attended by a Nazi delegation. Shouts of "if Luther were here he'd throw you out," and "Go to the rabbi and let him pay you your blood money" led to a disturbance great enough to force the police to close the meeting. The Nazis, having made their point, walked out.[57]

These tales—of ritual murders, of missing persons and slit throats, suspicious foreigners and loitering strangers with "Jewish" faces—seem at best the kind of sensationalism that could hardly influence anyone with an intelligence level above low-normal. Particularly in the countryside, however, they produced a fair number of anxiety reactions. Even before the campaign reached its peak, one village girl told her father that a Jewish butcher proposed to show her his big refrigerator in the cellar. As she prepared to descend the steps she saw him pick up a huge knife. He explained that it was only to cut meat. She became frightened and ran to her father. He in turn complained to the police that the Jew had planned to ritually slaughter his daughter!. The angry butcher immediately filed suit—understandably enough, since any dishonorable intentions embodied in his offer probably involved sex rather than murder.[58] The threat, however, remained before the public eye, as the Nazi vote continued to increase.

5 | The Jew as Businessman

For Julius Streicher the Jew's hatred for Christianity was concealed only for one reason: business. On one level, money was the Jew's god. To secure it he would become a usurer, a traitor, a murderer—even a wholesaler of candies marked with the swastika. On another level, however, Jewish economic activity was a means to an end. The Jew gained power by first pretending to tolerance and brotherhood, then trapping Christians in a web of compound interest, notes of hand, and similar unnatural pieces of paper. He used that power to challenge and destroy the true wealth of a nation: the productive capacities of its people. Indeed, *Der Stürmer* argued, Jewish competition had so successfully ruined even the greatest German captains of industry that the workers had no one left to fight. The time had come to shed Marxist illusions and focus on the real enemy. Any German engaged in business dealings with a Jew must remember that the Jew's forefathers had given him a heritage of two books: the Talmud, that he might follow its commands, and the penal code, that he might evade its contents.[1]

1

This approach faced a major challenge: explaining away the philanthropic Jewish merchant. For *Der Stürmer*, an epitome of this Jewish type was the Fürth meat dealer and canner August Bauernfreund. Bauernfreund, according to Streicher, was the kind of Jew who always knew the right people. He expanded his business during the war, adopted modern advertising techniques, and now honest German butchers and farmers stood by with clenched fists and tears in their eyes as customers flocked into Bauernfreund's to buy American-made steam lard labeled "genuine German pork fat." His offenses ranged from keeping two sets of books to allowing vegetables to be prepared for canning under unsanitary conditions. "Bauernfreund's Beans," Streicher declared, were prepared in rooms ridden with lice, roaches, and infant excrement, at three pfennigs per pound. Eat and enjoy yourselves, customers—just don't allow yourselves to think during the meal.[2]

In the depression summer of 1931, Bauernfreund opened a soup kitchen. The menu was not particularly elaborate: it featured soups made from assorted meat remnants. But in July, 1931, *Der Stürmer* ran a sensational article accusing Bauernfreund of deliberately poisoning even the meager food he served to Fürth's poor. Over thirty people had suffered saltpeter poisoning from eating the sausage soup which had given this Jew such a reputation for charity. Streicher also accused the mayor of Fürth and several other officials of deliberately conspiring from political motives to conceal the facts. When *Der Stürmer* published a poem satirizing Bauernfreund and his alleged cronies in the city government, police response was prompt. The paper was banned for two weeks—not because of its attack on Bauernfreund, but because of elements in the poem described as a deliberate attempt to undermine confidence in government. This was forbidden by the law of March 28, 1931; *Der Stürmer* was therefore ordered to suspend publication.[3]

The facts supporting Streicher's charges involved a report on July 15 by the Fürth ambulance service of several cases of food poisoning. The only common source had been Bauernfreund's soup kitchen. Investigation revealed no soup on the premises. The kettle from which it had been served had been cleaned and was being used for other purposes. The next day Bauernfreund said that the "soup" at issue was not sausage soup, as alleged, which would have made saltpeter poisoning a likely possibility, but broth made from boiled cattle heads. To date he had received no complaints, but he agreed that it might be wiser to stop distributing the broth during the heat of summer. It was not, Bauernfreund declared, always properly kept by the recipients; bacteria could easily breed in July heat. That same day, however, the Fürth city council received a report that in no case had bacteria been a factor in the poisoning. On July 25, the final medical report was presented: the patients of July 15 were indeed victims of saltpeter poisoning.[4]

This was more than enough to encourage Streicher to appeal his paper's suspension. Bauernfreund *did* serve the soup. A child *was* diagnosed as suffering from saltpeter poisoning. Over thirty people of all ages and sexes displayed similar symptoms. All of them had eaten the broth in question. Besides, "anyone" who knew anything about meat or chemistry was aware that saltpeter was often used to remove the smell from rotten meat. Its use was forbidden in butcheries. How, therefore, could anyone suffer saltpeter poisoning if Bauernfreund was running a strictly legal operation? The poem for which *Der Stürmer* had been banned was a satire, a general description of the differences between Jews and non-Jews in these hard times. And was the versifier so wrong? On one side thirty people came close to death. On the other, the officials of the Weimar system ignored it. Not only were Jews ubiquitous; they got special treatment.[5]

The police commissioner stood by his decision and forwarded the complaint to the Bavarian Ministry of the Interior. This agency too saw no reason to lift the ban, but passed the issue to Berlin. The *Reichsgericht* at Leipzig considered the case and rendered its decision on August 27. Streicher's appeal was rejected. It was true, the court declared, that eating Bauernfreund's soup had put people in the hospital. It was true that the poem was a satire. But the author also attacked police and legal officials for shielding a guilty man for political reasons—one of the worst charges possible against an official, who was expected to be above party considerations. The court ruled that even if the poet's main intention was to attack the place of Jews in German life, he could not plead ignorance of the implications of his attacks on Fürth's *Beamtentum*. The decision was a good illustration of Weimar's legal positivism in action. Satirizing Jews was not illegal, nor was questioning their place and influence in Germany. Criticizing officials, however, was covered by an appropriate paragraph, and justified suspending the offending newspaper for two weeks.[6]

Unfortunately for Streicher, Beauernfreunds were few and far between. Attacks on Jewish sexuality might depend heavily on unprovable innuendo. But simple customer service was difficult to deny convincingly. A workman who bought a winter coat for thirty-nine marks, then saw the same store advertise it for twenty-nine marks a few days later, filed a complaint. The manager of the store said the ad was an error, but refunded ten marks. To anyone but a Nazi, the store's behavior was a response to a customer willing to make waves in a competitive environment. To *Der Stürmer*, the refund proved that the ad was not an error, that the Jew was a conscienceless liar, caught for once in the act.[7]

Acts of public service forced *Der Stürmer* into even more transparent casuistry. When a Social Democratic newspaper praised a small-town capitalist's good will, this suggests that his generosity and his attitude alike made a generally favorable impression. All Streicher could do was to argue that the man's gifts were nothing but a subtle form of advertising. When some of Nürnberg's department stores offered five-mark gift certificates to poor families during the Christmas season of 1928, this was dismissed as a trick to draw stupid Germans into their stores. A lottery in 1929 was a similar fraud; the winners had to take their certificates to Jewish-owned department stores. Simple charity got the same treatment. When the League of German War Invalids, Widows, and Orphans staged a Christmas party in 1928, a Jewish-owned firm donated money for cake and coffee. Streicher juxtaposed his report of the incident with descriptions of the "Talmudic" command to be charitable in public in order to improve the public image of Jewry.[8]

As depression bit deeper into Franconia's economic structure, Streicher's arguments became even more imaginative. When a paint firm in Würzburg gave the city several hundred certificates, each good for a few cans of paint, *Der Stürmer* asked why no one who praised the Jews' charity could evaluate a simple fact. The small amount of paint offered was useless by itself. In order to do anything with it, the unwary recipients would have to buy more paint from the firm which made the original

gift! This philosophy, prefiguring Robert Heinlein in its insistence that there was no such thing as a free paint job, was a bit
more difficult to apply when during the hard winter of 1931, a
Coburg firm announced its intention to donate part of the proceeds of its December sales to Winter Relief. When a Jewish
clothing firm offered to sell the Nürnberg *Elternvereinigungen*
children's clothing at a discount for donation to needy children,
Streicher could do no more than grumble that Nürnberg had
enough German businessmen to meet her needs. And when the
Schocken chain of department stores offered to donate three hundred thousand marks for emergency relief, only the most fanatical Nazis suggested the money be rejected.[9]

Probably no element of *Der Stürmer*'s anti-Semitic propaganda campaign drew more consistent reader criticism than its
attacks on Jewish philanthropy. The argument that it was a Talmudic trick to increase business or camouflage conspiracy was
unconvincing even to hard-core adherents of the *völkisch* movement. In 1924, one writer declared that he was the last man in
Germany to say a good word for Jews; most of them were bastards. But the target of one of Streicher's recent attacks was a
true exception. This man helped everyone regardless of religion;
even donating to the Student Relief Fund despite the fact that
most of the recipients of his charity were known anti-Semites. He
was a good employer who paid well. Truth, the correspondent
concluded, was after all truth. The letter remained unpublished.
So did another written seven years later by a Buxtehude businessman who asked how Streicher could run an article on the swindle
of artificially reduced prices by Jewish firms, yet simultaneously
feature ads from a Gentile-owned clothing store announcing
rebates as high as 50 percent. I am a good Nazi, the writer
declared, but a swindle is a swindle whatever the ancestry of the
confidence man. He concluded by advising Streicher to check the
content of his ads more thoroughly in future.[10]

These letters reflect two characteristics of German popular
anti-Semitism often mentioned by contemporaries and historians
alike. First, even hard-core Nazis often had their "decent"
Jew—the one they had known for years, who simply could not be
fitted into certain aspects of an ideological model. Second, many
Germans seem to have assumed that the worst things done to or

alleged against Jews were the products of error, misunderstanding, or some kind of anonymous bureaucratic process.[11] By 1931, Streicher's reputation as National Socialism's leading anti-Semite was firmly established, yet the writer of the second letter mentioned above seemed perfectly sincere in his belief that *Der Stürmer*'s editor had merely failed to check the nature of his advertising correctly, or at worst had let a desire for profit temporarily blind him to the demands of *völkisch* integrity.

2

Stripping away the Jew's philanthropic mask enabled the exposure of his true approach to business relations. Fips's cartoon "Überfahrt," featuring a Jew declaring that he had gone bankrupt in Germany and was now joining his money overseas, symbolized a theme repeated in article after article: the Jewish businessman who exploited his German victims without mercy. *Der Stürmer*'s generalized descriptions of Jewish control of the press or the film industry tend to be sterile. Jewish "smokestack barons," like "Goldschmidt of the Darmstadt Bank" with his "hundred directorships," were simply too remote from the average *Stürmer* reader to arouse indignation.[12] Streicher and his staff were far more effective in describing the fate of small investors ruined by smooth-tongued speculators. *Der Stürmer*'s account of two poor sisters, basketmakers, bilked of their pitiful savings by a Jewish wholesaler, was calculated to strike chords in the breasts of every pieceworker in Franconia. Small businessmen who went into debt to expand found their accounts taken over by merciless Jews who sent their creditors into the street or threatened them with arrest for debts of a few marks. Accepting goods on consignment was also a serious risk, as proved by the fate of a woman who accepted a contract selling linen goods on the promise of a 25 percent commission. She found, like many of her sisters before and since, that the only profit in this kind of business goes to the wholesalers. When she broke the contract, her employers took her to court. Her four-month jail sentence was only overturned on appeal.[13]

Contracts were no protection. In 1924 *Der Stürmer* described the fate of an Aryan businessman who bought shirts wholesale from a Jew only to have them fall apart at the first washing. The German's irate customers forced him into bankruptcy. The Jew sat back and counted his profits. A cattle dealer ran up a bill of 114.89 marks for a rented car, refused to pay, and then said it was no use trying to impound his property since he owned nothing in his own name.[14]

Business dealings with a Jew could be fatal. In 1928, Nürnberg's newspapers reported the suicide of a furniture-maker, his wife, and their child. *Der Stürmer* described the tragedy as a result of business failure through practicing the old-fashioned virtues. In its pages the victim was presented as descending from an old Nürnberg family, a good craftsman but a poor speculator who fell into debt during the great inflation of the early 1920s. His capital exhausted, he borrowed from a Jew. When he tried to pay his dept by delivering furniture, the Jew declared that the prices set were too high. Work which cost twelve hundred marks to produce was arbitrarily valued at seven hundred. As the craftsman's debts deepened, his creditor began impounding his private property. After writing one last letter pleading for mercy, the desperate Aryan finally sought in death the peace denied him in life by Jews and a Jewish-dominated system.[15]

Streicher further appealed to the economic fears of the little man with an increasing number of descriptions of failed banks whose Jewish owners, managers, and depositors somehow always seemed to escape the consequences of collapse. The legalisms of bankruptcy offered other ways of deceiveing hard-working Gentiles. The employer who paid only a small percentage of due wages, the creditor allowed to discharge debts at ten percent, might be within his rights. But to men and women of limited means Streicher was not completely unreasonable when he described the process as legal robbery. Not everyone was able or willing to imitate the debtor who told such a cheat to pay in full or find himself in traction. If he got his money, dozens of others did not, and could relate to Streicher's accusation that a Jew who filed for bankruptcy neither made restitution to the best of his ability nor exerted every effort to repay his creditors. The *goyim* could content themselves with empty regrets. The Jew accepted the maximum living allowance any court was willing to grant. One hundred fifty marks weekly might seem a small sum to one of these speculators. To a clerk on the dole, it was wealth beyond counting. Fips's cartoon contrast of fat Jews dining on lobster with German workers spooning thin soup at a factory gate was not merely an appeal to wage earners.[16] Given the increasingly shaky economic conditions in predepression Germany, combined with the growing anxiety over jobs and businesses among the lower middle class, such material was well calculated to deepen the fears of anyone who owed money or had debts to collect.

Jewish exploitation could also be indirect. *Der Stürmer*'s overlapping campaigns against Jewish methods of luring customers amounted to a traditionalist critique of twentieth-century marketing methods. When a fast-talking wholesaler attempted to charm an employee into showing his goods to her boss, even offering her a job and asking if she had a boyfriend, this might be dismissed as a common salesman's ploy—to anyone but Streicher and the indignant woman who reported the incident complete with the name and address of the overly aggressive salesman. When a textile dealer hired a pilot to cover the countryside with handbills, the novelty of this paper bombardment may have improved his business, but also resulted in a *Stürmer* attack on pollution of Bavaria's environment. When a hosiery firm in Siegen held a "leg parade," displaying their wares on the winners of a "lovely legs contest," *Der Stürmer* took time out from condemning short skirts to notice that no *Jewish* women appeared among the contest participants.[17]

The Christmas season provided a focus for *Der Stürmer*'s attacks on Jewish business practices. A favorite opening was a quotation, sometimes presented anonymously and sometimes attributed to one Rabbi Wise in the *Kasseler Sonntagsblatt*. Its content, however, never varied: "It is better to have Christmas than smallpox. Besides, it's lucky the Crucified One came to give the Jews their biggest money-making season. If only Mary had had two sons, one born in the summertime, to give us two such profitable holidays!"[18] A striking Fips cartoon featured "The German Christmas Angel" bound in a safe by a Jewish businessman and given over to a rabbi for flogging. Another juxtaposed an Aryan Santa, complete with swastika pin, and a Jew wearing a Santa mask. The caption asserted that two thousand years ago, Jews murdered Christ on Golgotha. Now they made his birthday a source of profits.[19] No true Christian, Streicher declared, should buy Christmas gifts from Jewish shops. Aryan businessmen were modest in their seasonal advertising, using natural and traditional symbols like fir branches and candles. Jewish firms, on the other hand, featured huge trees and electrically lit Stars of Bethlehem to lure customers into their webs. What they really thought of it all was reflected in one firm's suggestion to "give practical Christmas gifts." In the economic context of 1927 Nürnberg, this was sound advice for any consumer. For Streicher, it was a subtle mocking of the unthinking generosity which characterized German Christians at this most sacred season of the year.[20]

A final *Stürmer* indictment of Jewish business practices involved the sale of foreign merchandise. Anyone needing proof that Jews had no sense of national identity only needed to walk through a Jewish-owned store. A candy and perfume company not only advertised French goods; it hired a French employee— and this in the depths of the depression. *Der Stürmer*'s readers were also enjoined to avoid barber shops which recommended French toiletries and cosmetics. And what needed to be said about the allegedly "German" department stores which sold watches and pencils clearly marked "Made in Russia"? Streicher only remained uncertain whether to concentrate his criticism on German consumers too indifferent to read the fine print, or to ask rhetorically how even a Jew dared to sell alien pencils when workers in Nürnberg, the center of Germany's pencil industry, were unemployed.[21]

The image of the Jew as a dishonest businessman was kept alive by dozens of reports, letters, and complaints from all over Germany. Some of the material was psychopathetic, like the rambling claim of a man that a particular Jewish businessman cheated him, violated legal closing hours, and then bought off witnesses. The NSDAP refused to listen to his grievances, the writer declared, but he was a good nationalist whose nerves had been destroyed during the war. That point at least is supported by the tone of the letter. Similarly, it is difficult to see how the Jewish owner of a toilet-paper factory, even if it was the largest industry in a small town, was able to cut electricity to the radio station whenever "a good German piece" was being presented.[22]

Other letters inspire more sympathy. A correspondent forwarded a three-page description of conditions among independent Munich shoemakers. The letter, written by a man who did not want his name made public, was desperate in tone. Cheap foreign shoes sold by the wagonload were driving Germans out of business. No one cared for the men, whether in the trenches or in the workshops—even Cardinal Faulhaber was sympathetic to the Jewish wholesalers. Streicher's correspondent offered to circulate the letter if *Der Stürmer* would only print it in pamphlet form. This man claimed to have five children and no income. His sincerity and his naiveté alike are indicated by his request that *Der Stürmer* send him the leaflets at reduced price, or gratis.[23] Streicher was never in the free-sample business.

Buying from a Jew might be dangerous, but working for one was slow torture. In the world of *Der Stürmer*, no one but Jews paid low wages or employed strikebreakers. No one but Jewish employers hired seasonal workers at slave wages. When Streicher sought concrete examples, *Der Stürmer* was never without descriptions of Jewish directors and foremen who behaved like prison wardens. One such man, apparently an advocate of Taylorism, was described as removing all the clocks to prevent clock watching, and cutting holes in toilet doors to discourage loitering. Another company forbade its workers to smoke or speak on the job. If anything went wrong, the best the women could expect was to be called "geese," "animals," or "hysterical broads." A third firm, one of its employees declared, paid its women workers so little that they were forced to moonlight as prostitutes. A protest delegation was received by the Jewish manager with the suggestion that they sit down promptly. Otherwise, he declared, they might drop dead and he'd have to call a hearse.[24]

Obtaining even such degrading positions could prove a challenge. When a firm advertised for seamstresses, the women who appeared at 8:00 A.M. on the announced day were informed all the positions had been taken. In the economic context of late 1929 this could hardly be described as "trick advertising"; enough Nürnberg women were unemployed to provide plenty of surplus candidates for any job. But *Der Stürmer*'s report was well-calculated to focus diffuse fear and hostility on Jewish employers and their empty words.[25]

Jewish exploiters could hound their victims to the grave. A "pretty blonde," asked to work on All Saints' Day by a Jewish shipping firm in Kitzingen, refused. Her employer gave her two months' notice; then she disappeared. Her gloves and a note were found on the riverbank; her corpse was recovered from the Main. Whether having to work on a Catholic holy day is a motive for suicide is highly unlikely. The incident, however, offered an excuse to attack Jews for their contempt of Christian feasts and their general lack of human feeling.[26] And the office worker who felt above the battle might take note of the Jew who made his two clerks empty his privy in broad daylight, then pour the buckets on his garden. The story was perfectly designed to appeal to the status anxieties of Germany's little men in soiled white collars.[27]

Much of Streicher's information on working conditions came from employees. Some of Franconia's enthusiastic National Socialists were equally enthusiastic purveyors of office gossip. One series of letters, written in the spring of 1924, described the fate of a woman who worked long years for a Jewish boss, yet regarded it as "the highest good" to hear the truth from the lips of Julius Streicher. Then, after a quarter-century's loyal service, she was kicked onto the street. The case interested Streicher enough to lead him to phone for details—not his usual practice. If he was hoping for a story of a faithful German nationalist dismissed for political reasons, he was disappointed. What he got was an account of a quarrel between a senior employee and the office manager. When the debate grew acrimonious enough for the manager to say that the two could no longer work together, the woman left without a reference after twenty-seven years of loyal service, with the "cowardly Jew" asking her not to make too much fuss over her resignation. The incident is cast in some doubt by the informant's request to be left out of any account of it if at all possible, and Streicher eventually decided this particular episode was not "*Stürmer*-ripe."[28] He could always count on new contributions from frustrated secretaries and discharged bookkeepers.

In the blue-collar world, small brush and pencil factories

were particularly fruitful sources of letters and reports complaining about low wages, rude treatment, and long hours. Many of these plants seem to have maintained the kind of working atmosphere where cross-conversation of all kinds between labor and management was possible. It was not always clear when humor became something more. When a manager suggested that a woman who was habitually late could compensate for her tardiness by being a bit friendlier, was he making a crude joke or a serious pass? When an offer of a new dress brought a rejoinder that with higher wages a girl could buy her own clothes, was the respondent defending her virtue or stating an economic fact? Streicher, at least for public purposes, had no doubts.[29]

As the depression deepened, *Der Stürmer* featured an increasing number of articles describing the dismissal of employees with a quarter-century of service, or employees just on the verge of collecting their pensions. Here too Streicher did not have to rely entirely on invention. His files include, for example, a letter from a local pencil firm written in September, 1932, informing one of its pensioners that it was cutting employee pensions in half and cancelling widows' pensions entirely. No matter how hard the times, what elderly couple could contemplate such a step with equanimity? And if one were even a casual *Stürmer* reader, "The Jew" was easier than ever to blame for an empty wallet. The forty-seven-year-old master tailor who had been out of work for two months, then took a job in a Jewish-operated firm whose ancient machinery and low pay shocked him, was no Nazi crackpot. Even in the columns of *Der Stürmer*, he emerges as an honest man, trying to feed his family as best he could. And when he complained about his working conditions, as a craftsman of his age and position might be expected to do, he could not understand why his new boss not only fired him, but made it look as though he quit voluntarily, in order to prevent him collecting unemployment. The tone of the letter is that of a man who has suddenly come down in the world and in his own eyes, who cannot understand circumstances in which protest by a wounded veteran means summary dismissal. Such men were not automatic recruits to the Nazi camp. But they were angry enough to support change—any kind of change.[30]

3

Another mixed bag of grievances against the Jew as businessman and employer focused in Der Stürmer's campaign against department stores.[31] These stores had begun appearing in German cities during the third quarter of the nineteenth century. By 1914 a network of branches had spread into the larger towns. The stores manifested four general characteristics. First, everything in a given store, from counter placement to management organization, was designed to encourage business. Second, the department stores advertised heavily. This was a major departure; retail businessmen, particularly in the "home towns" of central and south Germany, believed in the tradition that the quality of one's goods and services should speak for itself. Third, department stores emphasized self-service, with limited contact between clerks and customers. If one could find what one wanted, the only sales person needed was a cashier. Finally, department stores offered new patterns of employment and career development. They were too large for one or two people to supervise the entire plant. This made it possible for a salesman with ability and experience to become the equivalent of a factory foreman, supervising a section of the store and controlling his own staff of subordinates. And an increasing number of those subordinates were likely to be women. The post of junior sales clerk in a department store could not, in any previous sense of the concept, be regarded as skilled labor. No matter how low an employer's opinion of woman's intelligence might be, it was clear that clerking made virtually no demands beyond reading price tags, remembering where items were located, and relating to customers. Besides—probably the most decisive point—women were usually willing to accept low wages in return for employment that was respectable, offering an opportunity to wear clean clothes to work and—who knew—perhaps even to charm an eligible young man with one's personality and appearance. For the daughter of a struggling artisan or an ambitious laborer, lacking the education and address for more refined employment, a job in a department store could represent a desirable intermediate career on the way to a home and children of her own.

By the end of the nineteenth century the department stores of Germany were firmly established. Their golden age, however, began under the Weimar Republic. The new state's refusal to socialize private business combined with a general reduction in local fees and taxes levied on department stores to increase profits. Chains such as Tietz and Schocken built new subsidiaries and purchased independent stores. In 1926 the first "one-price store" opened in Germany and proved an instant success. These "extracts of department stores" featured fixed price steps, emphasized high and rapid turnover of low-priced goods, and depended on their customers' willingness to accept a limited range of choices. They existed in most large cities by the end of the decade, the most familiar being links in the Woolworth chain.

Even before World War I department stores had been successful enough to generate substantial opposition from more traditionally organized retail business. On one level this hostility was expressed in moral rather than economic terms. Department stores, their critics argued, depersonalized the relations between buyer and seller. Whole networks of human exchanges were disrupted by turning customers into numbers to be processed in and out as rapidly as possible. It was the factory system translated to the world of buying and selling. This echo of the home town, a nostalgic regret for a vanishing commercial arcadia, was repeated in the common accusation that department stores specialized in cheap, low-quality wares. Any savings they offered were ephemeral. The unwary purchaser would find his suit wearing out, his crockery breaking, and his furniture collapsing beneath him before he finished paying for his bargains. And for those who believed woman's place was in the home, it was easy to describe the ill effects on young girls of long hours on one's feet —to say nothing of the total dependence of female employees on male supervisors.

Though it was common enough before 1914 to describe department stores as "Jewish-oriental," resembling a bazaar, with customers pawing through piles of tacky goods, anti-Semitism was not a major factor in the initial attempts of small and middle-sized businessmen to limit the role of these stores in German economic life. The National Socialists, however, argued from the beginning that department stores epitomized the Jewish influence in German life. Department stores were useful symbols of big business and unfair competition. It was, moreover, relatively easy to find individuals who had had some form of unpleasant experience at Schocken's or Woolworth's. One rude clerk, one poorly sewn blouse, or one inaccurate bill, could remain in memory precisely because it was so difficult to find anyone in the store to whom a customer with a grievance could appeal and get any real emotional satisfaction. Even a complaint department was staffed by underlings. If one did see the manager, what was he but just another employee? To Weimar's little man, the department store could be presented as the embodiment of his fears of depersonalization, of becoming part of an amorphous mass of taxpayers, voters, and customers.

Der Stürmer's role in the offensive against department stores has been accurately described as the systematic pouring of poison into one of Germany's open wounds.[32] Streicher's paper did not, however, seriously begin the process until 1926. Earlier attacks on department stores were occasional, connected more with other kinds of anti-Semitic grievances than with department stores as such. Many of the references to "false Jewish advertising and cheap Jewish goods" were reprints of pieces originally run in other Nazi or *völkisch* papers. Editorial comments seldom went beyond vague threats and suggestions that such criminal activity should be appropriately dealt with.[33] A copy of a letter to the Tietz store in Nürnberg complaining that what the store's lunchroom served for roast veal "stank," and the gravy was "simply indescribable," never even moved from Streicher's files.[34]

Der Stürmer's active campaign against department stores began when the Schocken firm opened a branch in Nürnberg. The fact that the store timed its opening for the Christmas season of 1926 was an added incentive to attack its "Broadway architecture" and its low-quality goods. Glorified junk stores, Streicher declared, were replacing honest German merchants who waited behind their counters until quality goods and services brought them customers. Streicher also emphasized the capitalist nature of the Schocken chain, with its two dozen branches. And yet Socialist politicians and Socialist newspapers supported the extension of a tentacle of this octopus into Nürnberg. What but a racial connection could inspire such cooperation? Schocken enterprises might call itself German, but *Der Stürmer* could prove it was Jewish-owned and operated.[35]

Part of the reason for Social Democratic enthusiasm was the location of the new store in a blue-collar district of the city, where its prices and convenience rapidly attracted customers—and criticism from outflanked competition. *Der Stürmer*'s editor became convinced that an intensified campaign against department stores would increase readership, sales, and support for National Socialism. Department store chains, he declared, had one thing in common. All were owned by Jews. This meant that anyone shopping in a department store was digging his own and his country's grave. Yet in Nürnberg, newspapers which proclaimed themselves defenders of the *Mittelstand* showed no scruple in accepting advertisements from any department store with money.[36] It was once again *Der Stürmer*'s task to expose the scandal and the swindle.

By the spring of 1927, Streicher regularly featured articles on "Salman Schocken the King Jew," whose prosperity was based on speculation during the inflation, and who now sought to buy respectability through philanthropy and legitimacy by paying high taxes. Streicher attacked the right of Jews to decide the wages of Germans. Everything was for sale in a Jewish store, he declared, including German girls. When a Jewish clerk "helped" his customers try on dresses, he was seeing Aryan women as he liked them best—in their underwear.[37]

Sexual behavior was, however, less significant than business practices. One could stroll through Nürnberg and see nothing but Jewish-owned stores which, despite their claims to serve the little man, persisted in tantalizing him with window displays of a good life far beyond the means of any honest German. Where was the old Christian merchant, the man who was honest, fair, just to his apprentices, who was never open to reproaches about his goods? He had been replaced by department stores whose aims were to ruin German businessmen by cutting prices, to destroy German morals by selling dirty books, to empty German pockets by replacing the old *Trachten* with fashions which changed annually and at random, to advertise "good German wares" but peddle imported trash.[38] Department store sales involved nothing more than juggling prices so that the unsuspecting customer paid more—a trick learned from the "relativity Jew" himself, Albert Einstein.[39] Their grocery sections specialized in wormy cherries, rotten fish, and similar thinly disguised garbage. Their managers and supervisors periodically ordered employees or customers suspected of shoplifting to undergo body searches. *Der Stürmer*, interestingly, itself provided evidence that the suspicions were sometimes justified when it declared that the low salaries paid by the chains drove "honest people" to theft in order to supplement their pay.[40]

Streicher's fulminations against one-price stores focused on the Nürnberg branch of Woolworth's. As times grew harder, an increasing number of *Nürnberger* shopped there to save money. Streicher's attacks on "the Jew Woolworth," who issued 70 percent dividends to his Semitic stockholders by exploiting domestic workers like the Thuringian dollmakers, no longer seemed enough. Instead he switched to science, declaring that the Municipal Electrical Company had informed *Der Stürmer* that the light bulbs Woolworth's sold so cheaply were of a type outmoded for two decades because they used too much electricity for the light they gave.[41] He also tried poetry, publishing a set of verses in which a man warned his wife against buying "Jewish junk" no matter how hard the times or how low the prices, and concluded by threatening the lady with divorce if she continued undermining her *Volk*. The piece is an interesting foretaste of divorce suits brought and granted under the Third Reich for just such reasons.[42]

If small firms were open to accusations of vulgar or misleading advertising, department stores, with their huge budgets and comprehensive campaigns, were even more obvious targets. Few *Stürmer* advertisers had the wit to match the clothing store which informed the ladies of Nürnberg that they could *not* be served better and less expensively by a Jewish store than by one owned by National Socialists.[43] In 1930, a Nürnberg department store attempted to overcome a summer slump by announcing a "St. John's Children's Day" and sending out advertisements featuring the coming of the *Johannesmännchen*, who fulfilled the wishes of good boys and girls. It was at best a feeble attempt to provide an imitation Christmas in July, hardly likely to succeed during a depression. But to Streicher it represented an attempt to turn St. John into an advertising symbol—an outrage made worse by the fact that the *Johannesmännchen* had flat feet, a crooked nose, and lived in a department store! When the Tietz branch in Bamberg presented a window display featuring monkeys dressed as firemen, Streicher proclaimed this an unbearable and deliberate libeling of German officials. Another store ran a newspaper advertisment showing a customer chained to a doghouse with the caption: "be on the watch"—for a big sale. To *Der Stürmer* this simply illustrated the Talmudic assertion that all *goyim* were criminals and animals who belonged in shackles forged by the Chosen People.[44]

On January 15, 1930, the city of Nürnberg doubled the municipal taxes on department stores. This decision, though frequently connected with the fact that Nürnberg was Streicher's headquarters, probably owed more to a shrinking tax base than to latent National Socialism on the city council.[45] Streicher's campaign, however, did provoke letters and comments not always easy to dismiss as manifestations of the lunatic fringe. A Franconian villager protested the action of a teacher who, as part of a class excursion to the big city, took the children into a department store. Another correspondent protested the insertion of advertising plugs into children's theater programs, illustrated by the character in *Cinderella* whose lines called for a statement of hunger, but who added an intention to eat at Tietz! A concrete indication of the effect of *Der Stürmer*'s campaign was the readiness of Nürnberg department stores to wrap packages in plain paper instead of the usual wrapping with the store's name highly visible. Streicher was not far from the mark when he described this as reflecting an increased belief that anyone who did business with Jews was a traitor to his own people—or at least ran the risk of being insulted by someone whose consciousness had been appropriately raised.[46]

4

Substantive business disputes continued to provide material for Streicher's columns. Anti-Semitism was less important in their origins than questions of warranties, unpaid bills, or damage liability. The sums involved were often minuscule, even by the standards of small businesses in the 1920s. But if the exchange of letters and phone calls was long enough or acrimonious enough, epithets began flying and Streicher was likely to be notified of another incident of Jewish dishonesty or Jewish sharp dealing.

An angry correspondent described the behavior of a firm which sold a fur coat on time for ten marks a month; then eight months later demanded a balloon payment of a hundred marks within a week. Perhaps this was simply another illustration of the truth that no one should sign an installment contract without reading the fine print. To the letter writer it was an example of "Jewish trickery." So was the offer of a Frankfurt firm to all officials to buy cloth at a discount in November with no payment until the next year. This stock device of contemporary American businessmen in the holiday season was sufficiently unusual in Germany to arouse suspicion. An argument between a housewife and a door-to-door salesman produced another angry letter. The incident reads like a sequence by Chic Young: a harried woman attempting to get rid of an overly persistent peddler. When she declared she would never buy from a Jew, and boasted of her ability to recognize one five kilometers away, the salesman shifted to the familiar form of address and the argument became political. In other times and places, it would have made conversation over the breakfast and coffee table. By 1932, it was prominently featured in *Der Stürmer*.[47]

Sometimes this process could be profitable, at least for the gentile party to a dispute. In 1927 Streicher received a cheerful letter from a reader who thanked him for his indirect help in recovering part of a twenty-mark debt from a Jewish customer. After a year of unsatisfactory correspondence, the mere threat of exposure in *Der Stürmer* combined with the pressing of legal action to produce a payment of five marks. If the sum at issue seems hardly worth the postage involved in its recovery, the aggrieved party left no question that payment had become a matter of principle.[48]

Becoming too deeply involved in these kinds of disputes carried its own risks, illustrated by the statement of a creditor that anti-Semitism was neither an excuse for late payment nor security against a libel suit.[49] Streicher checked his facts reasonably carefully before publishing these stories. In 1924, for example, *Der Stürmer* received a letter from a wholesale firm stating that they had purchased a new truck from a Jewish dealer. The truck had given them nothing but trouble; after nine months and many repairs the Jews had begun charging the outrageous rate of two marks an hour for labor. The author wanted Streicher to use this material to show deluded workers the difference between the prices Jews charged and the wages their employees received.

On the surface the story seemed a tailor-made front page item. But the auto dealer also submitted a statement. In it he informed the angry truck purchaser that his vehicle had been badly damaged by overloading and had to be fixed in overtime. The dealer concluded his reasonable and conciliatory letter by saying that a truck could not be consistently and massively overloaded without expensive damage to springs and suspension, and in this respect was drastically unlike a horse-drawn wagon. Streicher was no mechanic, but even he could see the limited possibilities for scandal offered by this issue.[50]

As a rule, *Der Stürmer*'s attacks on the Jew as businessman were designed to skirt the edge of legal liability. Like most nationalist and *völkisch* periodicals, *Der Stürmer* regarded it as vitally important to keep its readers informed of Jewish businessmen and Jewish professionals in its areas of circulation. Baptized or not, Streicher warned, the Jewish doctor, lawyer, or tavern keeper remained a Jew. When a Nürnberg merchant announced a quitting-business sale, and *Der Stürmer* recommended that all good Germans avoid the sale no matter how low the prices, this was interpreted by the courts as a call for a boycott.[51] It was, however, legal simply to describe a firm as Jewish and let readers draw their own conclusions. Streicher's files contain letter after letter asking if *Der Stürmer* could print a list of *German* businesses, or whether a specific firm was Jewish-owned or employed Jews. After all, one bewildered correspondent said, the individual under discussion did not *look* Jewish![52]

Here again *Der Stürmer* depended heavily on informers. One party member replied to an inquiry by declaring that he had worked for a certain firm in question for two years and could say unequivocally that its owners were pure German, with no Jewish employees, and even looked favorably on his National Socialism. A small businessman responded to an allegation that he employed Jews by denying that he hired anyone but Aryan Christians.[53] On some occasions the implications were more serious. In the spring of 1924 *Der Stürmer* ran several articles accusing the "Jewish" firm of Himmelsbach Brothers of selling wood to French dealers at a time when Germans were freezing. In June, a friendly letter from the firm described Streicher's allegations as simple nonsense. The firm was Christian and employed no Jews; surely *Der Stürmer* would correct the error. A month later, the firm took a much stronger line, demanding a full retraction. Clearly brotherhood was not regarded as good business, at least in south Germany in the 1920s.[54] Neither *Der Stürmer* itself, the *Streicher Nachlass*, nor the *Stürmer-Archiv* contain any letters remotely equivalent to that sent to the *Schwarze Korps* in 1936 declaring emphatic support for a Jewish employee.[55] Instead, firms and their employees were commonly at pains to deny any Jewish connection whatever. After all, *Der Stürmer* made lists of Aryan businesses available at ten pfennigs a copy.[56]

The ideal result of Streicher's campaign against the Jewish businessman is manifested in a letter submitted by a housewife whose husband was unaware of her action. The couple owned a small granite quarry. To keep it open in the face of increased competition required mechanizing the operation, but the business was so heavily indebted no bank would risk making them further loans. The husband, a veteran of twenty-two years in the army, was in such despair that he wanted to take a Jew as a partner. The wife described herself as a maid of all work, on her feet from five till midnight, caring for her mother and her niece as well as attempting to help keep the family business afloat. But she was also aware, thanks to *Der Stürmer*, of the risks involved in accepting help offered by a Jew.

The letter's significance lies in its suggestion of the impact of fear on ordinarily decent people. The writer emerges as neither fanatic nor crackpot, but rather as a person driven to the edge of despair by economic forces she could not comprehend. She concluded by wrapping herself in what remained of her pride, telling Streicher that she wanted neither charity nor publicity. Her only desire was that he be made aware of the way innocent people were being drained by "alien parasites."[57] Of such people too was the Third Reich made.

6 | The Jew as Bad Neighbor

The material of this chapter is a mixed and frustrating bag. It concentrates on the day-in, day-out irritations that Streicher assembled and reported to convince his readers that Jews were bad neighbors. A common observation about German "national character" is that Germans tend to suffer from a collective inferiority complex. Even if one denies the possibility of fixing psychiatric terms on an entire culture, it is legitimate to argue that many individual Germans after 1918 did feel the vicarious humiliation of defeat multiplied by postwar dislocations. This in turn generated free-floating hostilities—which could focus, or be focused, on extremely unlikely targets. In *Der Stürmer's* pages the Jew as sex criminal provided titillation. The Jew as businessman generated fear. The Jew as bad neighbor made even the word "Jew" an insult. This involved a process of presenting information in four different contexts: Jews simply being Jews, Jews interacting negatively with Gentiles, Jews behaving as bad citizens, and Jews benefiting unfairly from the Weimar system.

1

For a believing Nazi, the fact that Jews and Aryans were different required illustration rather than demonstration. A favorite *Stürmer* comparison involved Jews and lice. Both were vermin from the east. Both stank. Both sucked blood. Initially one did not notice either of them; then suddenly there were too many to get rid of. Article after *Stürmer* article presented Jews as a mixture of black, Mongol, German, and ape. The simian heritage, Streicher declared, was shown by such characteristics as hairy bodies and anthropoid jaws, torsos too long for legs, and abnormally shaped feet. And if German medical students had access to Jewish corpses, the world would know exactly why Jewish bodies were abnormal, why Jewish brains were different from those of other people, why so many Jews were insane. Instead the Jews deliberately concealed their dead. A dead Jew, Streicher declared, was surrounded by noisy women until other Jews put him in a crate and buried him in a separate cemetery as quickly a possible. This community took no risk of having its racial secrets exposed.[1]

Aside from imaginary fears and exaggerations, behavioral differences between Jews, particularly observant Jews, and their Gentile, Christian neighbors did exist. In this context intermarriage and conversion could be less significant than such mundane issues as funeral customs. One vitriolic letter, for example, attacked a Jewish cattle dealer who allegedly let a cow with a broken leg suffer throughout the Sabbath without either destroying the animal himself or violating the holy day by calling a Gentile butcher to perform this act of mercy. The connection between this incident and the New Testament's comment on rescuing an ox from a pit even on the Sabbath is obvious enough to make the letter suspicious. As so often with *Der Stürmer*, however, generalized plausibility reinforced the credibility of the specific incident described in the letter. It could have happened the way the correspondent described it. A Jew with a strict and literal approach to Sabbath observance might have let an injured animal suffer rather than perform the "work" connected with destroying it. Similarly, when an observant schoolboy on a class excursion aroused the curiosity of his classmates by stopping in the midst of the day's activities, facing east, and reading gibberish from a book printed in incomprehensible characters, he might impress some observers by his piety. He was likely to convince other onlookers that Jews were in fact different from Christians. And to many of Streicher's correspondents, different could easily be synonymous with dangerous.[2]

Food also played a role in *Der Stürmer*'s image of the Jew as bad neighbor. The paper cited ads for kosher food as proof that Jews regarded "their" food as superior to that eaten by Germans. Streicher also stressed the "fact" that Jewish butchers were allowed to sell "offal"—that is, nonkosher parts of the animal, or the whole carcass if the slaughter was unacceptable to a supervising rabbi, to Gentiles. This involved a bit of semantics. The word "offal" was used in rabbinic literature in a highly technical sense: to describe parts and carcasses ritually unfit for consumption by observant Jews. But Streicher used the word itself in its literal meaning to reinforce another image: Jews deliberately selling filth to their neighbors.[3]

Since the Middle Ages German folklore had incorporated tales of poisoned wells and polluted food. *Der Stürmer* occasionally ran such a traditional item, describing a frustrated dry-goods peddler, enraged over failing to make any sales in a busy farming village, who threw cloth scraps into the village well. Caught in the act, he tried to deny that he knew it was a well, then offered his observers bribes to keep silent. On another occasion the paper went modern, describing the behavior of a Viennese nightclub employee who had contracted venereal disease and must therefore "ritually" wash himself. The filthy Jew used a champagne glass for this process, then put it back with the other glasses used to serve unsuspecting Gentile customers. A three hundred schilling fine instead of a rope was an insult to all Germans everywhere.[4]

Given Streicher's editorial hostility to nightclubs, such a story was likely to be limited in its impact. Decent people, after all, should have nothing to do with such places in any case. A more effective argument involved assertions that Jewish butchers deliberately polluted the food they sold to *goyim*, in accordance with the "Talmudic" injunction to feed filth to Gentiles. Since the 1880s this accusation had been made periodically, often in connection with legal charges of selling spoiled meat. The *Stürmer* archives, for example, contain a pamphlet of the stenographic report of a trial held in Würzburg in 1901, in which a Jewish butcher was accused of deliberately urinating on the meat he sold.[5]

Since this particular pamphlet was in its eighth printing, it can be assumed to have had a wide circulation, at least among anti-Semites. Its essential allegation certainly remained durable. In the summer of 1930, for example, a village Nazi declared that he saw the daughter of a Jewish baker urinate into a baking trough. This was hardly surprising, Streicher declared; Jews were known to pollute meat, why not bread as well? In this instance, however, the baker filed suit for libel. The result was another endless small-town lawsuit, with the baker's lawyer declaring small children often urinated in any handy object and the Nazi defendant bringing in a witness who swore he had seen the baker himself urinate into a milk can. The judge dismissed the case. What effect the accusation had on the town's customers remains unknown, but itcan hardly have been positive.[6]

Constant repetition made it at least possible for an unintelligent or unreflective person to ask if there might not, after all, be something to *Der Stürmer*'s allegations. And once the seeds were planted, Streicher fertilized them with a line of reasoning designed to prove that Jews were not only different; but that they regarded their German neighbors with contempt.

No item was beneath notice. When an eighty-three-year-old in Würzburg entertained a "lady" in her twenties, and the "guest" said she would enjoy herself more if the window were left open, two eavesdropping gossips were shocked enough at the resulting noises to spread the news throughout the neighborhood. *Der Stürmer* reported the event as an example of Jewish indifference to public decency by a man who should be old enough to know better—if he were indeed human. A Jew forbidden by a streetcar conductor to jump from a moving car answered "what can you do when the dog blocks the gate?" Everyone in the car laughed—except "Heimdal," who asked the conductor why he tolerated such an insult. When told it was just a joke, he broke into rhetorical rage and asked when Germans would ever learn the true nature of their real enemy? On another occasion Streicher printed a letter describing a women's bridge club which played every evening from 7:30 to the small hours of the morning. The chairman was Jewish, declared the writer, and the rest of the club must be Jews as well. For one thing, the game continued even on Christmas night. For another, what German woman would play cards so regularly in these hard times? A dedicated bridge player in Streicher's entourage might have been able to supply an answer. What *Der Stürmer*'s readers got instead was a cartoon showing four Jewesses sitting at a bridge table, one of them saying that it was impossible for a Gentile woman ever to learn to play bridge properly. *Goyim*, after all, had to care for their own children.[7]

These and hundreds of similar items were presented to strengthen *Der Stürmer*'s image of an unbridgeable gulf between alien species. The more innocuous an incident seemed, the greater was its significance. For it was in his unguarded moments that the Jew showed his true colors and became most quintessentially Jewish. One of the stranger incidents featured in *Der Stürmer* began when a Jew saw a couple with a little dog and talked them into selling it. Shortly afterward he wrote the former owners, telling them the dog was a joy and could not be treated better. He slept like a little god and, like all dogs, communicated with God in a special way. The communication as quoted bears all the marks of that exaggerated fondness for animals similar to that characterizing some leading Nazis and many ordinary Germans. Even Streicher had to say that on the surface nothing seemed wrong. But, he reminded his readers, the Talmud also said that it was better to feed a dog than a *goy*. Properly interpreted, the whole transaction was simply another reflection of Jewish contempt for Gentiles—a contempt which in this case involved ridicule rather than overt hatred, but which was no less real for that.[8]

The Jew was also a Jew when it came to recreation. *Der Stürmer* frequently deplored the spectacle of sports fanatics persuing their Sunday papers to see whether Bayern or Eintracht won its game. It was nothing but a Jewish plot to distract the attention of Germans from important matters like elections. On the other hand, the paper noted the mismanagement of the Ulm Football Club by a Jew who had the effrontery to hit an Aryan member of the team in front of other players. When the South German Football League decided to forbid Nazis to use its fields for open-air rallies, Streicher described this decision as a manifestation of Jewish dominance. And when Nürnberg lost its league championship 0:2 in 1932, *Der Stürmer* ascribed the defeat to the club's Jewish trainer. No Jew could show a German how to play football, Streicher declared. Jews were not "built" for the game. Since the club had had the same trainer for over three years, and had a winning record over that time, for once Julius the anti-Semite ended by sounding like any ordinary, disappointed fan.[9]

When it came to local organizations, *Der Stürmer* felt itself on firmer ground. Whether a *Verein* listed a Jewish religious service in its schedule of activities or allowed Jews to dance at its annual ball, such lapses from grace were always worth a few lines and a suggestion that "real Germans" should hide their heads in shame.[10] *Der Stürmer* was particularly incensed at the participation of Jews in gymnastics clubs. Gymnastics had been founded by a true German, Vater Jahn. But the existing clubs and their parent organization, the *Deutsche Turnverein*, were willing to admit anyone. Jews were on boards of directors. Jews were allowed to participate in competitions, even at Christmas. The Jewish Gymnastic Society Bar Kochba, named after a murderer who was a forerunner of Trotsky and Zinoviev, even shared German club facilities. It was no wonder that the *Deutsche Turnerschaft* complained that more and more of its members were becoming politically active—and bringing their political convictions into the meetings and competitions.[11]

Like gymnastics groups, choral societies were more interested in talent than ancestry. Sometimes they were also interested in money. One village choir aroused Streicher's particular ire by singing at a Jewish wedding instead of a Nazi rally. After the massive Nazi electoral victory of 1930, another singing group was split by an altercation which developed between a Jew and a Gentile member of the group—political affiliation unrecorded —during a dance. An overheated room, alcohol, and two men interested in the same woman seem to have produced "kiss my ass" on one side and "Jew pig" on the other. Since neither of the aggrieved parties was interested in resigning, the society took sides. The incident is typical enough, particularly in a group whose common denominator was pitch. Its significance is that as late as 1930, the *Verein* divided evenly.[12]

If the Jew as footballer, gymnast, or singer frequently remained a hidden Jew, carnival allowed him to remove his mask.

German misery only heightened the gaiety of Jews who did not know how to get rid of their money. One way they made it was by paying the insulting sum of one pfennig for each finished carnival cap made by families thrown out of work by the depression. And the same Jews who paid these low wages bought champagne to ruin German girls. Streicher's description of women refusing drinks and rejecting dance partners because of *Der Stürmer*'s enlightening work probably embodied more wishful thinking than reality. The paper had better success attacking what Streicher liked to call *Faschingsjuderei*. Each carnival season brought a quota of letters from outraged moralists and people who had been unable to make their own connections for the night. *Der Stürmer* professed to be scandalized when a Jewish woman attended a ball whose theme was "eternal youth" dressed as a first communicant, with white dress, candle, and rosary. Streicher's report of a party held in Aschaffenburg in 1932 makes one sorry to have missed the fun. With one man declaring that he was autumn and inviting the women guests to take off their leaves, with couple after alcohol-stimulated couple seeking side rooms for "privacy," it was natural for town gossips to send full details to *Der Stürmer*—accompanied by a list of women who sought or accepted Jewish company for the evening.[13] Even a party to celebrate the end of the winter term at a *Gymnasium* generated an angry letter accusing Jews of trying to corrupt the morals of Bavarian teenagers with dirty jokes and pictures. Given Adolf Hitler's riotous behavior at one end-of-term celebration, Streicher could hardly make massive capital of this particular incident.[14]

2

Even a *Stürmer* reader might be inclined to treat Streicher's interpretation of such incidents as an exercise in editorial paranoia. *Der Stürmer* could, however, also rely on a steady flow of reports, many extremely detailed, of directly unpleasant personal encounters between Jews and Gentiles. Some speak volumes about their narrators. One such story began with two Gentile girls greeted "in a way not to be misunderstood" by two Jews.

One of the girls protested the familiarity, apparently couching her objections in ethnic terms. She received the reply that she could kiss the ass of her would-be cavalier until he turned Christian. Her answer was, "you can kiss mine until I turn Jew." Or what can be made of the report from a "soldier's widow" that one of the women with whom she worked asked her Jewish supervisor what a *shiksa* was and received the answer, "you are"? The account also describes the widow's rage at a "younger woman" for dating the same supervisor, and ends with a despairing account of her dismissal for being seen with *Der Stürmer* in her hand. Is it reading too much between the lines to see anger, frustration, perhaps even jealousy, transforming a remark almost certainly intended as a joke, and at worst a joke reflecting bad taste and no judgment, into proof of a Jewish conspiracy to insult Gentiles to their faces?[15]

A disproportionate number of unpleasant encounters occurred in streetcars and trains. Modern transportation seemed to strain German privacy spheres to the breaking point A *Stürmer* report from train or trolley could involve something as innocuous as a Jewish passenger reflecting on the differences between Jew and Gentile and concluding that the Jew kept his nose to the ground while the German preferred to have his head in the clouds. Or it could involve a mother's complaint that she and her two sons were riding the streetcar home after a long day's hike. When two Jewish women boarded the crowded car, a Jewish man told her boys to give them their places. The mother said they were just returning from a six-hour hike and were tired, only to be told that it made no difference. She became angry enough to write Streicher. I believe my boys should usually give their seats to ladies, she declared, but this was too much.[16]

Physical exchanges under these circumstances were not unusual. A Jewish woman physician in a Hamburg streetcar took a second seat for her armful of packages and was politely asked to move them. She complied, but grumbled about it to the woman sitting next to her. When she received no sympathy, she lost her temper and declared that all Germans were alike: clods without class. The reply was a suggestion that if she were unhappy, she should go back to Palestine. The doctor lost her temper and slapped the other woman's face. She was promptly ejected from the car, fined three hundred marks, and required to pay her victim a further two hundred marks damages—an average set of penalties for that kind of offense in 1924, but to Streicher a sad indication of the degeneracy of Germans who turned to Republican justice instead of holding court in a streetcar.[17]

More to *Der Stürmer*'s liking was the fate of a Jew "accosting" a German girl in a streetcar, who found his intended victim strong enough to slap his face and push him off the platform into the street. Another desirable result of such encounters, at least in Streicher's pages, was illustrated when one of the passengers in a train compartment idly asked if Salman Schocken, the department store magnate, was really Jewish. A young man wearing a swastika said yes. Another passenger denied Schocken's Jewishness and said that he himself was a Jew. "I see that," the swastika wearer replied. The two men began exchanging insults. Then the Nazi slapped the Jew and invited him to step onto the platform and settle the matter physically. The Jew refused. Objectively this was a sensible enough decision, since even *Der Stürmer*'s article conceded that he had not begun the argument, and stressed the difference in age and weight between the potential adversaries. But to Streicher refusal to accept a physical challenge was only to be expected from a race of born cowards and weaklings.[18]

The Jew as landlord was able to indulge his true nature to the fullest. The Germans unfortunate enough to rent accommodations from a Jew could expect nothing but the most cordial treatment *until* they made their initial payment. Thereafter it was a different story of unmade beds, unclean linen, poorly cooked food, and constant harassment. One couple described their life as made a "living hell" by noise. Another complained that their Jewish landlady stole their firewood—even on Easter Sunday. Trouble could also occur when the roles were reversed. When a German landlord's dog drank some milk belonging to a Jewish renter, she retaliated a few days later by pouring boiling water on the dog.[19]

A German who had the misfortune to rent a house or apartment from an absentee Jewish landlord could expect to be martyred legally, as opposed to being persecuted directly. Typical of many reports *Der Stürmer* featured was the account of a crippled war veteran forced to go to a sanitorium to maintain what remained of his health. When as a result he fell behind in his rent, his Jewish landlord got an eviction order and had his furniture thrown into the street. Even the municipal government responded to this ex-soldier's sacrifices for the fatherland and his decorations for valor. It allowed him to store his furniture in the town mortuary. Only the Jew remained indifferent to everything but his money. As for seeking redress in court, the German might as well seek instant admission to paradise. A Nürnberg midwife who could not pay her rent sought to improve her financial status by taking her childless daughter and son-in-law as subtenants. When the owner of the building refused, the midwife took her case to the law. A Jew called as an expert witness said that though the couple was now childless, they were young enough to have children, and the owner did not have to allow "rabbit breeding" on his premises. The remark, tasteless at best, was for Streicher another indication of Jewish contempt for Germans, for their closest family relationships, and for their intimate life.[20]

The significance of such stories in *Der Stürmer*'s pages is twofold. The correspondents themselves frequently insisted on their white-collar status. They were men and women who, for whatever reason, had come down in the world sufficiently to move from apartments to furnished rooms, or who had been constrained to move to lower-rent districts. Their letters, moreover, acted as a warning to *Der Stürmer*'s bourgeois readers. In the miasma of anxiety covering Weimar Germany, a miasma deepening by the month during the early 1930s, even men and women who had jobs and decent lodgings were insecure enough to project themselves into Streicher's columns—into the world of rude landladies and unemptied chamber pots. The Jewish question took a clear third place to issues of life style and social status.

Other questions of status involved domestic service. In the face of a widely held public belief that Jews paid and treated their domestic servants well, *Der Stürmer* lost no opportunity to argue that Jews preferred Gentile help only because they could abuse and insult *goyim* with impunity. Verbal attacks could be combined with physical mistreatment ranging from reading private mail to forbidding a housemaid to visit the dentist until her teeth had rotted away. And if one could collect even part of one's wages without recourse to the courts, this was accidental. It had nothing to do with the honesty of a Jewish employer.[21]

These situations, typical of many in *Der Stürmer*'s columns, are characterized by their plausibility. Servants could be underpaid and overworked. Landlords and tenants might find each other mutually distasteful. Employers could be inconsiderate or incompetent. In the final analysis, many of these incidents are not likely to have been invented, if for no other reason than the discredit they so often reflect on the narrator. The author has described, for example, the altercation mentioned at the beginning of the section to Germans ranging in age from eighteen to seventy-three, including many *Nürnberger*. The most common response has been a rueful grin, a shake of the head, and the words "typisch Deutsch" or "echt Bayrisch"—not because of the anti-Semitism, but because of the manners displayed by the major participants. Streicher's art lay in interpreting these events as part of a pattern: the biologically determined insolence and shamelessness of a minority which should be humbly thankful for the temporary right to breathe German air.

Streicher's treatments of the direct clashes between Jew and German in a minor fashion support the argument that German Jews on the whole felt comfortable and secure in their environment. People constantly looking over their shoulders are not likely to exchange crude insults or public face-slappings with members of a majority community perceived as directly dangerous. Physical retaliation was a more common Jewish response to insult or provocation than is generally accepted. *Der Stürmer*'s columns frequently featured colorful and plausible descriptions of violence inflicted on Germans—particularly Nazis—by Jews. Such incidents were presented to show Jews as cowards. For this reason the Gentiles involved included a disproportionate number of old men, cripples, and children—people against whom physical force could be used in safety. At the same time, this particular behavior indicates a correspondingly high degree of perceived social integration. A typical report began with an illegally parked car blocking the entry to a courtyard. When the seventy-nine-year-old *Hausmeister* asked the Jewish driver to move the vehicle, he was greeted with a volley of insults. The *Hausmeister* replied with the epithet "Jew sow" and was promptly knocked

141

down. When a Gentile child told a Jewish playmate that "everyone" knew Jews killed Christian children, the father demanded that the children's teacher punish this lie. When the teacher refused, on the legitimate grounds that the incident happened out of school hours, the Jew sought to inflict punishment himself. A lawyer struck the husband of a client for calling him a "Jewish sow," and defended his action on the grounds that such an insult required quicker redress than legal action was likely to provide.[22]

3

Der Stürmer's attack on the Jew as bad neighbor incorporated four forms of contact best described as showing Jews as bad citizens. The first and most important involved Jewish patriotism—or its absence. In particular allegations of Jewish shirking during World War I had been a staple of anti-Semitic propaganda since the fall of 1914. The Jewish community's angry response has frequently been described. Even Jewish pacifists were known to argue that a hundred thousand Jews had worn Germany's uniform. Twelve thousand of them had died under Germany's flag. Perhaps the cause had been ignoble. Perhaps the deaths were meaningless. But by the nationalists' own standards, they should at least pay the dues of full membership in the German community.[23]

Streicher responded with a mixture of jeers and logic. If the Jews kept dedicating war memorials to their fallen, he declared, there would soon be more monuments than dead Jews. In Munich alone, 13,000 Germans had fallen for the fatherland, but only 175 Jews. A reunion of Jewish veterans from all of the principality of Waldeck attracted only four hundred, despite heavy publicity. Some truly German villages could field as many combat veterans. Any patriotism these parasites had demonstrated was nothing but camouflage. They sought safe jobs in one of Walter Rathenau's proliferating agencies. They dug themselves into offices and orderly rooms, even mutilating themselves rather than face the trenches. Streicher often reminded his readers of the 1916 order to count the number of Jews actually in the front lines—and of what he called the Jewish-inspired re-scinding of that order. What the Jews really thought of the war was shown by their constant sabotaging of war loans. Just how they did this *Der Stürmer* never explained, but the constant reiteration of the argument may have had some effect on Germans who had put their savings into Imperial promises and saw both vanish on November 11, 1918.[24]

The Jewish community, Streicher argued, never published in one place all the names of its alleged dead. Of the names they published, many were not Jewish. Many others could not be traced through military records. Where names could be traced, the deaths "suspiciously often" occurred after the war, and could be ascribed to natural causes. If a Jew who spent his uniformed years at a replacement depot in Berlin died of influenza on November 10, 1918, how could he legitimately be considered a war casualty? Finally, Streicher asserted, a high proportion of Jewish casualties were listed as missing in action. Given the nature of the Jew, it was highly likely that these "missing" men had in fact allowed themselves to be captured, then settled after the war in Poland, Russia, or France, probably under new identities, and done as well for themselves as Jews always do.[25]

The parallels between these arguments and those advanced by such pseudo-scholars of the Holocaust as Arthur Butz are striking—particularly the suggestion that the missing Jews simply absorbed themselves into whatever communities their fates took them. Whether Streicher's points by themselves convinced many people that Jews had behaved as cowards and shirkers is debatable, and probably unprovable. They did, however, contribute their share to an expanding myth that the German Jewish community had fulfilled the "Talmudic injunction" to be the last to go to war and be the first to return home.

With the establishment of their Republic, the Jews showed their colors openly. Their daughters refused to sing patriotic songs in Nürnberg's schools. A Jewish instructor at Heidelberg declared that German soldiers had fallen on the field of dishonor and deserved no more than a single turnip as their monument. The Jews at the University of Erlangen translated theory into practice. The school was unable to fund a war memorial, but maintained a museum commemorating a Jewish writer. In a similar vein, Streicher argued that postwar opposition to dueling was Jewish-inspired. Any thought of men measuring their strength on the field of honor frightened a race of born cowards.[26]

Given the images of jingoism and chauvinism generally borne by veterans' associations of the Weimar era, it is interesting to note how often such organizations inspired Streicher's anger by stubbornly refusing to discriminate against "their" Jews. The veterans of at least one small town chose a Jew to unveil the municipal war memorial. Regimental ties could also outweigh prejudice. When the Third Bavarian Train Battalion held its reunion in Fürth in 1925, its Jewish ex-officers shared the podium with Crown Prince Rupprecht himself. And when a Nazi growled that Jews had no business there, he was promptly advised to shut his mouth or be silenced with a fist. As late as 1930, when a Nazi proclaimed his intention to resign from a regimental association which admitted Jews, he was informed that the Jews of the Nineteenth Bavarian Infantry had done their duty like everyone else. Streicher's comment that the committee which issued the statement must have done its soldiering at headquarters, where Jews *were* to be found, elicited no reply. To the men of the Nineteenth, their record spoke for itself.[27]

Arguably more effective, certainly more forceful, were *Der Stürmer*'s attacks on the Jew as automobile driver. If the subject may initially seem trivial, the relationship between the German and his auto runs deep. The car has been described in scholarly and popular analyses as a direct extension of personality, an identity symbol whose driving involves constant tests of ego and sexuality. And *Der Stürmer* featured many a column complaining that when an honest man could not cross the street safely because of heavy traffic, all he needed to do was look for a luxury auto driven by a Jew—particularly a Jewish woman who liked to drive with flair. It was still a debatable *Stammtisch* issue whether women were physically or psychologically suited to drive cars at all, but certainly the Jewish community had no compunction about turning its womenfolk loose on the streets of Nürnberg.

Jews were the ones who could afford to belong to auto clubs —auto clubs which were too good to have local bands play for their dances and parades, preferring to import talent from the big cities. And who but a Jewish driver would insult a traffic policeman by using the familiar form of address when stopped at an intersection, call him names, strike him in the face, and cap the incident by filing charges of verbal brutality. *Der Stürmer* presented a lyrical description of the hard life of the modern traffic officer, a life no Jew would choose, one which deserved recognition by everyone who used the streets. Two hundred years ago, Streicher declared, a Jew who behaved in such a fashion to a public servant would have been killed on the spot and thrown into the river—an interesting suggestion, given Streicher's own propensities for reckless driving.[28]

Another reliable form of attack was to describe the Jew as a driver completely heedless of pedestrians and cyclists, particularly if they were Gentiles. Here again Streicher had a bit of sociology on his side. Aside from the normal truck and auto traffic, Franconian cattle dealers, who included many Jews, were likely to drive at odd hours in areas where, even in the 1920s, a motor vehicle was a relative rarity. Nor were their vehicles likely to be in the best mechanical condition. When these facts were added to post-accident shock, *Der Stürmer* often had the material for a feature story. An Ansbach cattle dealer ran over two small boys who darted into the road, then tried to drive away after the accident. As a crowd gathered, he first said "things were not serious" —with one child lying dead and another hopelessly crippled! When the peasants talked of lynching, the cowardly Jew took shelter in a *Gasthaus* until the police arrived. In court his Jewish lawyers blamed mechanical failure, carefully overlooking their client's two previous convictions for careless driving. The Jew received the laughable sentence of three months in jail. Even that was preferable to the three-week penalty imposed on another Jewish cattle dealer who tore through a village at 6:00 A.M. and ran down an eighty-three-year-old woman on her way to church.[29]

Any lingering doubt that Jews translated the Talmudic injunction to treat *goyim* like animals into their driving habits should have been removed by *Der Stürmer*'s descriptions of the aftermath of Jewish-caused accidents. Typical was the behavior of the Eichstätt trucker who ran down a man in his seventies, then denied any knowledge of the affair. He was brought to justice only by the intervention of three cyclists—naturally, Gentiles—who had seen the accident and were able to identify truck and driver. The Jew served a short jail term, and out of the alleged goodness of his heart gave the meager sum of eighty marks to the widow of his victim. In the context of such stories it was natural for a Fips cartoon captioned "The day of vengeance is coming" to feature a German, with bloodied child cradled in his arms, shaking his fist at a disappearing car full of Jews.[30]

With this kind of active hostility to human beings, what did Jews do to four-legged animals? Ritual slaughter had traditionally been a favorite point of anti-Semitic attacks. With the emergence of organizations for the prevention of cruelty to animals in the nineteenth century, the issue acquired new life. These groups were overwhelmingly urban and middle-class in composition, and hardly anti-Semitic in orientation. Their initial purpose was to limit or eliminate the grosser forms of animal abuse visible in the growing cities of Europe: overworked, underfed, and beaten draft animals. But as the passage and enforcement of municipal laws in the last quarter of the nineteenth century increasingly removed overtly abusive behavior from the public view, the German Animal Protection Leagues needed new outlets for their energies. One of them involved investigating the conditions in slaughterhouses. And here animal lovers began interacting with anti-Semites. Apart from its political overtones, Jewish ritual slaughter could prove shocking to the uninitiated. Cutting a conscious animal's throat with a single slash, then permitting the blood to flow freely until death, is arguably no crueler than other methods in general use during the 1920s. But to someone who had never seen a large animal actually killed, the process could seem like nothing more nor less than ruthless and inhumane torture.

The issue of ritual slaughter generated a degree of early empathy between humanitarians and such racist groups as the Nazis who sought to limit or abolish the practice. The campaign against it inspired loud complaints in lurid detail, some of them expressed in bad verse. School children were taken on excursions to the municipal slaughterhouse, with *Der Stürmer* taking careful note of their reactions. When one child wrote that ritual slaughter was so cruel that only an animal in human form could practice it, Streicher made approving comments about little children being wiser than their elders.

Even before the Nazis began overtly working to mobilize the *Mittelstand*, Streicher was soliciting bourgeois support on this issue. The Jew, Streicher declared, was a born tormentor of animals who joined Dumb Friends' Leagues for the same reason he joined any other organization: to deceive the public as to his true attitudes and intentions. If proof were required, all that was needed was to examine attitudes whenever ritual slaughter was discussed. Docking horses' tails was worth whole columns in the Jewish press. Cutting cows' throats, on the other hand, was not a subject for debate. When Nürnberg proposed to introduce electric shock into the municipal slaughterhouses to stun the animal before killing it, Streicher wanted to know why the Jews wished this method practiced only on hogs? And why were Jews so strongly opposed to the introduction of legislation in Bavaria requiring the numbing or stunning of all animals before their slaughter?[31]

A fourth source for illustrations of the Jew as bad citizen involved tourism. On one occasion *Der Stürmer* did attack the German tourist industry as a whole for acting "like Jews" in overcharging and otherwise exploiting travelers. Particularly in rural Bavaria, Streicher declared, summer visitors were too important to the economy to risk driving them away.[32] This suggestion, however, was an exception. *Der Stürmer*'s usual approach was to attack the alien and rude behavior of Jews on holiday. Once again Streicher was developing a familiar theme. Since the last quarter of the nineteenth century, the Jewish tourist in Bavaria had been an object of jest, contempt, and outright hatred. Sometimes the attitude had more to do with residence than race. One article described the "swinish" behavior of the *Deutsch-Jüdisch Wanderbund Stuttgart* who descended, sixty strong, on the town of Oettingen one Pentecost. They cavorted nude on meadows—a fact eagerly reported by the local children. They roamed the town in bathing suits, even entering the local Protestant church in such undress. And when they bothered to wear clothes, "one broad's dress was so lowcut that, as the immature young men say, 'her whole heart hung out'."

In short, the group behaved like stereotyped big-city tourists on a Sunday excursion, perhaps even enjoying shocking the locals a bit. Nude gymnastics were not a universal feature of these hiking groups, but neither were they uncommon. As for the "bathing suits," the difference between hiking shorts and swimming trunks is not always obvious to the naked eye. Newspapers in any tourist center in the western world receive similar letters every summer. Reports of nude swimming, mixed or not, in the sight of impressionable children were more likely to arouse emotion among foes of the *Wandervögel* as a class than among anti-Semites in particular.[33]

Hotels, *Gasthaüser*, and restaurants provided more useful material for this aspect of Streicher's campaign. *Der Stürmer* frequently reported in revolting detail the filthy conditions in Jewish-owned or operated restaurants, with their kitchens overrun by mice and vermin. More effective, however, were descriptions of offensive Jewish behavior in such public places as *Gasthäuser* and small hotels. *Der Stürmer* reached as far as Austria to report the complaints of resort owners against orthodox Jews, particularly Hasidim from Poland, who even brought their own food into hotel restaurants. "Anyone" on vacation, Streicher declared, knew how badly Jews behaved. They abused employees, demanded repulsive entertainments such as jazz bands, and in general were such unwelcome guests that it was no wonder proprietors tried to get rid of them.[34]

Relatively few of *Der Stürmer*'s readers could afford to take regular cures. But enough of them enjoyed modest vacations or ate meals out to provide an interesting cross section of letters describing Jews as insulting, hard to please, and above all, poor tippers. That Jews made passes at female employees was obvious. In some cases it could involve attempted rape: an early wake-up call; the Jew lying in wait; the desperate girl breaking free; a stableboy who conveniently belonged to the SA driving off the cowardly assailant with a pitchfork. This was the stuff of melodrama. More common were such letters as that describing a party of Jews who entered a garden restaurant early one summer evening, demanded house utensils and ice water, then produced their own food from paper bags. Every German knew that such restaurants were crowded on hot days: they ate and left. But

Jews could be expected to sit for hours over a single glass of beer or cup of coffee, ordering nothing else, occupying tables with vacant seats even at rush hour, and leaving five-pfennig tips.

The alleged cultural differences lay chiefly in the eyes of the observers. It was not, and is not, uncommon to see Gentile Germans bring bag lunches to a beer garden as an economy measure. Nor is the German a proverbially lavish tipper. But many of Streicher's correspondents seem to have accepted the dictum that anyone who watched Jews in a public eating place could see that they were alien, unfit to associate with Germans under any circumstances.[35]

It was natural enough, then, that German resorts, hotels, and restaurants should protect their human patrons by refusing to accept Jews as guests. Again, this pattern of exclusion was a half-century old when Streicher began publishing *Der Stürmer*. It was so common that Jewish organizations and newspapers had long made a practice of issuing lists of establishments which refused Jewish guests—partly as an encouragement to proprietors to mend their ways, partly to protect readers and members from humiliation. On several occasions Streicher simply reprinted the lists of such papers as the *Israelitisch Familienblatt*. Sometimes he accompanied them with letters from pensions or *Gasthaüser* "thanking" the group for inclusion. But always he had praise for the fighters, those proprietors who understood the battle between Jew and Aryan in all of its ramifications, and who forbade Jews in their resorts as part of an ongoing campaign to remove this alien group from German life entirely.[36]

4

Jewish infiltration of the "Weimar System" was a favorite *Stürmer* theme, well illustrated by a Fips cartoon, "The New Instructor," showing a *Stürmer*-Jew urging his "class" to leave the church and learn Esperanto, to favor abortion and become pacifists.[37] This, Streicher declared, was the logical result of the Bavarian *Kultusministerium*'s order that school excursions not be scheduled on Fridays or Saturdays so as not to conflict with the Jewish Sabbath. Once no Jew in Germany had rights. Now the

Graf Zeppelin, symbol of Germany's mastery of the air, celebrated the Sabbath when aloft. Public slaughterhouses and cattle markets were closed for Yom Kippur.[38] A Jewish-dominated government lent huge sums to banks and insurance companies run by Jews and Socialists. It hired increasing numbers of useless bureaucrats. Particularly in the election campaigns of 1932, *Der Stürmer* exhorted its readers to "send a message" to those who encouraged waste in government. In articles whose tone resembled that of some of the literature in California's 1978 Proposition 13 campaign, Streicher argued that a Nazi government would save money by trimming fat, not muscle.[39]

Surprisingly, *Der Stürmer* paid relatively little attention to actual Jewish criminal activity. White slavers, rapists, speculators, and profiteers all had their place, but usually in other contexts. At least part of the problem, from Streicher's perspective, lay in the fact that statistically Germany's Jewish community was law-abiding. The most notorious cases of government corruption involving Jews, the Barmat scandal of 1925 and the Sklarek case four years later, occurred in Berlin, too far from *Der Stürmer*'s usual hunting grounds to be useful front-page material. When *Der Stürmer* did highlight an actual criminal case, it was frequently in order to emphasize the contrast between races even in their criminality. A German evildoer, caught and convicted, never crawled before the bar of justice. He accepted his sentence like a man. Jews, on the other hand, began pleading for mercy from the moment that it became plain that they could not escape the prosecution's net—even though they could count on a striking contrast between penalties imposed for similar offenses on Jews and Aryans.[40]

An early issue of *Der Stürmer* told of a telephone operator sentenced to a month in jail for illegally passing stock market information to a Jew who went scot-free and collected his profits. Or Streicher would juxtapose the release of a Jew who allegedly poisoned two girls for refusing to submit to his "Asiatic lusts" to the eight-year prison sentence imposed on a front-line veteran for threatening a farmer's wife with a knife when he was refused food for his hungry family. Jews could commit parricide, or shoot a schoolmate in a fit of "oriental rage." They could even murder their own children, yet still be released for lack of evidence. And if peoples' justice was not allowed to run its course and lynch the criminals, Jews could always find Jewish psychiatrists to declare them insane, Jewish newspapers to support the contention, and purblind judges to confine these criminals in comfortable hospitals instead of putting them on death row. The Leopold/Loeb case, seemingly well-reported to *Der Stürmer* by a combination of wire services and letters from Chicago's German community, offered a perfect illustration of the kind of justice Jewish money could buy. And if by some unusual combination of circumstances a Jew were convicted of a capital crime, bleeding-heart, Jewish-controlled Leagues of Human Rights were certain to press for pardon or early release.[41]

The law and order elements of *Der Stürmer*'s message probably carried more weight in this particular area than its anti-Semitism. Streicher perceived the average *Stürmer* reader as sufficiently hostile to the Republic to believe that it allowed criminals of all races and religions too many easy escape routes. Here too, *Der Stürmer* benefited from the combination of increased education and improved mass communications. Many a newspaper reader likes to consider himself an amateur of the law, and follows local or national criminal trials with something of a sportsman's interest. Whenever possible, Streicher cast himself as the detached observer of the process, offering insight into the underlying workings of the system.

He began with the argument that Germans disliked courts, particularly those of the Weimar Republic, whose "paragraph system" subordinated justice to procedure. The Jew for his part was correspondingly at home in legal proceedings. His Talmudic training, with its emphasis on juggling and twisting evidence, gave him an inborn advantage. One only had to walk into a courthouse and observe the self-confident air of the Jewish lawyers who proliferated there to see that the Jews felt themselves masters of the legal system. And why should they not feel confident, since an increasing number of their racial fellows had been allowed to become judges since the Revolution? Jewish judges, according to *Der Stürmer*, came in two types. One was hostile to Gentiles in any trial that involved Jewish interest, however peripherally. The other was the false friend who questioned witnesses in such a way as to make them believe he was on their side, then deceived them. Judges and lawyers alike maintained an enduring interest in extending the length of trials, especially civil processes, as far as possible. No matter which side gained the final decision, his victory was likely to prove barren emotionally and financially. Only the Jewish lawyer laughed all the way to the bank.[42]

Any legal system is likely to seem forbidding to someone not regularly involved in it. A small businessman pursuing a civil suit or a motorist in traffic court is liable anywhere to feel that he is caught in a machine whose workings he does not understand, a machine which operates by its own rules and has only marginal relevance to an outsider's interests. It is usually easy to find agreement with the suggestion that everyone needs a lawyer to protect himself from other lawyers. In the courtroom itself, common sense often seems at a discount even to an observer with some knowledge of how the system is supposed to function. The legal positivism which dominated Weimar courts could make it extremely difficult for an uninitiated observer—to say nothing of someone with a direct interest in the proceedings—to follow the course of events. And since German courts did not operate on an adversary system, it was not necessarily proof of layman's paranoia for a "civilian" to wonder if judges and lawyers were not in some kind of unholy collusion. All that remained for *Der Stürmer* to do was provide the Jewish connection—to "prove" that here, as in so many areas, what one did not understand really did reflect conspiracy intstead of ignorance.

III

Der Stürmer
AND THE WORLD

Der Stürmer offered its readers more than a farrago of anecdotes drawn from daily life. Chapter seven presents its interpretation of international, national, and local politics: a revealing mixture of *Judenkoller* and populism. Chapter eight addresses the question of *Der Stürmer*'s popular appeal: Streicher's attempts to incorporate homely touches designed to make the reader feel he belonged, to integrate various classes and interest groups into the emerging Nazi community. Finally, chapter nine deals with *Der Stürmer*'s position under a government of laws by establishing the legal framework within which Streicher and his paper operated, then discussing the responses of the group and the individual who were *Der Stürmer*'s principal targets: the Jews and Nürnberg's mayor Hermann Luppe.

7 | The "Universal Jew" at Work

Der Stürmer's strong orientation as a local anti-Semitic sheet is clearly shown by its coverage of international and national affairs. Here the paper probably reached its intellectual nadir. The episodic, unsophisticated treatment of issues and events, unusually poorly executed even for the Nazi party press, were used primarily to illustrate Streicher's position on the Jewish issue. The points discussed and the images projected in *Der Stürmer* were important not in themselves, but as links in a chain of evidence illustrating Jewish conspiracy to control Germany and the world.

1

The pattern of developing this theme varied slightly from country to country. Julius Streicher's Austria differed little from his Bavaria in the sense that the same kinds of crimes and scandals reported in Kitzingen and Nürnberg happened in Linz, Salzburg, and Vienna. Jews seduced gentile women, plundered municipal treasuries, and operated degenerate nightclubs with monotonous regularity. Switzerland, the other "Germanic" state to which Streicher had easy access, tended to be criticized for its tolerance of Jews and its hospitality to international conferences and organizations. Not until 1932 did its image improve, and then only because of the alleged rise in anti-Semitism accompanying the increasing number of Jews fleeing to Switzerland in anticipation of a National Socialist triumph in Germany. All anti-Semitism needed to flourish, Streicher declared, was enough Jews. Let Switzerland have her turn, and see how the "real" Swiss liked the experience of living with soulless parasites.

In *Der Stürmer*'s pages, France and Britain alike had sold whatever souls they once possessed to the Jew. Jewish merchants grew rich exploiting the natives of India and Africa. Jewish swindlers penetrated every level of the British government and the English aristocracy. Jewish intellectuals preached Franco-German brotherhood while a Jewish-controlled French government recruited German youths for the infamous Foreign Legion and sent them to Morocco as cannon fodder.[2] In 1924 *Der Stürmer* published its version of an anecdote current in the German popular press to the effect that during the war a French general declared that were he to shake hands with a Boche, it would be necessary for him to wash afterwards. The general in question, Streicher declared, was of Jewish heritage. His original family name of "Levi" had been changed to "de Metz." Five years later *Der Stürmer* featured an even stronger version of the same story. In this version, an order allegedly signed by one Major General Levi declared that if he ever touched the hand of a Boche, he would immediately purify the offending limb by plunging it into excrement. To Streicher, both anecdotes made the same point: France was dominated by Jews, who, as the Talmud required, regarded Gentiles as lower than filth.[3]

The United States came off no better than its ex-allies. Occasionally it might produce a Lindbergh—a born hero who "looked Aryan," acted like a gentleman, and performed feats impossible for Jews, Indians, or Mongolians. On the whole, however, America was a land where Jewish-owned banks devoured the substance of Europe with ruinous loans. It was a land where Jewish stock speculators played ducks and drakes with German businesses, and foolish Germans seeking the alleged opportunities of the new world were cheated, robbed, or raped by Jews and their bastards.[4]

The Jew was everywhere. Plutarco Calles, president of Mexico, was alleged to favor trial marriage—and Calles, of course, was of Jewish ancestry. From Brazil, an expatriate *Stürmer* reader described his successful use of Streicher's paper to drive a

Jewish land speculator from the very doors of a Catholic church.[5] But *Der Stürmer*'s favorite source of this kind of material remained the states of eastern Europe. Even Poland, a country which Streicher ordinarily despised, at least knew what to do about the Jews. Jewish medical students were driven from anatomic institutes. Ritual slaughter was forbidden in Warsaw. In Lemberg, a Jew who attempted to rape an eight-year-old girl was beaten to death by the child's outraged neighbors. In Poland charges of ritual murder were not dismissed as paranoid nonsense. They were carefully investigated by the proper authorites, whose activities were in turn closely supervised by an aroused and enlightened people. Surely this was an instance of the last being first; Germany had some catching up to do.[6]

The results of failure to perform this racial duty could best be seen in Soviet Russia—*Der Stürmer*'s constant horrible example of a Jewish-run state. Jews had run the liquor industry under the Tsar. They operated state-controlled vodka shops under the Communists, and with the same goal: the destruction of whatever racial value the Slavic Russians still possessed. Jews desecrated Russian corpses for ritual purposes. Jews fostered the deportation of German farmers from their land on the Volga. The government could not even create the appearance of prosperity. High taxes and no luxuries, state-fixed wages and no fringe benefits—this was life in the so-called workers' paradise. Any German who needed further proof should try living there. By 1931 Streicher had gone so far as to print a call for "A Crusade against Soviet Judea." Though it was presented in Aesopian style, as the dream of a simple village schoolmaster, the message was plain. Only an army fighting under the swastika, led by Adolf Hitler and Julius Streicher, would be able to destroy this plague spot.[7]

Der Stürmer also paid close attention to the Jewish settlements in Palestine. Initially, and somewhat surprisingly, Streicher congratulated the Jews' efforts. Every Jew mired in the swamps of Palestine was one less to oppress Germans and Europeans. But this was still the same race that had destroyed the Aryan peoples of ancient Egypt. Streicher grew fond of quoting British administrators to the effect that the Jew could never be a farmer. He cited Zionist statistics indicating an increasing migration of Jews to Palestine's growing cities. As for the agricultural settlements of which the Jews boasted, these were founded, Streicher declared, not by Jewish settlers but by Jewish capitalists flourishing through the exploitation of Arab labor. Any doubts of the validity of this analysis were dispelled by the Arab rising of 1929. To *Der Stürmer* this was still another example of Aryan ability to make a true land of milk and honey, only to see it corrupted by the Jew. The Arabs knew their enemy. And this enemy was not Christianity, despite the age-old rivalry between the faiths. Nor was it the British, the current rulers of Palestine. It was the Jew, and only the Jew. If Poles and Arabs recognized mankind's real enemy, how could Germans remain so blind?[8]

2

Der Stürmer's coverage of national events depended even more heavily on anti-Semitism. All the Weimar Republic did for Germany in *Der Stürmer*'s pages was expose it completely to the machinations of international Jewry. The much-vaunted constitution grarranteed free speech—but what happened to the Nazi who attempted to exercise that right? The same vaunted constitution promised to support the interests of the *Mittelstand*. And what was the place of that group in a world of department stores and ruinous inflation, high taxes and government regulation? The eight-hour day remained a carrot held out to deluded workers by Jews and their tools. Officials attempting to serve their new masters were pushed aside by political appointees who were the only ones likely to draw the inflated pensions offered by the extravagant Republic.[9]

The Jew's hand was everywhere in the Weimar system. One of Streicher's favorite sources of fury and bathos was the occupied Rhineland. Youths in search of work and freedom were forced far from their fathers' graves and their mothers' care, to soulless urban swamps like Hamburg or Berlin. No one under twenty would ever know the old, beautiful Germany of the Rhine and Moselle valleys. Yet when the Republic negotiated the withdrawal of allied garrisons, *Der Stürmer* explained the process as a result of demands made by the Jewish-controlled French press, which in turn feared Italy's pressure on Jewish-controlled French North Africa. And it was well known that Mussolini despised Jews. The occupation, moreover, had borne Jewish fruit. The French might be gone, but fifteen thousand of their bastards remained behind—fifteen thousand living embodiments of racial pollution, fifteen thousand cuckoos in German nests.[10]

The sophistication of Streicher's analysis of the evacuation of the Rhineland was almost matched by his approach to the Dawes and Young Plans. The Dawes Plan offered many opportunities to illustrate the sweeping away of German wealth by Jewish international financiers.[11] Except, however, for an occasional attack on Germans for being their own pimps, Streicher focused on a single aspect of the plan: its influence on Germany's railroads. The extension of mortgages on the railway network became for *Der Stürmer* an explanation of every train wreck in Germany. The nation's railway system had once been the envy of the world for its safety and efficiency. As such it naturally aroused the fury of the Jew, who could create nothing and was terrified by machines of every sort. Now, in order to maximize profits for the "Dawes Jews," repair gangs were reduced in number. Train crews were overworked. Equipment was operated without regard for safety margins. The price was paid in blood, but when had Jews regarded German blood as having any importance?[12]

The Young Plan was similarly described as sixty years of slavery imposed on Germany by its Jewish-dominated government. Streicher's unwillingness to exploit systematically this aspect of the reparations issue may have reflected his own dislike of Hitler's sudden alliance with the Hugenberg right, dominated by big business and big landowners. It also indicated his belief that his prospective readers were not likely to be attracted by the kinds of complex questions of transfer payments and chattel mortgages basic to the Dawes and Young Plans. General indictments of "Dawes Jews" and "Young Slaves" were useful to foster a sense of indignation, but anything much deeper made poor propaganda.[13]

Until 1930 *Der Stürmer* seldom featured elections prominently. Parliaments were presented as dominated by Jews, to be purified only by the proverbial lieutenant and his file of musketeers. Parties, particularly the Democrats, were Jewish-financed. Elections brought to power only those weak enough to serve a race of born criminals. Even President Hindenburg, target of vicious Jewish-inspired attacks before his election, became the subject of their flattery once he took office.[14]

The Nazi landslide in the elections of September, 1930, justified Streicher in expanding his coverage of national politics. Not until 1932, however, did *Der Stürmer* go much beyond occasional attacks on such specific legislation as the Emergency Decrees instituted in 1931.[15] Only Hitler's standing for president in 1932 finally brought Streicher into the front lines of national politics. *Der Stürmer* was editorially incredulous at the behavior of Hindenburg, the one-time national hero who now depended on Jews and Socialists. In the final vote, the Jews and "all thirteen" of their parties supported Hindenburg. But this decaying monument had become nothing but a ventriloquist's dummy.

The fall of the Brüning government in May gave Streicher renewed hope. At least, he reasoned, the new Chancellor Franz von Papen was cordially hated by the Jews. But this point in Papen's favor soon gave way to editorial disgust at the new government's continued refusal to enlighten itself on the Jewish question. Through the balance of 1932, Streicher's paper continued to stress Hindenburg's dwindling support from the "red-black coalition" which had elevated him to his second term. Abandon Jewish help, Streicher encouraged the president. Your true friends, the saviors of Germany, stand under the long-despised swastika. Translated into practical political terms, this was a call to appoint Hitler chancellor of Germany.[16]

3

Streicher's approach to local politics was both more sophisticated and more effective. He was particularly fortunate in his primary opponent: Nürnberg's mayor, Dr. Hermann Luppe. The conflict between these men is frequently cited as a symbol of the struggle between Weimar and its *völkisch* opponents. Luppe, the man who accurately described his life as a battle for democracy and German unity, is juxtaposed to Streicher the destroyer,

Streicher the Jew-baiter. In the process he frequently becomes a man whose motives and behavior are as automatically subject to positive interpretations as Streicher's are to negative ones.[17]

This approach dehumanizes one of Germany's greatest mayors by putting him on a pedestal. Luppe was undoubtedly an able man, with a distinguished record in the municipal adminis-tration of Frankfurt and a developing career as one of the leaders of the new Democratic Party. His problem was that he knew it. From the day in 1920 when he took office, Luppe faced a daunt-ing spectrum of challenges. From the Kapp Putsch to the *Mach-tergreifung* he was attacked both by the Socialists who felt he did too little, and the bourgeoisie who criticized him as a Marxist in DDP guise.[18] It is, however, also true that Luppe consistently de-pended on his abilities alone to carry him through situations demanding political intelligence as well as technical skills. His behavior as Nürnberg's mayor combined progressive planning and assertive leadership with a marked capacity to give offense. His memoirs describe the city's institutions as inadequate, ana-chronistic, or prehistoric; his subordinates as intellectually limited, reactionary, or timid and unreliable. His approach seemed almost calculated to build walls instead of bridges. Tell-ing his new fellow citizens that they would fall for the promises and programs of any charlatan rather than listen to the voice of reason was hardly likely to increase support for the Democratic Party and the Weimar Republic.[19]

Streicher almost certainly would have attacked Luppe under any circumstances. In addition to the argument that Luppe inspired Streicher's jealous hatred by being educated, cultivated, sophisticated, respected—everything Streicher was not—Luppe was also Weimar's symbol in Nürnberg. Streicher was shrewd enough to spot the mayor's increasing vulnerability. He had another reason for selecting Luppe as a primary target. A combination of anti-Semitism and attacks on *völkisch* politicians whose names were only marginally familiar even in Nürnberg was not likely to sell enough papers to establish *Der Stürmer* as a profit-making enterprise. An unpopular mayor, however, was another situation entirely.

Streicher was attempting more than a simple exercise in showing up the powerful. Even before 1914 a broad spectrum of conflicting communal pressures had been building in Nürnberg. War and defeat increased these pressures. The city government, which since 1914 had exercised an increasing amount of control over its citizens' daily lives, was a visible target. Its workings were comprehensible even to someone without an *Abitur*, and could be felt at every turn. By the early 1920s enough free-floating hostility existed in Nürnberg that Streicher could raise some echoes by shouting in meeting halls, in courtrooms, and in the pages of *Der Stürmer* that the "decent people" of Nürnberg were mad as hell, and were not going to take it anymore.

Since his appointment Luppe had been attacked in Nürnberg's press from left and right alike. Nothing, however, prepared the city for *Der Stürmer's* "Drumfire" against its new mayor. Particularly Streicher emphasized Luppe's alleged Jewish ancestry. But *Der Stürmer* worked even harder to create the image of Luppe as a coarse party politician given to personal abuses of power. Streicher's Luppe kept a restaurant open past closing hours. He used city-owned autos for private purposes. He punished officials who criticized his behavior. *Der Stürmer* regularly featured accounts of Luppe's efforts to deny the paper its legal right to print the news, or rhetorical essays asking how long the city of Dürer and Hans Sachs, the treasure-house of Germany, could tolerate such a man as mayor.[20] The half-dozen Nazis on the city council after 1924 followed a consistent pattern of disrupting meetings, then responding to expulsion by noisily accusing Luppe of suppressing views which challenged his own.[21]

Luppe initially considered Streicher a ridiculous figure with a primitive mind, and mocked him to his face. He came to regard him as an extremely dangerous psychopath, a wallower in perverse filth. But Luppe was trapped. To ignore Streicher's attacks was impossible for him as a public official and a man of honor who was anything but cold-blooded. To respond, on the other hand, risked alienating those respectable citizens who believed, at least for public consumption, that their governors should be outside the political process.

Luppe fought Streicher on public platforms and in the city council. He took his tormentor to court in a series of spectacular lawsuits. But the man who as late as 1929 dismissed Adolf Hitler as nothing but a "miserable babbler" never quite understood that legal condemnation did not mean automatic discreditation. Courts rendered favorable judgments. Democrats throughout Germany offered sympathy and support. Indeed, even some of Streicher's supporters occasionally suggested that enough was enough, that Streicher's tactics were making Luppe seem a victim of persecution.[22] Yet Streicher continued to wheel freely through the beer halls of Franconia, drawing applause as a man who bowed before no one, while Luppe continued to express his bewilderment at the number of people, even those educated people, who heard Adolf Hitler, were completely inspired by him, but never seemed able to remember what he had said.[23]

Practically every non-Nazi city councillor and municipal official in Nürnberg came under *Der Stürmer*'s fire at one time or another. To Streicher, Max Süssheim had three points against him: he was a Jew; he was a Social Democrat; and he was a lawyer. He was also successful and prosperous. Particularly during periods when *Der Stürmer* was concentrating its appeal on the working classes, Streicher delighted in portraying Süssheim as the kind of proletarian leader who refused to defend a worker unable to pay in advance. *Der Stürmer* attacked him for everything from refusing a challenge to excessive use of a spittoon. [24] But despite Mayor Luppe's description of him as a "soft, labile Jew," Süssheim proved among Streicher's most formidable legal adversaries during the *Kampfzeit*. Indeed, Streicher's first conviction came in 1922 from a series of attacks on Süssheim published in the *Deutscher Volkswille*. Both on his own behalf and as Luppe's attorney, Süssheim fought Streicher to a standstill until his death in 1933, just after the *Machtergreifung*. His success indicates the potential of legal action properly and determinedly applied.[25]

City Councilman Hermann Heimerich was less successful. Early in 1924 *Der Stürmer* began attacking him for abusing his office, violating regulations designed to minimize Nürnberg's housing shortage. Heimerich was anxious to leave Nürnberg for a higher appointment, and had limited interest in damaging his prospects by engaging in a series of libel suits against a man who had a reputation for being a dangerous adversary in a courtroom. When he moved to Kiel in 1925 as deputy mayor, he handed

Streicher a victory by default.[26]

Criticism of Heimerich's decision to relocate rather than fight is muted by the fate of Finance Councillor Julius Fleischmann. *Der Stürmer* culminated a series of attacks by describing him as a line-dodging shirker who stole clothes from his comrades' baggage. Fleischmann sued for libel. The trial, an example of Weimar's hurrah-patriotism at its worst, vindicated Fleischmann on paper. Streicher was fined nine hundred marks. But *Der Stürmer*'s editor was not exaggerating when he declared that the trial had convicted Fleischmann of cowardice in the public press. Even the court sententiously described Fleischmann's wartime behavior as "unsoldierly." Such results hardly encouraged Streicher's future targets to seek legal redress if they had anything at all worth concealing in their pasts.[27]

In addition to its attacks on specific individuals, *Der Stürmer* consistently accused Luppe of importing officials from outside Nürnberg. These draft-dodging Jews, lazy and incompetent, depended on relatives and ancestry for promotion. It was, for example, a disgrace to the city that a Jewess whose parents were named Kohn and Levi had authority over four thousand German orphans and foster children. *Der Stürmer* also attacked the Nürnberg *Volkschochschule*, founded in 1921 to provide evening courses and similar programs for working people, as Jewish-dominated—a charge reflecting the fact that many Jewish teachers felt such new institutions offered greater professional opportunities than traditional schools dominated by traditional administrators.[28]

Luppe did in fact seek talent where he could find it, and made no secret of his conviction that too many municipal appointments in Nürnberg were made on no sounder grounds than possession of a proper regional accent. Periodic Nazi attempts to fix charges of corruption on these new people were usually thwarted. Here if anywhere, *Der Stürmer* suffered from its sources. Disappointed office-seekers, Nazis in subordinate posts, and simple office gossips could not provide the kind of material necessary to force accusations of malfeasance through the city council—particularly if the people under fire were doing their jobs properly.[29] *Der Stürmer*'s only major success involved the forced resignation of the director of the Nürnberg *Volkshoch-*

schule. He was caught in a hotel room with a young woman to whom, according to Streicher, he had promised a job as a kinder-garten teacher. *Der Stürmer* delighted in publishing the details of the "special instruction" offered by this symbol of the new republic. The accused man lost his job and left the city rather than risk a trial.[30]

4

Policies made better targets than did personalities. Par-ticularly in the mid-1920s, the paper's slogan might well have been "no item too small." Streicher ran a pathetic feature story on a veteran of 1866 and 1870 sentenced to three days in jail for begging. What kind of government, *Der Stürmer* asked, can let its old heroes starve? The fact that the beggar was carrying over a hundred marks when arrested never appeared in Streicher's pages. When in 1923 a brewery provided beer at reduced prices to a police station, allegations of bribery were promptly raised—particularly since the beer was donated through a tavern frequented by Nazis. *Der Stürmer*'s answer was to ask how anyone could call it illegal to offer underpaid officials beer at yesterday's prices in these times of inflation. Was it bribery to give a thirsty man a drink? When the city council voted to refuse to continue leasing municipally owned land to small farmers, the decision emerged in *Der Stürmer*'s pages as an effort to replace a free peasantry with a collective farm. The city farm itself came under fire for being a source of free food for councilmen and free clothes for tramps. The next year, *Der Stürmer* described the same farm as "Luppe's Penal Colony," whose workers were paid less than German POWs in French camps. Luppe's government was accused of raising the prices of city-owned utilities as part of a deliberate attempt to destroy the *Mittelstand*. It was charged with neglecting the graves of its fallen warriors. When renters of city property were forbidden to keep pigeons, the administration defended the decision on hygienic grounds. For Streicher, it was one more proof that Luppe cared nothing for the poor people who might depend on the money they made raising and selling pigeons to supplement inadequate pensions and welfare checks.[31]

All of these attacks, whether involving beer or birds, had a common denominator: defense of the little man against the anonymous "they" who ordered his life. Nazi city councilmen introduced resolutions calling for higher taxes on neon and billboard advertising. They called it a "luxury tax" whose proceeds could be made available to the men made jobless by the Jewish businesses which would be hardest hit. Nazis proposed a tenfold increase on department store taxes. They advocated allowing small shops to open before the legal hour of 7:00 A.M. to encourage the patronage of workers who would otherwise have to buy food in factory canteens. In 1926, when the council voted to give Luppe and his wife a silver anniversary gift, Karl Holz asked why the money should not instead be donated to the unemployed. In 1927, when a new streetcar line was opened between Nürnberg and Fürth, the city staged a dinner to commemorate the event. How, *Der Stürmer* asked, can Nürnberg waste two thousand marks on a party when thirty thousand of its citizens are jobless?[32]

These were the kinds of issues to which the everyday reader, whatever his social or economic standing, could presumably relate on a visceral level. It is a political cliché that petty corruption is more likely to arouse public indignation than exchanges of six- or seven-figure sums. Two million marks would be an ungraspable figure for most *Nürnberger*. Two thousand marks, on the other hand, was a sum small enough to be emotionally meaningful. When Germany was still Germany, *Der Stürmer* declared, no one objected to a hard-working city council having a dinner or standing itself to a few drinks. But under this administration fifteen geese at a time were roasted in the *Rathskeller* for the benefit of councilmen, many of whom claimed to be proletarians.[33]

In *Der Stürmer*'s pages Nürnberg's government was as incompetent as it was greedy and unresponsive. The public health service was a favorite Streicher target. When *Der Stürmer* published allegations that female clinic patients were tended by male nurses and that workers' families were treated like dirt, Streicher could reasonably expect to strike a response from anyone who had had to wait an hour or two for a doctor. Why, Streicher asked, were Nürnberg's workers unable to earn enough to choose their own physicians? With the onset of the depression, the municipal health program began, gradually and reluctantly, to charge for its services. Fifty pfennigs for a prescription or for a certificate entitling doctor's care might not seem like a large sum. To *Der Stürmer* it was one more step in the process of pauperizing the unemployed and dependent. Health care, Streicher declared, should be above partisan politics and removed from the "loud-mouthed Jews" who controlled it and enjoyed humiliating their Aryan clients.[34]

Once again *Der Stürmer*'s primary appeal was to psychic realities and visceral images. By any standards Nürnberg's public health services functioned well before 1933. But they were public services. Long waits, occasional rudeness, a sense of being treated as a set of detached organs rather than a person—these are usual, if not inevitable, elements of such services. By calling attention to them, *Der Stürmer* could appeal both to the actual grievances that might be entertained by those who used the clinics and to the fears of the underemployed, the citizens on fixed incomes, and anyone else who felt that they might find themselves reduced to using the municipal health care facilities.

A similar approach characterized *Der Stürmer*'s attacks on Nürnberg's housing policies. Even before 1914, the city suffered from the effects of rapid increases in population accompanying rapid industrialization. Events after 1914 combined to transform a problem into a crisis. The construction of private housing for all practical purposes ceased during the war. In the immediate postwar years, defense workers who preferred to stay in Nürnberg competed for living space with an increasing number of refugees and émigrés, most of them from German Austria, specifically Vienna, and the Sudetenland. While some of the new residents listed their previous addresses as being in territory ceded to Poland, very few listed their religion as "Mosaic." If Nürnberg was being overrun by anyone in the immediate postwar years, it was being overrun by Catholics. But Catholic, Protestant, or Jew, refugee from peace treaties or defense worker who liked the big city, everyone was competing for an increasingly scarce resource. The competition was intensified after 1918 by two internal factors: a rash of marriages postponed during the war, and an increasing number of single women, working for a living, who sought to establish their independence by finding their own rooms or apartments.

Most of these housing-seekers lacked money. Wartime savings had been eroded by inflation. Refugees and immigrants brought few negotiable assets with them. Young couples and underpaid women could afford only the cheapest accommodations. And overshadowing all was the rampant inflation pressuring landlords and tenants alike. Luppe regarded himself as a housing specialist. From his first days in office he labored to enforce rent controls fairly, to regularize the construction of shantytowns which had sprung up everywhere in Nürnberg, and above all to combat the chicanery and downright corruption which inevitably accompanied such a situation.[35]

Luppe's best efforts nevertheless made slow progress. *Der Stürmer* picked up an alleged quotation of the mayor in response to his critics: "now everyone is sheltered somewhere," and contrasted Luppe's comfortable house with the shabby apartments of the factory workers the broken-down railway cars and converted gypsy wagons of the less fortunate taxpayers. Luppe's ready acceptance of responsibility in this sphere left him open to Streicher's charges of a "secret dictatorship" conducted from city hall—conducted for the benefit of Jews. On one hand Jews avoided municipal housing regulations by converting taverns and similar buildings to lodging-houses. On the other, they used the courts to expel even long-standing Aryan tenants unable to pay inflated postwar rents.[36]

The results could be seen in any walk through Nürnberg's poorer districts. Pensioned noncommissioned officers of the Imperial Army found themselves on the street. Eviction notices were served in the middle of winter, with women, children, and household goods piled in the streets in driving rain. Even those families escaping eviction faced inhuman living conditions. A crippled war veteran returned from long hours in a factory to spend his nights in an old backyard laundry. A worker's ten-person family was crowded into three rooms, with a girl of twenty sleeping in the same bed with two teenaged brothers while two other boys slept in the toilet. A man, his wife, and three children were packed into two rooms with only one window. What kind of socialism was this? asked one despairing woman. The gulf between rich and poor was greater than ever. The city was talking about a twenty-year building program to remedy the situation. But what would happen in the meantime? A Jew, fat with money acquired during the inflation faced no problem. A path of gold would open the way into any house or apartment in Nürnberg. And where was the government that should have been taxing these fat cats? It was busily evicting a man with nine years' military service because his desperate wife had tried to commit suicide. This made them undesirable tenants in a building where a Jewess lived alone in a seven-room apartment. But what was to be expected in "Luppe's paradise," where everyone had "somewhere" to live.[37]

Throughout 1926 and 1927, *Der Stürmer* continued its campaign of contrasts. Jews like Süssheim lived in a twelve-room apartment; a war-crippled worker existed in a goat shed. And even this disgraceful accommodation had been achieved in defiance of city authorities who wanted to separate the family, sending the wife to a shelter for the homeless and the children to an orphanage. By 1928, the housing shortage had abated enough to reduce *Der Stürmer*'s campaign to an occasional cartoon presenting the eviction of a Gentile family as making more room for Jews, or to an occasional communication from a man protesting that a dispute with his Jewish landlord ended with himself, his sick wife, and eight children being put onto the street—with the connivance of a Jewish doctor who declared that a desperately sick woman could be moved despite her condition. The depression, which intensified once more the housing crisis, did not inspire a campaign to equal that of 1923–1925. One of Fips's most effective cartoons, "The Way Out," portrayed a poor family which turned on the gas in final response to their miserable living conditions. The ghastly expressions on the faces of the half-dozen corpses of all ages do credit to Ruprecht's abilities as a sketcher.[38] But as the party gained strength locally and nationally, specific issues like housing shortages gave way to a general appeal for workers with their muscles and workers with their brains to unite against those men and institutions who had made Germany a poorhouse. And in Nürnberg, that meant Luppe and his gang.

The impact of *Der Stürmer*'s political appeals is impossible

Der Ausweg

Nichts von dem ist in Erfüllung gegangen was ihnen die Novemberrepublik versprochen hatte

THE WAY OUT. "Nothing the November Republic promised them has been fulfilled."

to document accurately. On balance, the unmodified *Juden-koller* which was the paper's basis for discussing national and international affairs almost certainly reinforced existing convictions more than it changed minds. On a local level, constant attacks on the real and alleged shortcomings of Nürnberg's municipal administration seem to have helped focus voter anxieties and hostilities. Throughout 1932 Nürnberg's Nazis pressed for a dissolution of the city council. New elections might give the National Socialists an absolute majority. Even without such a majority the beleaguered Luppe might well resign. *Der Stürmer* campaigned heavily for a referendum on the issue, printing sample ballots, arguing that the existing council no longer represented the will of Nürnberg and Germany, and demanding changes. The council finally capitulated. A three-fifths majority was required for dissolution. When the referendum was held on July 31, 1932, one hundred five thousand of Nürnberg's voters supported the resolution. One hundred twenty-seven thousand rejected it. On one level, this was a Nazi defeat. On another, *Der Stürmer* was justified in its boast that it had taken seven parties working together to keep the council in office. When the paper bragged that soon the Nazi colors would wave from city hall, it could be seen no longer as an idle threat.[39]

8 | *Der Stürmer* and Its Public:

The Politics of Transcendence

In the decade between its founding and the *Machtergreif-ung, Der Stürmer* incorporated positive appeals to almost every definable interest group in Nürnberg, Franconia, and Bavaria—except, paradoxically, that petty bourgeoisie which provided so many Nazi voters. Streicher enjoyed mocking what he considered the spineless, pettifogging mind-set of the respectable middle classes. A *Stürmer* series titled "Schildbürgerstreiche," described a town whose citizens made fools and criminals their leaders, saw their money made into paper and their wealth taxed away. When the *Schildbürger* sought justice, they found the courts in the hands of their enemies. And when they returned home, they found their sons and daughters had been seduced by the newly arrived *Schweinhünde* who now ran the city—so the grand-children of the *Schildbürger* were half *Schweinhünde*![1]

Streicher regarded himself as issuing a call to battle. This chapter concentrates on four groups he considered important enough to seek as converts to the cause of National Socialism and the ideology of anti-Semitism: farmers, workers, educators, and women. *Der Stürmer*'s approaches to them reflected the varying mixtures of criticism, encouragement, and scapegoating Streicher considered appropriate to win support from different sectors of the population. They indicate that the paper was more than an undifferentiated hate sheet. Yet at the same time these approaches illustrate a different aspect of a common theme: anti-Semitism as an instrument of social and political integration.

1

In its appeal to the farmers of Bavaria *Der Stürmer* manifested a greater degree of evolution than in any other area. Streicher may have begun his career as a village schoolmaster, but by 1923 he was as much a man of asphalt and carbon monoxide as any born Nürnberger. His paper's initial references to peasants described greedy farmers who sold watered milk to suburban housewives, then hired Jewish lawyers to befuddle the courts. They contrasted villagers who grew rich during the war, yet refused to donate to funds for maintaining the graves of German dead in foreign countries, with factory workers who were as generous with their money in 1923 as they were with their blood in 1914.[2]

This attitude, a fairly sharp departure from the official Nazi party line of blood and soil, continued through the middle 1920s. Despite occasional success in distributing copies of the paper at cattle fairs and markets, when *Der Stürmer* seriously addressed itself to agricultural questions it did so from an urban perspective.[3] Its primary use of rural material was as a source for anti-Semitism, and the primary focus of that material involved cattle dealing.

Not every livestock trader in Franconia was Jewish. Enough Jews, however, were in the business to make them visible. Over years, and sometimes generations, their relationships with their customers had developed to a degree of complexity baffling alike to courts and historians. Cattle trades involving money to boot, notes of hand, cash loans to help through hard times, small-scale speculations—all reinforced a pattern of mutual haggling, jockeying for advantage, and loud complaints on encountering a more skilled cheat. Dealers and farmers alike frequently regarded their negotiations as a test of skill, as well as a business. Thus the *Stürmer-Archiv* includes an undated copy of a *Phrase-Book for Farmers*—a pocket-sized guide to the jargon of cattle dealers. The pamphlet bears no trace of anti-Semitism. It is rather a straightforward guide to an argot similar to *Gaunersprache*, mixing Yiddish, Hebrew, and German. The number one is Oleph, two is Bes, three is Gimmel, twenty, Kaff, and so on. "Bankrupt" becomes "machulla." "Sick" is "kühle." Such jargon, spoken in a rapid undertone, would enable dealers to discuss prices and sales in front of prospective customers without exposing too much of their hand. *Landwirt* K. Roth merely proposed to redress the balance.[4]

It took *Der Stürmer* to make the game a symbol of Jewish exploitation of Germany's farmers. Even then the paper did not begin emphasizing the issue until 1927—in part apparently because Streicher had not established a network of rural correspondents who could give him the kind of information he needed. Some of the stories are dated enough to be amusing. It is a bit difficult, for example, for a modern holder of bank credit cards to sympathize heavily with the "poor sick farmer" who purchased a calf with "usurious" interest charges of 1.5 percent monthly on the unpaid balance of three hundred fifty marks. The dealer who, when buying a cow by weight, declared that he himself was four pounds lighter on the post office scales than on those of the village market probably knew his farmers all too well. The calf buyer who brought with him a boy whose task it was to let the calves suck his fingers in order to keep them still on the scales, then instructed the child to lift the animals by their gums in order to reduce their weights, was hardly an exemplary businessman. It is also difficult to imagine a farmer sufficiently stupid to be deceived by such an obvious trick.[5]

If Jews were smart enough to cheat Bavarian peasants in direct negotiations over livestock, when paper was involved there was no contest. As early as 1924, *Der Stürmer* announced the recruiting for the *völkisch* movement of a peasant who had obtained money to pay his taxes by signing a note at usurious interest.[6] Interestingly, most accounts of similar incidents before 1930 give a different impression from the one Streicher intended. They describe farmers ready and able to defend their interests in court when they felt that the notes they signed were being misused. *Der Stürmer* might urge peasants to call their dogs whenever a Jew approached with an offer to trade livestock or loan money on a signature, but the accompanying minatory accounts usually end with the would-be swindler paying a significant fine or disappearing behind prison walls.[7]

The national elections of 1928, in which the Nazis suffered a disastrous defeat, led Hitler to order the concentration of organizational and propaganda efforts in the countryside. A rural population suspicious of the Republic, and concerned with steadily declining farm prices, seemed to offer fruitful recruiting grounds for National Socialism. Streicher, however, initially found some difficulty in reaching this audience. Peasants seeking specific answer and specific information on farm problems were unimpressed with generalized anti-Semitic rhetoric.[8] Then Streicher found two specific issues that he could exploit in the countryside.

The first involved hops. The hop market of Franconia originally involved a cash crop grown by a large number of small farmers for sale to regional brewers. By the end of the nineteenth century it had become an international business. The major buyers were no longer individual breweries but large wholesale firms. Conflicts between farmers, who felt themselves victimized by the vagaries of a market only dimly comprehended, and wholesalers, who were attempting to reestablish commercial networks disrupted by war and inflation, existed well before Streicher discovered the issue.

In January, 1929, *Der Stürmer* began publishing detailed reports of hop dealers mixing cheap foreign hops with the native product. Something had to be wrong, *Der Stürmer* declared, when every employee of Jewish-owned hop firms was putting in overtime during what was usually a slack season. And the Jews who ran the businesses were perfect specimens of their race. Even though many of them had been involved in the hop trade for generations, moved in the best society, and kept riding stables, they were no different from the newest Galician immigrant. For years they had attempted systematically to reduce the hop farmers to peonage by cutting prices. When this failed, they imported foreign hops and sold them to brewers as the native product.[9]

The economic background of the hop crisis is less important than Streicher's use of it to appeal to the bread-and-butter grievances of Franconia's small farmers, particularly after several hop dealers were in fact convicted of the offense Streicher described. Then *Der Stürmer* generated another scandal when it accused Jewish meat packer August Bauernfreund of ruining small farmers under the protection of high officials in the Bavarian

Ministry of Agriculture. It took over two years before Streicher was finally convicted of slander for his allegations in this matter.[10] In the meantime *Der Stürmer* continued to accuse the Weimar Republic of "slaughtering" its farmers by levying taxes on rural insurance cooperatives, or by allowing the import of French fertilizer which could grow only the incomes of French businessmen. Falling milk prices were part of a plot to eliminate small dairymen. The Young Plan was a special burden on farmers already heavily indebted. A bad harvest or a few sick cows, and the "Young Jews" could count on destroying another German holding. When the government made a desperate effort to help find buyers for rye in the spring of 1931, *Der Stürmer* declared this to be no more than a protective cloak for Jews who, as usual, would buy cheap and sell at high prices.[11]

By 1930 the tone of the stories describing direct relations between Jews and farmers had also changed. The new background suggests a pattern of mutual desperation. Crop failures, cattle plagues, and depressed markets combined with a sharp decline in the availability of commercial credit to make an increasing number of peasant farmers desperate for ready cash. If the depression itself had not yet hit the countryside full force, fear of it was tending to make small-town bankers increasingly cautious about making new loans and correspondingly insistent on prompt repayment of outstanding notes. The livestock dealers, Jewish or Gentile, were caught in the middle. In some instances, old and valued customers came to them for the credit they could no longer obtain elsewhere. In other instances, doing any business with a farmer obviously going deeper into debt each year necessarily involved correspondingly greater requirements for security. It must also be said that the livestock trade was hardly a breeding ground for altruism. More than a few men who had spent their business lives in petty trading for small profits saw an opportunity to capitalize on the misfortunes of others.

Der Stürmer provided full reports on all three behavior patterns. The "honest Jew," trusted by his business associates, who encouraged farmers to sign notes of hand for small amounts of cash in hand, with high rates of interest and a final, impossibly high balloon payment, became a stock villain in Streicher's pages. The stories convey an impression of small businessmen, themselves pressured by a deepening economic crisis, often forced to sell farmers' paper at a discount to keep themselves afloat. Even then, the list of bankrupt livestock dealers grew longer and longer.

Local prosecutors rarely found evidence either of criminal intent or culpably bad management. A three-month jail sentence here, a minor fine there, were usually the highest penalties imposed. Even then the courts seemed to accept the line of argument that the "dishonesty" involved desperate juggling to keep a declining business from collapsing, rather than deliberate long-term attempts at fraud. The businesses and individuals involved were almost without exception well-established, well-regarded, and honestly managed. Even in *Der Stürmer*'s pages the men who went bankrupt in 1930 or 1931 were seldom the men who sold sick cattle in 1926. Indeed it might be argued that they were victimized by their own optimism and their own good will. Believing times had to improve, finding it difficult to deny the appeals of old customers, they extended credit to the point of their own financial collapse. But the independent peasant, who may never in his life have borrowed substantial amounts, or who had never needed credit of any kind for longer than a few months, found it difficult to accept the explanations of the authorities who came to seize his crops and cattle, or to sell his farm at auction in settlement of debts or taxes. Streicher's explanation that this was part of a Jewish conspiracy might not be intellectually convincing, but it could be extremely emotionally satisfying to a farmer seeking a concrete outlet for his rage—particularly when the message was absorbed on top of a few drinks.[12]

Once the hypothetical farmer recovered from his hangover, he was likely to find that life in his village had changed in ways that further reinforced his new feelings. Throughout the late 1920s businessmen from towns like Ansbach, Leutershausen, or Regensburg had been purchasing farms on speculation, sometimes bringing in strangers to work the land, on other occasions retaining the former owners as tenants. This loss of independence, even when reflecting the bluntest economic necessity, was painful to the victim and shocking to his neighbors, who saw themselves as likely candidates for the same fate. In particular forced sales offered ample grounds for misunderstanding even given good will and honesty on both sides. If a dealer made a cash offer, the peasant was likely to call it too small. If the farm was auctioned, charges of excessive commissions, or of collusion between auctioneers and purchasers, kept rural courts busy in 1930 and 1931. *Der Stürmer* was even busier. Lead articles described "Throat-slitters" and "Oppressors of the Peasant." Cartoons showed a poor farm family watching in anguish as a Jewish auctioneer sold their home from under them, or depicted a peasant, gun in hand and a bloody hole in his temple, dead eyes fixed on the harvest he would never reap.[13]

Increasingly the farmers of northern Bavaria began turning to the kind of self-help that had earlier proved effective in Schleswig-Holstein.[14] One result of this process can be summarized by police reports on two speeches with almost the same lines of argument delivered by Karl Holz in villages with roughly similar demographies. An open-air meeting near Rügland "found no special echo among the farmers" in 1926. In 1930, at Wassermungerau, Holz received "general applause"—and received it at the expense of another speaker from an organization which claimed to be the true representatives of Bavaria's farmers in the Weimar Republic.[15] The *Bayerischer Landbund* and similar organizations had initially tended to ignore Nazi propaganda. By 1932, however, agricultural depression combined with constant Nazi attacks on existing farmers' organizations as unable to cope with the crisis began to take effect. According to *Der Stürmer*, at least, the *Landbund* and its sister organization the *Landvolk* were becoming organizations without members. Farmer after farmer was instead joining the NSDAP. Offers to cooperate, at least on a local level, were met with the reply that the Nazis had no use for "*Landbund* clowns" who allowed Jewish department stores to sell imported frozen meat and accepted reduced prices for milk.[16]

Streicher enjoyed calling for drastic action by the farmers against their Jewish oppressors. A 1932 article, for example, attacked Jews as born rogues and encouraged farmers to reach for their whips and unchain their watchdogs when a Jew approached their gates.[17] Yet despite Streicher's rhetoric, *Der Stürmer* tended to report more threats than violence from the Bavarian countryside. Periodically an angry farmer would

Deutſche Ernte 1931

German Harvest 1931.

describe his intention to horsewhip a persistent dealer, yet these lively debates usually ended in nothing more serious than flourished sticks and mutual recriminations. On one occasion at least, a debate over the sale of a cow led to an Aryan peasant being pelted with dung, then beaten by two Jews. The police wrote off the incident as typical of the kind of business disputes that were a regular part of rural life, usually to be settled by mutual bandaging, a round or two of drinks—and, one hopes in this particular case, a bath.[18]

Der Stürmer's appeal to the farmers was also significant for what it did not include. The paper reported a surprisingly small number of sex scandals involving Jewish peddlers or livestock dealers, and even then their offenses seldom involved more than attempting to steal a kiss from a farmer's daughter, or making passes of the kind characteristic of traveling-salesman jokes in all languages.[19] Another reasonable indication of the relative absence of the kind of anti-Semitism Streicher wished to encourage is the shortage of specific descriptions of National Socialist involvement in the relationship of peasant and Jew. The antagonism that existed between these groups was traditional, with the Nazis frequently playing an instrumental role. A dispute over the sale price of a cow, for example, ended with a group of farmers informing the Jewish purchaser that they were going to see to it that his name was published in *Der Stürmer*, then accepting his offer to buy fifty litres of beer in exchange for silence![20]

National Socialism could prove instrumentally useful in other ways. When the farm of one party member was ordered to be sold at auction, the most likely bidder was a Jewish land dealer named Aal. *Der Stürmer* gleefully described a room crowded with brown shirts and swastikas. When Aal and his "coterie of Jewish speculators" failed in their effort to have the Nazis removed, the auction began. Aal then had the gall to offer fifty-one thousand marks for property valued at over three hundred thousand marks. He paled, but refused to increase his offer, when a Nazi in the audience loudly demanded that the farm's sawmill be sold separately, since wood was going to be needed for a gallows. Aal initially got the farm at his price. The biter, however, was bitten when the town council, which had been forced to order the tax sale, demanded an immediate down payment of eight thousand marks, which Aal could not produce. His bid was therefore rejected and the farm sold to neighbors of its legitimate owner.[21]

Der Stürmer's story parallels closely the accounts in a series of official reports. Aal, who had left the auction under a barrage of threats from pursuing Nazis, filed a complaint. His description of events might have been a bit more credible had he not concluded by declaring that once he learned that the original owner wished to keep the farm he withdrew his own bid out of sympathy. But his claim that he had not been given proper protection inspired the Bavarian Ministry of the Interior to order a full investigation.

The gendarmerie's report was objective in words but hostile in tone. The responsible officer said he had been present with two of his men. They had escorted Aal in and out of the auction hall. Aal in fact had made a bid on the farm without the down payment he knew was required. And how, the policeman asked, could three men clear the hall of a crowd of men who had a legal right to be present? Keeping order was the auctioneer's job. The clear implication was that the gendarmerie had better things to do with its time than participate in the dispossession of honest citizens who had fallen on hard times. The ministry accepted the report and reprimanded the auctioneer—though how he alone could have controlled a room full of brownshirts remained unexplained.[22]

It is probably legitimate to suggest that in such cases, from the Ministry of the Interior downwards, the sympathy of an overwhelming majority of officials rested with the farmers. Anti-Semitism was a contributing factor, but in the context of the depression, nobody loved a land speculator. Aal, who seems to have possessed more determination than common sense, had this point reinforced three weeks later when he appeared at another auction. This time a crowd of farmers, many of them Nazis, simply blocked his way into the hall. When he appealed for help, the notary conducting the auction said he was not responsible for public opinion. When another would-be purchaser, presumably a Gentile, presented a bid, the crowd made noises like a lynch mob until he withdrew the offer. The final outcome of the auction was the sale of the property to the community, which promptly installed the previous owner as the new tenant.[23]

The villagers took care of their own. But as late as the fall of 1932, a village teacher was pilloried in *Der Stürmer* for his refusal to associate with "Nazi gypsies" in a tavern—one of many indications that National Socialism was still not seen as universally respectable in the countryside. It remained a means to an end. As for *Der Stürmer*, as a sex-and-scandal sheet, it had its share of rural admirers. As a fighting newspaper appealing directly to the interests, concerns, and prejudices of the peasantry, it seems never to strike quite the right set of positive chords despite Streicher's efforts.[24]

2

National Socialism's interest in Germany's workers was practical as well as doctrinal. From its beginnings the party labored to win members and votes among the proletariat.[25] For Streicher this campaign was particularly important. Elsewhere in Bavaria it might be possible to concentrate heavily on the *Mittelstand*, the shopkeepers and small farmers, while using organized labor as a bogey. But the situation in Nürnberg itself was different. Through the 1920s a strong and militant Social Democratic party was able to describe loftily the "*völkisch* plague" of hysterical women, youths who grew up without proper parental guidance during the war, and clerks and petty officials who falsely thought themselves superior to honest working men.[26] In Streicher's home city this was both a bitter pill to swallow and a challenge to change the situation.

Streicher constantly reiterated that the proletariat knew not what it did. It was misled rather than malevolent. *Der Stürmer* made the point anecdotally. A farmer was vainly trying to get his ox to move when a well-dressed man walked up and whispered in the beast's ear. The ox promptly began pulling its load. To the astonished farmer's question, "how do you know so much about dumb animals?" the man answered that he was a union secretary.[27] And behind the unions stood the Social Democrats, and behind the Social Democrats stood the Jew.

Der Stürmer borrowed one of its principal arguments more

or less intact from the Communists: whatever integrity the Social Democrats once possessed had been sacrificed to their participation in the November system. Nürnberg's workers, argued Streicher, had spent half their lives following bosses who betrayed them in 1918 and continued the betrayal under the Republic. Before 1914 the *Bonzen* promised a paradise, with workers earning twelve thousand marks a year and owning their own cars. Under the Republic, Socialist leaders were men of property, whose revolutionary rhetoric concealed wealth earned from German sweat. Even during the anarchic days of the Bavarian Republic, the reds had protected banks. *Der Stürmer* urged its readers to compare the salaries of Socialists in public offices with hourly wages in factories. Simple arithmetic, argued Streicher, would demonstrate the emptiness of Socialist slogans of equality. Anyone who sought further proof needed only to look at the allegedly "Socialist" cooperative businesses which flourished under Weimar. Far from being Marxist in their ethic, *Der Stürmer* declared, they were big businesses—rich enough to make six-figure loans to cities; capitalist enough to go bankrupt whenever the Jews running them saw a chance of profit.[28]

The depression gave *Der Stürmer* other pegs on which to hang charges of Social Democracy's betrayal of its promises. Despite its open opposition to Brüning's government, the SPD either supported or was silent in the face of government-inspired cuts in pay and work hours. It accepted emergency legislation restricting what the Nazis considered freedom of expression. Above all, it drew closer and closer to the Jews.[29]

Locally, Streicher pilloried the Socialists on the Nürnberg city council as indifferent to the fate of the little men who voted them into office. To *Der Stürmer*, Social Democratic support of cutbacks in the Municipal Insurance Fund was a deliberate attack on public health. An attempt to limit the practice of early retirement of city employees on full pensions for health reasons was a desire to exploit the last labors of dying men. And when Socialist councilmen voted to increase the city tax on beer, *Der Stürmer* asked why alleged leaders of the people were increasing the price of a peoples' beverage.[30]

A major instrument of the workers' deception was the *Fränkische Tagespost*. This journal has been mentioned earlier as one of the largest, best, and most popular Socialist papers south of the Main. In it Streicher faced a formidable rival, one not nearly as vulnerable to simple vituperation as many of his institutional enemies. To call it the *Tagespest* was hardly likely to generate any significant effect. Personal attacks on its staffers as traitors and draft-dodgers were generally ignored. Once again, therefore, Streicher developed alternative approaches.

He began by asserting the Jewish connection. What was a working class paper doing publishing Jewish wedding announcements and advertisements from Jewish firms? *Stürmer* cartoons showed a figure labeled *Tagespost* cleaning the mud of scandals from the shoes of a leering Jew, or a Jew taping a *Tagespost* bandage over the eyes of a muscular worker. Articles attacked the *Tagespost* for hypocrisy in supporting Nürnberg's bourgeois mayor, or for trying to conceal the plain facts that Jews had cost Germany the war and were now trying to separate the occupied Rhineland from Germany permanently.[31]

A second way of criticizing the *Tagespost* was for its alleged double standard of reporting—important in view of the paper's wide credibility as a news sheet. Its antimilitarism conveniently overlooked both Social Democratic support for the war and the fifty-three million Russians murdered by Bolshevik reds. When a worker in Roth died of sausage poisoning and charges were pressed against the owner/butcher of a local *Gasthaus*, *Der Stürmer* accused the *Tagespost* of keeping silent because the criminal was a Socialist and a regular *Tagespost* reader. When *völkisch* leader Dietrich Eckart wanted to purchase a country house, Streicher declared, the *Tagespost* responded with proletarian horror. But it ignored similar houses owned by local and national Social Democratic leaders, and certainly never thought to ask where these apostles of equality got the purchase price in the first place.[32]

The Social Democratic self-defense organization, the *Reichsbanner Schwarz-Rot-Gold*, is commonly described as more or less innocuous compared to the SA. Its principal historian, however, concedes that the organization also used violence and the threat of violence to break up opposition meetings—in fact, the *Reichsbanner* began the process of street marches and demonstrations which the Nazi storm troopers perfected. Nürnberg's left wing in particular included many men who were not intimidated by the sight of a brown shirt, and who could handle beer mugs, chair legs, and knives as well as their Nazi rivals.[33] Perhaps for this reason, Streicher's treatment of the *Reichsbanner* was ambivalent. When *Der Stürmer* could report on a member of the organization receiving a three-year sentence for incest, or another one intervening in a schoolboy fight in order to beat an adolescent whose father's politics he disliked, the paper seized the opportunity. At the same time *Der Stürmer* could attack Socialist leadership for its alleged failure to decorate the grave of a deceased comrade. The man in question, Streicher declared, was an honest, upright fighter, respected even by his enemies. His grave should be a monument. But only a single woman stood by the freshly turned earth. No flowers or wreaths marked the passing of this comrade. How different was the behavior of the Nazis, who on at least one occasion stood to attention as a Social Democrat was carried to his last rest.[34]

The image of the rank and file *Reichsbanner* men as deluded victims was sustained in several other ways. Letters from allegedly repentant Socialists described how they were encouraged to lie about their encounters with Nazis. Essays described efforts by "reds and Jews" to pit worker against worker in Nürnberg's factories, turning honest Germans into spies watching for swastika insignia. Ridicule was another useful weapon. When the *Reichsbanner* held its national meeting in Nürnberg in 1926, *Der Stürmer* wanted to know why the city was wasting money on decorations. Why not show the reds something they would appreciate, like the municipal torture chamber? *Der Stürmer* challenged attendance figures, offering an exact count of 11,253 participants in one parade, as opposed to socialist estimates of 80,000. The reporter did not say how he arrived at this figure. Perhaps he counted legs and divided by two. But *Der Stürmer* never described a *Reichsbanner* meeting in the Nürnberg area without stressing its low attendance and lower tone—though why the "stink of beer and cigarettes" should be presumed repulsive to a *Stürmer* reader is a bit puzzling. To Streicher, nevertheless, any *Reichsbanner* assembly was as amusing as a carnival— only the participants were unaware of the pathetic figures they made to an enlightened German of any social class.[35]

Der Stürmer had even less sympathy for Socialist youth groups. One of the paper's first issues suggested that the adolescent participants in a recent Socialist political demonstration would have been better advised to get haircuts and jobs to earn money to buy soap. Whenever youth-oriented gymnastic competitions or sport festivals were sponsored in or near Nürnberg by left-wing organizations, Streicher proclaimed them nothing but political activities involving innocent children—at best, an excuse to skip school for a day, at worst, excuses for offenses against public decency.[36]

Such head-shaking despair seems designed to appeal to the dislike many respectable parents felt for youth groups of any kind. An alternative approach involved describing the immorality and corruption of Socialist leaders. A mayor forbade the laying of a wreath bearing a swastika at the village war memorial. A councilman "socialized" his neighbor's tree. Another lured a four-year-old girl into the village's Catholic church and molested her—hardly surprising behavior from a member of a party which had no fear of God's wrath.[37] When a Socialist official anywhere in Bavaria developed anything which might remotely be interpreted as a case of sticky fingers, *Der Stürmer* made as much of the swindle as possible. It might be something as minor as an ex-cabinet minister allegedly arrested for hunting without a license. It might involve the disappearance of funds from a municipal bank. It might involve sweetheart contracts, or favoritism. Social Democrats who became municipal officials after 1918 were described as "party book experts," using influence to push aside men of ability and experience. Whatever the incident, *Der Stürmer* did its best to fit it into a pattern of betrayal at worst, culpable incompetence at best.[38]

Given the average level of skills in German village administration, combined with the number of men and women inexperienced in managing anything but personal budgets who did in fact assume local office under the Republic, the surprising fact is not that *Der Stürmer* could unearth evidence of bad judgment and attempted coverups, but that it found so little material on which to base its attacks. This is even more significant because the virulence of political antagonisms tends universally to be in inverse ratio to the size of the stakes. Criticism of Socialist leadership, however, could be useful in two ways. It might persuade an occasional proletarian that he was being deluded. It would almost certainly appeal to bourgeois fear of the red menace.

Der Stürmer inevitably described socialism as a Jewish movement. However, from Lasker and Lassalle to Liebknecht and Luxemburg, the connection was not only obvious, but frequently taken as a source of open pride by the German left.[39] *Der Stürmer* therefore labored to show its readers that this link was for appearances only. Whatever party they might support for their own advantage, Jews remained Jews. Their synagogues were used to determine the disposition of the Jewish vote at each election—sometimes for the SPD, sometimes for the middle class, always for the Jews. To them, Gentiles were "voting cattle," sheep to be bred only as needed to work and pay taxes.[40]

Anyone who doubted this truth need only ponder the fate of the small-town *Reichsbanner* leader who accused Nazis of desecrating a Jewish cemetery, but was silenced when police dogs traced a suspicious scent from the cemetery to his house! And this was only a beginning. According to *Der Stürmer*, the rash accuser came to the Nazis within weeks, tears in his eyes, to tell them that he had purchased raw material for his small ropemaking business from a Jew on credit. The Jew thereupon promptly went bankrupt and sold the notes of exchange to a third party who was pressing for immediate repayment.[41]

The story itself is almost certainly imaginary. It is unsupported by evidence in Streicher's files, and too pat to be plausible, even by *Der Stürmer*'s standards. Its pattern of false accusation, betrayal, and forgiveness has more relationship to fairy tales than politics. Nevertheless, it makes its point. The fate of this broken man, *Der Stürmer* warned, awaited any German blind enough or stupid enough to become a front man for Jewish leeches hiding behind the mask of socialism. Neither business ethics nor proletarian solidarity nor party loyalty would protect him from inevitable betrayal. The proletariat must indeed unite—but only under the swastika.

3

Among *Der Stürmer*'s editorial idiosyncracies, none was more peculiar than a continued interest in education at all levels. On the surface, the only appeal *Der Stürmer* might seem to have to the academic establishment would involve schoolboys' fondness for smut. Streicher raved about the dangers of allowing a race determined to destroy what it could not control to have any influence at all over the education of German youth. How, he asked, could one speak of a "German" Academy which included aliens like Theodor Wolff and Georg Bernhardt? How could one speak of "German" Parent-Teachers' Organizations which kept inviting Jewish speakers? Jewish teachers favored Jewish students. They brought politics into the classroom. They used racial and political connections to push themselves ahead of colleagues with longer service and better qualifications. The sexual precocity of Jewish children endangered their German classmates.[42] Nevertheless, enough wheat could be winnowed from this anti-Semitic chaff to encourage academicians to believe that they had a friend at court—a man who, for all his intemperate outbursts in other areas, understood the essence of their problems and could get others to listen.

Julius Streicher never ceased to consider himself a teacher as well as a party fighter. Throughout the Weimar era, he continued to agitate for educational reform—often using styles and arguments highly inconsistent with his usual manner. Give the elementary teacher a better, more complete education, Streicher urged. Help the young instructor learn his job instead of merely criticizing his shortcomings. Reduce the large class sizes, which particularly in the villages meant that too many teachers were too overworked to become part of the community. Too many students found themselves in a root, hog, or die situation with no one to help them through academic difficulties. Streicher movingly described his own father's valiant efforts to instruct by himself 130 children annually. That he was alive at the age of eighty-four was no fault of a system which tried to work him to death! Germany needed teachers who enjoyed children, who knew how to laugh, to bring sunshine into the classrooms. Since the war, however, inflation had created a teachers' proletariat, forcing them to spend more time fighting for their rights than shaping Germany's new generations.[43]

These sentiments, no matter who uttered them, were difficult to challenge. Streicher's frequent criticism of confessionally oriented educational material and his defense of the common school, which emphasized German nationality over religious affiliation, were more debatable, but still defensible. Conservative teachers could applaud *Der Stürmer*'s unfavorable comparisons between the old-style upright pedagogue and his modern counterpart, weakened by Marxism, defending such degenerates as Erich Maria Remarque. And Streicher spoke to practical experience in his frequent defenses of corporal punishment. Children, he declared, were difficult enough at best to raise, and the times called for hard men, not mothers' darlings. Successful instruction required order and respect. The colleague who could achieve this through sheer force of personality was to be admired. But when physical discipline was necessary, only Jews who wished to soften their future victims dared object.[44]

For all of Streicher's efforts, *Der Stürmer*'s general reputation discouraged any significant public support for the paper from teachers. On the other hand, the nature and tone of Streicher's public statements on education might well have made him something less of a bogey than he deserved, particularly among elementary instructors. These people, with normal school educations and back-breaking teaching loads, were regarded as of lower caste than the Ph.D.s who taught in the better secondary schools. They bitterly resented both their lack of status and what they perceived as public indifference to the importance of primary education. Even for *Gymnasium* teachers, presenting the same subjects year after year in an environment fostering the notion of teacher and student as natural enemies, a movement offering the opportunity to build bridges instead of barriers could be attractive.[45]

German students were quicker than their teachers to begin climbing on the Nazi bandwagon, even when Streicher was driving. Anti-Semitism had existed in German universities since the last quarter of the nineteenth century. World War I did nothing to diminish it.[46] This was particularly true among students of law and medicine, who usually took the lead in calling for the exclusion or limitation of Jews in academic programs. German doctors in particular regarded themselves as members of an overcrowded, underpaid profession, forced to fight for every prospective patient, then forced to fight him for their fees. Anything that might reduce the competition was welcome, and *Der Stürmer* was well known for its attacks on Jewish doctors. Complaints that Germany had too many physicians were only part of a Jewish plot to discourage Aryans from entering the profession. German parents could pity their sons who were "workers of the brain," yet were barred from earning their bread honestly by their Jewish competitors. The paper reported every appointment of Jews to posts in the Nürnberg public health system. It described a Bavarian attempt to increase the fees paid by medical school students as part of a general plan to reduce the number of poor Germans able to become doctors. An honorable profession, Streicher declared, was becoming a career open to purses instead of talents. And everyone knew whose purses were the largest under the Weimar system.[47]

These kinds of appeals proved particularly effective to the students of the University of Erlangen. As early as May, 1923, Adolf Hitler spoke to a student rally. Five months later the National Socialist student group included 120 members. Medical student Fritz Hülf gave Streicher an entree to the Nazi students, served on *Der Stürmer*'s editorial board, and still managed to get his doctorate in 1925 for a dissertation on bowel resections.[48]

After Hülf's graduation, *Der Stürmer* reported with applause every demand for a *numerus clausus* and took every opportunity to inform its educated readers that only eight thousand of the four hundred thousand citizens of Nürnberg were Jewish, but fully half of the doctors and lawyers were practicing Jews. Jürgen Schwarz suggests that many German students distinguished between intellectual anti-Semitism and the physical, overt brand favored by the National Socialists, which was considered a bit too vulgar for a man with education and breeding. But by the time the Nazis won an absolute majority in the Erlangen Student Government, and when that body voted twenty-four to one to recommend restrictions on Jewish enrollment, Streicher could boast that his *Gau* had the first true National Socialist university in Germany. It was also one whose students had had every opportunity to study Nazi anti-Semitism in its crudest manifestation.[49]

A common belief about *Der Stürmer* is that its pornographic tone and strident anti-Semitism won its news a wide following among elementary and secondary-school students.[50] As early as 1925 an open letter declared that the most harmful aspect of *Der Stürmer* was the paper's popularity among half-grown youths. Immature adolescents could learn about homosexuality, prostitution, and every kind of perversion from a newspaper that presented pornography in the guise of politics. Did not even *völkisch* sympathizers worry when they saw *Der Stürmer* in the hands of primary school pupils? Did not Nürnberg's parents feel qualms when they saw *Stürmer* displays surrounded by children?

This attack was serious enough to inspire Streicher to address the question directly in the Bavarian *Landtag*. His critics, Streicher declared, said *Der Stürmer* harmed Franconia's youth and was passed from hand to hand even in girls' schools. Why did no one express a similar concern for the contents of the Jewish-controlled Berlin gutter press? Why not seek the real corrupters of youth, that race whose members once wore the yellow mark of the criminals and convicts they were?[51]

Parental misgivings about *Der Stürmer*'s moral impact were well-advised. However, Streicher's own evidence suggests that *Der Stürmer* and National Socialism were again often instrumental, serving as means to ends in conflicts of adolescents with adults and students with teachers. For example, a quarrel between schoolboys and Jewish adults over the use of a village swimming hole was decided in favor of the youth once they began shouting "Heil" in chorus and singing the "Horst Wessel Song" at their rivals. Nor did the harassed adults gain stature in the community when they demanded that the children be punished for such behavior. Streicher's correspondent gives the modern reader a shudder when he declares that the Jews involved in the incident would be "in the first transport" out of Germany when the Third Reich emerged. But the behavior of the students suggests a desire to plague adult interlopers who happened to be Jewish, and therefore highly vulnerable to certain kinds of harassment. It has the tone of Max and Moritz rather than the face of the Final Solution.[52]

Classroom behavior indicates similar patterns. Here much depended on the teacher. When an instructor in the Nürnberg *Volkshochschule* declared in class that Hitler could not pass Nazi criteria for suitable racial heritage and followed this with arguments from biology that mixed breeds were healthier and more intelligent than purebred stock, no one was prepared to challenge him openly. But in Nördlingen a student wit chalked a swastika on the window before class. The instructor entered and, suitably baited, responded by declaring that Germany would be better off without the Nazis. If Jewish businesses prospered, it was because their prices were cheaper, and besides, without the Jews there could have been no Christ. A student responded by asking why the Jews hated Christ. The three Jewish students in the class denied that they hated Him at all. By this time the teacher was angry enough to end the debate by calling Hitler a scoundrel and the class to order. A similar event occurred in Nürnberg, where students emerging from a history class talked loudly about the "Jewish race" in front of a quick-tempered mathematics instructor who punctuated his lecture on manners with a few appropriately placed slaps.[53]

Once again, the line between hard-core anti-Semitism and probing an instructor's weak spots is hard to draw. It nevertheless remains difficult to avoid the conclusion that one of *Der Stürmer*'s major values to its secondary-school readers lay in its potential for arousing the rage of adults, both Jewish and Gentile. The offender could then wrap himself in the mantle of political freedom and self-expression to avoid punishment—the kind of behavior practiced regularly by Streicher himself.

4

The attitude towards women expressed in the columns of *Der Stürmer* represented a unique and often amusing combination of *völkisch* advocacy of children, kitchen, and church with the swaggering machismo embodied by Streicher and imitated by his lieutenants, especially Karl Holz. When it came to calling things by their right names, neither man shrank from the test. Nor did plain speaking diminish the public popularity Streicher enjoyed among the women of Nürnberg and Franconia. It may even have enhanced the appeal of his speeches. At least one woman's *völkisch* feelings did not keep her from criticizing a Streicher lecture to a group of Fürth teenagers. "You proclaim innocence the highest good," she declared, "then elaborate on a suggestion that your listeners contrast in their imaginations two nude men, a German and a Jew. Your adolescent auditors," she continued, "probably went to the zoo and studied the anatomy of the orangutans to find out exactly what the 'thing' was to which you so frequently referred!"[54]

Needless to say, Streicher saw no reason to modify his speaking style. When the NSDAP scheduled a women-only meeting in April, 1926, the Nürnberg police forbade it on the grounds that its announced theme of "race pollution," when discussed by Streicher, represented a clear threat to public morals.[55] Streicher trod a consistently fine line between indictable obscenity and gross but legal admonitions on the need to protect German womanhood from Jewish pollution. Where once German maidens cast eyes of love on powerful Aryan men, he raved, now they took up with perfumed, silk-stockinged swine whose flat feet amply suited them to dance to the apelike tribal rhythms of the African jungle. According to Karl Holz, the earlier splendid militarism, when men were men and women respected them, had given way to the era of the Dawes Plan. Instead of admiring ranks of soldiers standing at attention, German girls danced in chorus lines to be ogled by Jews.[56]

In its attitude to working women, *Der Stürmer* closely followed the Nazi party line. The National Socialists never intended to remove women from the labor force entirely. Instead the party stressed their essential role in work involving nurture—teaching, welfare work, nursing—and conceded that single women, at least, were better off holding jobs suited to their nature and physique than sitting in cafés ruining their health and complexions.[57] What was important, particularly for young girls fresh from school, was providing honest work under employers who did not physically exploit the future mothers of the new Germany. For Streicher, this meant above all avoiding the siren lures of Jewish masters whose frequent offers of higher wages only concealed a desire to have Gentile girls available for bedding.[58]

Where married women were concerned, *Der Stürmer* made no compromises with the principle that they belonged to their homes and children. Like their men, however, they had a duty to combat the "Jewish Spirit" in their own spheres. A good Aryan woman could fight international Jewry while serving her beauty and health by refusing to smoke cigarettes. Or she could eschew changes in fashion which both weakened the financial structure of German homes by increasing their clothing budgets and diminished her sex appeal. The flapper look of the 1920s was for *Der Stürmer* a Jewish plot to masculinize Germany's female population. Similarly, Streicher argued that the slim-line styles of the 1930s might look well on a Parisienne, but German women were not "six-foot hop poles." Instead of looking elegant in the new mode, they merely looked fat—to the greater triumph of Jewish insolence. As for powder and lipstick, Jewish women might need them to conceal their ugliness. The German wife needed no other ornament than the swastika on her breast.[59]

No single fashion issue generated as much controversy in the pages of *Der Stürmer* as the introduction of bobbed hair. Streicher raged in article after article at this Jewish style, fit only for the degenerate womenfolk of a degenerate republic. When a suburban schoolmistress reported for the fall term sporting a shingle, local *völkisch* elements threatened a boycott. When a school doctor entered the debate by suggesting that short hair might be more hygienic than braids, *Der Stürmer* viciously attacked Jews who dared suggest that German parents did not know how to keep their children clean. This tempest in a beauty shop did not go entirely unchallenged. At least one self-described long-time reader declared that he could not seriously believe bobbed hair was part of a Jewish plot to defeminize German women. Yet even this lone voice of common sense expressed willingness to be shown how the new hair style harmed the German family.[60]

Der Stürmer's avowed concern for the moral welfare of German womanhood rapidly led it into a more serious field: sexual hygiene. Where could an editor better combine virtue and titillation than in articles on some of the controversial legislation involving the family which came under discussion in the Weimar Republic? Contraception, abortion, the status of the unwed mother, were controversial subjects which attracted a good deal of attention from all points of the political compass. Churchmen, Evangelical and Catholic alike, tended to maintain a hard line against anything which might encourage pre- or extramarital sex. And if abortion was legal in the Soviet Union, this only encouraged respectable Germans to unite behind Paragraph 218 of the penal code, making it a criminal act.

For *Der Stürmer*, of course, the Jew was at the bottom of it all. Since the days of Tacitus, Mohammed, and Seneca, Jews were known by the societies on which they preyed as born sex maniacs, whose Talmud allowed intercourse with three-year-old girls and whose unnatural drives could be checked only by the strictest application of the law. Now the Republic left them free to advocate homosexuality, sodomy, and every other form of perversion in the name of freedom. To a German, freedom depended on morality. To a Jew, companionate marriage, free love, or sexual intercourse without regard to age limits, were both natural expressions of his own character and subtle means of destroying the soul of the *Volk* he sought to destroy.[61]

Again and again *Der Stürmer* reiterated in word and verse the argument presented in Arthur Dinter's *völkisch* classic *The Sin against the Blood*. A German girl once bedded by a Jew was eternally polluted by the "dragon seed." Nevermore could she bear Aryan children; her fruit would be murderers and bastards, cursed eternally.[62] Similarly, a healthy *Volk* required healthy children in large numbers, and it was just this the Jew sought to prevent by legalizing abortion. Not only did it destroy life in the womb; it ruined women physically and psychologically. Only a Jew, Streicher declared, possessed the nerve to assert that a mother could collaborate in the murder of her child without compunction and without aftereffects. He illustrated his point with a series of cartoons so gross that the Nürnberg-Fürth police forbade the public display of one issue whose front page featured a leering Jewish abortionist.[63]

Der Stürmer believed in enlightenment. However, sex education in the schools, as advocated by Jews and their Republican

Versuchskaninchen

Na, wenn se och im Tierschutzverein gegen Vivisektion sind,
wofür haben wir die Gojims — —

GUINEA PIGS. "So what if the SPCA is against vivisection? What do we have
Gentiles for?"

servants, was nothing but a license to encourage degeneracy. When a doctor of medicine could describe masturbation as "normal" and generate no protest from Christian parents, even in a sink of iniquity like Berlin, then the nadir had been reached. Conservative Franconia offered few local opportunities for *Der Stürmer* to air its views on the subject. Occasionally a modern idea would arouse the local party faithful. For example, in November, 1929, the Nazi members of the Nürnberg city council requested the elimination of a series of lectures on "Today's Woman," presented at the *Volkshochschule*. The Nazis described the program as featuring an "eighteen-year-old slut's" discussion of "the sex life of the proletarian woman" in language better fitted for the brothel than the podium. When the council denied the motion, *Der Stürmer* seized the opportunity to deplore the waste of German taxpayers' money for immoral purposes.[64]

To the argument that sex education was effective in reducing the incidence of venereal disease, Streicher replied with a mixture of *völkisch* populism and his own interest in various forms of nature cures. The injection of German men with the "poison" of Salvarsan, the forcible testing for syphillis by the Wassermann method, were nothing short of criminal, he declared. There were many other ways to fight venereal disease, and the best method of all was to improve wages and living conditions. Only then would German men be able to support wives and families, gratifying their natural desires in a healthy, socially productive way. Only then would German women be in a position to resist the appeals of the Jews battening on their misery.[65]

Responses to these purity campaigns were not always quite what *Der Stürmer*'s editor might have expected. As late as 1933, one "critical German reader" suggested with a man-to-man leer, that Streicher ignored the fact that Jewish women had their own peculiar charm, something their Aryan sisters lacked—devilish, perhaps, but "extraordinarily enticing"[66] On the other hand, *Der Stürmer* could count on the support of such organizations as the *Deutscher Frauenkampfbund* of Eisenach. The good ladies were pleased to report the temporary thwarting of an attempt by "Berlin Marxists" to install condom dispensers in that evil city's toilets to the ruin of German youth, but what, they asked, of the future?[67] They could afford to relax. As long as *Der Stürmer* remained in print, public decency would never lack for challenge.

9 | *Der Stürmer* and the Law:
A Free Society's Limits

From Max Weber to Ralf Dahrendorff, social theorists have asserted the importance of conflict among self-serving groups as a necessary element of social cohesion, as opposed to being an abnormal or pathological manifestation. And in a state of laws such as Weimar Germany, the courtroom can be a major agency for resolving these conflicts. It offers redress and retribution. It determines, positively and negatively, the ideas and behavior a given system is prepared to tolerate.

Legal processes were particularly important in reacting to *Der Stürmer*. Direct, violent action against the paper or its editor was likely to be counter-productive. Attempting to discredit the sheet by political activity broadly defined, fighting Streicher from the hustings with his own weapons, tended to involve the necessity of outstinking a skunk. The nature and character of *Der Stürmer*, however, invited legal action. Precedents for public prosecution of politically oriented newspapers had been set in the Second Empire, with the Socialist press as the primary target.[1] Streicher's propensity to use individuals as symbols also facilitated efforts to recover damages or restore smeared reputations.

Evaluating *Der Stürmer* in a legal context offers a case study of the Weimar Republic's legal response to the threat from the right. This can be generally interpreted in one of two ways. The Republic may be shown as dying of a surfeit of procedural safeguards, ignoring warnings that a constitution cannot be a suicide pact, rejecting arguments that any system, however democratic, must protect itself against enemies seeking to use the safeguards of that system in order to destroy the system itself. On a more pragmatic level, Weimar is described as being victimized by a legal structure indifferent or hostile to republican principles, practicing an outrageous double standard when considering either political offenses, or attacks on the honor of the Republic, its servants and institutions.[2]

Reality was somewhat more complex, particularly when that reality involved Julius Streicher and *Der Stürmer*. In the abstract both the man and his newspaper were vulnerable to legal action. In practice, the potential for successful action in specific cases was frequently limited. This chapter demonstrates that point by first discussing Streicher's and *Der Stürmer*'s general relationship with the law, then concentrating on the legal reactions of two of the paper's major targets: Germany's Jewish community and Nürnberg's Mayor Luppe. This choice reflects the limits and prospects of both collective and individual action against Streicher's brand of National Socialism.

1

Julius Streicher's record of fines and prison sentences under the Weimar Republic was impressive, and he took as much pride in his convictions as in his acquittals. Certainly a privately printed, handsomely bound set of trial transcripts might seem an unusual kind of present, but Streicher seems to have valued the volume highly when presented it by a "nameless follower" after the seizure of power.[3] He was skilled at using the law as an offensive weapon, frequently winning civil judgments for libel or slander. He was well served by his attorneys, who combined technical skill with commitment to the Nazi cause. Above all, however, he benefited from Weimar's legislation providing immunity from prosecution for political activity to members of national or state parliaments. As a deputy to the Bavarian Landtag from 1925, and to the Reichstag after 1932, Streicher was close to untouchable. Since he insisted that all his activities, including his anti-Semitism, were based on his political convictions, attorneys and prosecutors were reluctant to press cases which had little possibility of coming to court.

Streicher consistently proclaimed his readiness to rely on free speech and the power of truth. All he demanded was a common standard: *no* parliamentarian should be able to claim immunity. His critics, Streicher declared, were in no hurry to abandon *their* special protection. National Socialists, on the other hand, could always count on having their immunity lifted whenever their attacks on the "November State" and its degenerate representatives bit too deeply.[4]

Streicher in fact relied heavily on his parliamentary status for legal protection. On the few occasions when it was lifted, he went to extreme lengths to secure its recovery. In 1929, for example, Streicher embarked on a series of attacks against Bavarian Minister of Agriculture Anton Fehr in the course of which he accused him of "passive bribery." The concept remained undefined, but the charge was serious enough to convince the *Landtag* to remove Streicher's immunity. The result was a formal apology to the injured minister—and the prompt restoration of Streicher's privileged status.[5]

A *Landtag* more willing to suspend Streicher's immunity might have succeeded in modifying his behavior. Most legislators, however, believed the worth of this privilege outweighed its abuse, particularly since opponents of the radical right in Weimar Germany persistently expected it to self-destruct before it could do any significant damage to the body politic.

Because Streicher himself was such a difficult target, the legal status of his newspaper was particularly important. The first copies were carefully examined by the administration of *Kreis Mittelfranken*, located in Ansbach. *Der Stürmer* reflected the political orientation of its creator—the necessity for fighting Jewish influence in German life. This was not a criminal position. On the other hand, Bavarian law allowed banning papers that only worked to poison public life. It forbade publishing falsehoods calculated to incite violence, or to set groups and individuals against each other. *Der Stürmer* did include such material. And if Streicher was unaware that the reports he printed were incorrect, this was legally actionable carelessness. *Der Stürmer* should therefore be required to suspend publication for at least three months.

Had the Nürnberg police followed this recommendation,

Der Stürmer might have become just another of the ephemeral *völkisch* sheets now disintegrating in various archives. Instead Streicher was summoned to police headquarters. He informed the interrogating officers, presumably with a straight face, that the first issues of his new sheet had been especially strong "only on tactical grounds"—to combat his party enemies, and presumably to attract readers. The Nürnberg authorities assured Ansbach that they would keep the paper under close observation and take action as soon as possible.

To assume that this attitude was simply a reflection of official sympathy for the radical right is an oversimplification. Streicher, like many another individual who constantly tests the fringes of the law, had by this time established a kind of mutual understanding with the Nürnberg authorities. He was a familiar figure, though not, particularly at this stage of his career, inevitably a sympathetic one. But the Nürnberg police were sensitive to criticism from a market town like Ansbach. What did paper-shufflers in a backwater know about the day-to-day problems of maintaining order among the political factions in a big city? This prejudice is reflected in the condescending tone of the report. Practical considerations were also involved. The Munich *Oberste Landgericht* had just lifted a ban on a Nazi paper similar in tone to *Der Stürmer*. With this precedent, any reasonably competent lawyer should be able to secure quick dismissal of any attempt to ban *Der Stürmer*. Pushing the issue was a waste of time and money.[6]

This did not mean that the *Polizeidirektion Nürnberg-Fürth* was prepared to give Streicher a free hand. Between August, 1924 and March, 1933, thirty-five issues of *Der Stürmer* were either banned and confiscated or suffered the less serious penalty of being barred from street sale. The reasons ranged from libel against public officials to publishing without permission statements of public officials involved in legal cases. Offenses against religion and challenges to public security were the most common justifications for suspension or confiscation.[7] On August 2, 1924, for example, Julius Streicher received an official notice stating that a special issue of *Der Stürmer* contained the sentence "Judaism is organized criminality." Presented without supporting evidence, the police declared, this statement violated Paragraph 4 of the Bavarian Press Code. *Der Stürmer* was therefore suspended for two weeks.

Streicher appealed the decision to Munich. He had, he conceded, used the phrase in question on many occasions. He believed that the Jews were a race living by its own laws. Those laws allowed the free use of lies, perjury, and deceit. But, Streicher declared, when he spoke of "Judaism" he spoke of it as an abstraction, the way one might speak of *Berlinertum*. This removed his statement from the category of inciting violence.

The *Oberste Landesgericht* remained unmoved by Streicher's juxtaposition of Jews and Berliners. It upheld the police decision and gave the Nürnberg prosecutor's office a clear signal for continued action against *Der Stürmer*.[8] On September 22, an extra edition was ordered confiscated for not containing the name and address of the printer—the kind of technicality police and prosecutors had grown expert in using against the Socialist press before 1918. Streicher replied that other previous issues of *Der Stürmer* had not included the printer's name, and he believed it was not necessary on this occasion. Particularly since the paper in question included the names of the publisher and the editor, Streicher argued, this omission was an oversight without criminal intent. Once again, the "paragraph justice" Streicher was so fond of pillorying saved his case. The prosecutor dropped the charges, saying that Streicher as responsible editor of *Der Stürmer* could be held to account only for violations of the press laws and not for police regulations regarding the press. As editor he was responsible for what was printed, not for the masthead. The punishment therefore fell on the publisher, Wilhelm Hardel, and the printer who set the type: a combined fine of thirty marks.[9]

The fine was not remarkably low for the offense, but could hardly be called a significant deterrent—particularly when juxtaposed with the events surrounding another extra of May, 1925. Issuing such extras first required police authorization; this one was on the street before anyone in authority was aware of it. Patrolmen were confiscating them from bewildered vendors before police headquarters issued any instructions. Karl Holz explained that he had telephoned for permission. The official he contacted asked for a copy of the proposed extra. Holz forwarded it and assumed all was well. The prosecutor loftily reminded him the law clearly stated that a newspaper must await permission to publish an extra edition. Merely submitting a letter of intent in no way fulfilled the legal requirements. The warning, however, seems to have been considered sufficient; no charges were filed.[10]

Two months later *Der Stürmer* again appeared on the prosecutor's desk. This time the case involved an article whose highlight was a graphic description of a girl allegedly forced to masturbate her Jewish employer. The prosecutor charged Streicher with spreading immoral literature through the press and ordered the confiscation of the offending issue of *Der Stürmer*. The police were ordered to act as quickly as possible, since the nature of the offending article was making *Der Stürmer* an instant bestseller. Once again, however, the prosecutor's office hit only half its target. When Streicher appealed, the court approved confiscating the offending issue. But Karl Holz filed a deposition that the article in question was taken from an Austrian paper. It had also been reprinted in an earlier number of another *völkisch* sheet which had sold several hundred copies in Nürnberg, and had not been confiscated there or anywhere else in Germany. This was enough to convince the Nürnberg prosecutor to drop the morals charge against Streicher. Apart from Streicher's parliamentary immunity, which would resume once the *Landtag* went into session, the chances for a conviction had become too remote to waste public money.[11]

By this time Streicher could be pardoned for assuming that he had found a workable legal formula for *Der Stürmer*. In a year's sustained effort the authorities had done virtually nothing to diminish the paper's impact or reduce its profits. The Nürnberg police were under increasingly heavy attack for their apparent softness on *Der Stürmer*. The Democratic *Nürnberg-Fürther Morgenpresse*, for example, criticized the authorities for banning posters advertising rallies of peace societies while allowing Streicher what appeared a free hand. In his report to the Ministry of the Interior, *Polizeidirektor* Heinrich Gareis responded that the critics overlooked *Der Stürmer*'s legal status. Laws pertaining to posters and leaflets could not be applied to a newspaper. And when individual victims of Streicher's vitriolic attacks sought redress, their lawsuits generally foundered on Streicher's parliamentary immunity—an immunity sustained because of Streicher's argument that anti-Semitism was the essence of his political activity.[12]

The real question was at what point did Bavaria and Germany decide that this brand of political freedom was too dangerous to exercise? The problem was compounded by the appearance of a number of other satirical anti-Semitic sheets during 1924 and 1925. None of these papers could match *Der Stürmer* either in the tone of their attacks or the quality of their graphics. They tended rather to resemble the comic papers of an earlier century, particularly in their cartoons. This very resemblance, however, enhanced their legal security. Germany had been historically sufficiently tolerant of this form of anti-Semitism to make banning such papers and prosecuting their editors virtually impossible under existing legislation.[13]

The guerrilla war between *Der Stürmer*'s editorial office and the authorities continued as long as the Republic survived. Streicher, like any successful Nazi, was expert at testing limits and baiting bureaucrats. For every official warning he received for such offenses as accusing judges of partisan politics, he could usually balance a propaganda triumph by encouraging the police to trip over their own regulations. For example, in May, 1932, *Der Stürmer* featured a Fips cartoon of a kiosk showing a Hindenburg election poster beside an ad for a patent medicine for strengthening nerves and virility. To the Nürnberg police this was a deliberate attempt to make the president look ridiculous. They promptly lent weight to the implication by banning the issue in question. Once again Streicher had free publicity. And ten days later, the prosecutor's office dropped the charges. In order to be an offense against the republic, the prosecutor declared, the cartoon had to attack the republic as an institution. The offending cartoon was, however, part of a political campaign. The Nazis too had a candidate for president and were therefore entitled to attack his rivals.[14]

The question of the attitude of Weimar's bureaucrats to *Der Stürmer* still remains open. Could the paper have been suppressed or crippled by a systematic campaign against it? Or was it encouraged through toleration by right-wing sympathizers in the police and administration? Critics of the Nürnberg authorities cite the Republic's demonstrated ability to harass Communist and other radical-left newspapers into oblivion. The comparison, however, has limited validity. Unlike the leftist press, and indeed unlike most of its *völkisch* rivals, *Der Stürmer* was financially strong enough by the mid-1920s to stand the expense of repeated court trials. Its editor was remarkably litigious, and his attorneys had grown expert at skirting the edges of press laws and police regulations regarding public security, offenses against religion, and similar matters that involved official legal action as opposed to private suits for libel.

Officially at least, the Nürnberg police and the Nürnberg prosecutor's office displayed little sympathy for *Der Stürmer*. Officially or unofficially, there was little they could do about the paper. In their professional opinion, harassment only increased sympathy for Streicher and his cause. Legal action simply provided publicity and increased circulation. In the final analysis, *Der Stürmer* had much the same position under Weimar that major Social Democratic papers held under the Empire. It had a sufficiently large cadre of readers, it had a sufficiently broad base of support, that it could not be destroyed except at apparently disproportionate cost to the legal system attempting the process. Perhaps the Nürnberg police had learned something of a lesson in their pre-1918 running battle with the *Tagespost* and similar sheets.[15]

Police and prosecutors, moreover, had other responsibilities. Hindsight tends to exaggerate the proportion of police time spent on political matters under the Republic. There were still murderers to be caught, traffic to be regulated, and forms to be completed. Julius Streicher was an ongoing problem to Nürnberg's authorities, and *Der Stürmer* was part of that problem. But only a certain amount of energy could be devoted to an essentially pointless effort to suppress a paper that an increasing number of citizens wanted to read. In this sense *Der Stürmer* was the journalistic equivalent of a victimless crime—or more precisely, a crime whose victims had to seek their own legal redress.

Paragraph 11 of the Weimar Press Code did require newspapers to recant "honest errors" of fact or judgment. However questionable might be the sincerity of a paper like *Der Stürmer*, the paragraph offered a useful opening for lawsuits. Streicher's files bulge with court orders to retract "baseless accusations" and letters from aggrieved private citizens or their lawyers. Most of the latter grievances were personal rather than political. A man might complain about being described as a Jew, when in fact he belonged to a Christian confession. A store owner might request his attorney to inform Streicher that, contrary to a recent article in *Der Stürmer*, his goods had become cheaper rather than more expensive—with the lawyer appending the suggestion that *Der Stürmer*'s reporters learn to be more careful with the truth. A legal firm might send a stuffy note defending its behavior in a divorce case. One man *Der Stürmer* described as having been "ruined" by his Jewish lawyers was, the attorneys in question declared, in fact ruined by his wife, who lived openly with another man and had borne his child. They had not solicited his business; he had come to them. Therefore they awaited a retraction under Paragraph 11.[16]

They had a long wait ahead of them. As a rule *Der Stürmer* ignored such letters, publishing retractions only under direct court orders or threats of massive legal action. As editorial policy it made good sense. The cost of a lawsuit relative to the probable judgment, even given a favorable verdict, acted as a natural deterrent to a firm or an individual proposing to take Streicher to court. Moreover, the nature of *Der Stürmer*'s readership suggested that on balance even a victory might well prove hollow. Who would read the retraction, much less believe it? And once printed, experience indicated that the retraction might well read like another accusation. Particularly for businessmen, overlooking a single attack or even a series of them often was simple common sense.

One notable exception to this rule occurred when a Passau department store gave a party for its employees. The mixture of alcohol and high spirits led neighbors to call the police and gave Streicher ample material to titillate or enrage those with less generous employers. *Der Stürmer* described the affair as a drunken orgy designed to give Jewish managers and floorwalkers an opportunity to seduce Gentile women. The store promptly sued for libel. The party, its attorneys stated, had been designed for no more sinister purpose than to foster staff harmony. Despite statements that 140 guests were provided with 70 bottles of champagne alone, despite a statement that at least one woman was seen drunk under a table, the local court decided that *Der Stürmer* was using a private party as an excuse to display its politics of "blind, fanatical Jew-hatred." Karl Holz, at the time *Der Stürmer*'s responsible editor, was sentenced to six weeks in prison for libel.[17] Such lawsuits, however, remained the exception. Nürnbergers and Franconians seemed to have learned their lesson well. A *Stürmer* trial increasingly tended to be a situation where the only winners were likely to be Streicher and his paper. Taking either to court required a sense of mission and a thick skin. However, many German Jews had both.

2

Images of the relationship between Jews and judges in Weimar Germany frequently juxtapose a passive community unwilling to make waves to courts unwilling to take action against even the crassest forms of anti-Semitism. Many Jews did adhere to their faith in Germany until loaded aboard trains for resettlement at Treblinka. This was not blind optimism. The Jews of Germany were no strangers to anti-Semitism. But it was the kind of anti-Semitism which could be fought in the courts more readily than in the streets. Bureaucrats might be unsympathetic, or ignorant of Jewish affairs, but they could by and large be trusted to enforce the law—particularly if prodded down the path of righteousness by well-prepared cases presented by good lawyers.[18]

In particular, the *Centralverein für deutsche Staatsbürger jüdischen Glaubens* from its foundation in 1893 kept a careful eye on all forms of anti-Semitism—including National Socialism. Its tactics essentially involved positive emphasis on Jews as full members of the German community, combined with social pressure and legal action against anyone who challenged this position. It readily adjusted to a republican form of government after 1918, and was joined by several new and more militant organizations.[19] Chief among these was the *Reichsbund jüdischer Frontsoldaten*; in defense of Jewish veterans' honor it aggressively pressed libel charges against speakers or newspapers accusing Jews of cowardice or shirking. But German Jews soon discovered that legal action in the Weimar Republic against the kind of anti-Semitism represented by men like Streicher faced problems differing from those met under the Empire.

Some indication of their nature is shown by legal action resulting from a Streicher speech in March, 1922. He discussed ritual murder, linking medieval anecdotes to the disappearance of three Nürnberg children in 1920. A Schweinfurt court decided that Streicher brought no proof of his allegations except legends. Whatever might have been the case in 1322, there were no grounds to believe anything resembling ritual murder existed in Germany six centuries later. Streicher was therefore sentenced to two weeks in jail. An appellate court reduced the sentence to a fine. The tone of the judgment indicates that the judges considered Streicher a crackpot. But to imprison every Bavarian with odd ideas might well empty the state in those times of stress. Attacks on the Jewish religion were liable to criminal penalties. Streicher, however, argued that his anti-Semitism was based on racial, not religious grounds. He had collected a mass of evidence from the Talmud and related sources that he believed supported his position. Charges of ritual murder had been frequently made in German history. The court saw nothing in the case requiring a legal ruling on the accuracy of Talmudic quotations. But one could not deny out of hand the possibility that if the kind of dark and criminal superstitions described by Streicher did exist, they might lead to cruel deeds.[20]

This equivocal approach was also embodied in a decision rendered by the *Schoffengericht* of Coburg on October 17, 1924. It acquitted Streicher on the charge of libeling the city's mayor by calling him a Jew. To call someone a Jew, the court declared, was not in itself a libel. The statement must be accompanied by attacks on the plaintiff's character or behavior. Admittedly Streicher declared that the mayor had flat feet. Since this was "known to the court" as a frequent Jewish problem, this statement could be interpreted as exposing the mayor to ridicule. On the other hand, Streicher was a leader of the Franconian *völkisch* movement. One of the major elements of this movement was its racially based anti-Semitism. To rule this opinion illegal would be an essentially political judgment. The court therefore decided the case by not deciding it. Since the Coburg town council had pressed the charges, the court concluded that they were claiming that the mayor was their employee. This not being the case, the plaintiffs had no standing.[21]

A strong case can be made that such a decision could have been reached only in Coburg. This community had been a Nazi-*völkisch* stronghold from the earliest days of the movement. It had become part of Bavaria only in 1920, and prided itself on a stubborn independence even by Franconian standards.[22] Certainly a town where a court could express the opinon that Jews were flat-footed can hardly be described as a center of enlightenment. The ruling, however, cannot be entirely dismissed as anti-Semitism thinly concealed as a legal decision. This small-town *Schoffengericht* had to grapple with an issue that was a key not only to the entire *völkisch* movement, but to the way in which the German Jewish community viewed itself and wished to be viewed under the law. Were German Jews a separate race? Or were they German citizens of the Mosaic faith? Existing laws protected the Jewish religion. However, to extend legal recognition to the Jews as a "race" could have unpleasant implications. The Streichers might be more easily punished, but their point would also have been conceded. Jews would be a separate racial community, arguably to be covered by laws differing from those governing the rest of Germany. And even militant individuals and organizations among Germany's Jews were frequently reluctant to accept the possible consequences of such a course of action.

Streicher, in short, had found a legal loophole he was able to turn to maximum advantage in the next decade. Perhaps it might be more accurate to describe it as a crawl space. Collective libel of the Jews as a race might not itself be a criminal act. Nevertheless, Jewish organizations or individuals seeking redress could argue that Streicher's anti-Semitism was expressed in ways violating laws already on the books. Letter after letter inquired into the possibility of pressing charges against specific issues of *Der Stürmer*, sometimes on the grounds of misrepresentation, sometimes on the grounds that its articles or cartoons incited to violence. As early as 1925 a merchant sent two copies of *Der Stürmer* to the Central Franconian Ministry of the Interior. It is a scandal, he declared, that this sheet is allowed to besmirch the honor of worthy men week after week, hanging in store windows where young and old can absorb the poison. If local police forces could not suppress it, then higher authorities must act. A sixty-eight-year-old grain dealer asked the Dinkelsbühl District Office to help prevent a *Gasthaus* across the street from hanging out *Der Stürmer* weekly. Its slogans and cartoons, the complainant declared, were damaging a business which had had high standing in the community since 1862.[23] When in February, 1928, Streicher spoke in Regensburg and declared that it was every good German's duty to break the necks of Jews "morally," the local rabbi suggested to the city council that the difference between moral and physical neck-breaking was too subtle for him. When the Regensburg prosecutor inquired into the possibility of pressing charges, he learned that the Bavarian *Landtag* was unlikely to lift Streicher's immunity for such a statement.[24]

Jewish efforts were frequently rewarded. In 1925 the Nürnberg police forbade a projected Nazi meeting in Fürth during the High Holy Days. Since the Fürth Jewish community was a large one, likely to be on the streets in its best clothes, the possibility of violent harassment by Nazi hooligans was used to justify the banning. When the Jews of Feuchtwangen attempted to get the district administration to stop a Streicher speech in 1926, the authorities expressed regret that the laws of freedom of expression protected even Nazis. They also sent a reliable official to observe the proceedings and report any possible illegalities.[25]

The courts too were active. *DS* 37/1924, for example, featured an article accusing a Jewish woman who had worked as a cook in a factory kitchen during the hungry months of 1917 of pilfering food for herself and her family. Her angry husband pressed charges; a year later the Nürnberg *Amtsgericht* declared that none of *Der Stürmer*'s allegations could be proven, and fined Streicher two hundred marks for slander. A decision of the Bavarian *Oberste Landgericht* rendered in May, 1926, stated that *Der Stürmer*'s comparison of Jews with insects and vermin exceeded all bounds of freedom of the press. An article in 1930 attacking the Jews of Leutershausen as an organized body of cheats and criminals gained Karl Holz a two-week sentence for libel. When he appealed the decision to the district court at Ansbach, he produced an assortment of witnesses describing

212

alleged seductions of servant girls and farmers' wives. The court sustained the original sentence and added a fine of six hundred marks.[26]

Such decisions essentially depended on individual initiatives, whether by citizens or officials. One possibility for systematic collective action involved Nazi calls for boycotts of Jewish businesses. Weimar's anti-boycott legislation dated from Imperial days. It combined the principles of laissez-faire liberalism with an anti-Socialist perspective. Provided with reasonable evidence that Nazis were encouraging boycotts of specific businesses or professional men, courts acted quickly and decisively enough to encourage even *Der Stürmer* to accentuate the positive, recommending buying from Aryans and taking care not to name names when encouraging avoiding Jewish businessmen, doctors, or lawyers. These actions, however, tended to reinforce an image of the Jew as interested only in money without challenging the basis of *völkisch* anti-Semitism. The *Centralverein* in particular preferred another approach—invoking Paragraphs 130 or 166 of the Weimar Legal Code, and filing charges of inciting class violence or committing offenses against religion.

Such cases were unpopular with police, prosecutors, and public alike. The *Centralverein* left itself exposed to criticism for trying to restrict free speech in a republic which to its enemies already restricted too many freedoms in the name of security. On a more technical level, German courts were aware of the difficulty of obtaining convictions carrying more than token sentences. Some prosecutors were in fact anti-Semitic. Others were reluctant to waste time on matters they considered more suitable for decision in the public forum than in the courtroom. And even when fines or prison terms were imposed, the possibility that they would deter repetition of the offense was virtually nil. The legal paragraphs and penalties involving blasphemy were aimed at village atheists, not politicized fanatics. Streicher was only one among many racists who boasted proudly of suffering for their beliefs, and announced their intention in open court of continuing their campaign.[27] But *Der Stürmer* was too vile a piece of work to ignore.

The *Centralverein* opened its direct campaign in 1926, demanding that the authorities take action against an issue of *Der*

Das geschächtete Polenmädchen

... Sie lockten das Mädchen in den Wald, fesselten und knebelten es und tranken aus den geöffneten Adern sein Blut ...

THE SLAUGHTERED POLISH GIRL. "... They lured the girl into the woods, bound and gagged her, and drank the blood from her opened veins ..."

Stürmer featuring an article on alleged ritual murder in Poland and a cartoon showing Jews butchering a nude blonde and drinking her blood. The *Centralverein* described the offending material as insulting the God of all monotheistic religions. Refusing to prosecute, whatever the reasons, meant that any libellous fanatic could besmirch the holiest beliefs of other groups and count on being shielded by the courts. What was the status of the Jewish religion when a Streicher needed only to say that he was referring to the Jewish "race" in his fantastic charges, and walk off scot-free.[28]

This powerful argument was met by Bavaria's best bureaucratese. The Nürnberg prosecutor asserted that neither Paragraph 130 nor Paragraph 166 could be used effectively in this case. Judges differed sharply on exactly what constituted a danger to public order. It was extremely difficult to prove that a specific newspaper article threatened the peace and safety of the community unless it contained a direct incitement to violence. The *Centralverein* might disagree with the court's interpretations of the religious content of a given article, but this only reinforced the point that questions of literary or theological interpretation were seldom subject to legal resolution.

Moreover, exactly who should be brought to trial? Streicher himself could not be prosecuted for the material, since he was already serving a jail sentence. Maximilian Hardel said he only published the paper, and had nothing to do with its contents. Philip Ruprecht stated that he was paid to make sketches based on a given article. Beyond that, Fips knew nothing. As for Karl Holz, he said he had adapted the article about the Polish murder from another newspaper. Mrs. Holz, like a good German *Hausfrau*, declared that her husband never discussed business matters with her. *Der Stürmer* had a responsible editor, as all papers were required to do. For the issue in question, the man was Otto Dietrich. But since he was in Berlin, serving in the Reichstag, was that body likely to suspend his parliamentary immunity? Even if it did, could the *Centralverein* hope for more than a token judgment—or any judgment at all? Holz was in fact eventually charged for his role in publishing that issue of *Der Stürmer* —but his case fell under the general political amnesty of 1928.[29]

The *Centralverein* was also beginning to discover something the citizens of Nürnberg had known for years. Court cases merely gave Streicher another public forum for his arguments. In the spring of 1928, *Der Stürmer* was charged for one of its monotonously semipornographic essays on "Der Jude und die Deutsche Frau." When a Nürnberg court returned a verdict of acquittal, the *Centralverein* appealed the case to Munich. Streicher seized the opportunity to proclaim in open court that the Jews were out to destroy him. When the prosecutor protested, Streicher declared that the trial was not being held at his instigation, and that anyone who tried to silence him had to be a better man than Streicher himself, who had fought for Germany while the prosecutor spent his war behind a desk. He concluded by proclaiming that if he had the official outside, he would give him a lesson in manners that anyone could understand. A day in jail for being ruled out of order was a small price to pay for such publicity.[30] Besides, one wonders how many little men, employees of every type, white-collar or blue, read Streicher's words with envy. *Here* was a man who cringed before no one and nothing!

By the fall of 1928, the *Centralverein* of Bavaria had decided that a more systematic offensive against *Der Stürmer* was necessary. Its legal department read the paper from April to October, then submitted its opinions. On the whole, *Der Stürmer*, with its piled-up farrago of falsified Talmudic citations, was both objectively inaccurate and an insult to peaceful Christians as well as Jews. To stop the sale of any newspaper unless it overtly incited to class hatred or high treason, or was clearly pornographic, was impossible. In any case, by the time the machinery of the law took effect, a paper like *Der Stürmer* with its limited and loyal clientele, was usually all but sold out. The best that could be achieved was the harassment of street vendors and small shopkeepers. On the other hand, if it were once possible to prove that a paper's overall tone was offensive to religion, street sales could be forbidden; stores could be required to check each issue for content. Therefore, the attorneys' advice, couched in cautious language, seemed to be to keep close watch on *Der Stürmer* for one major offense against Paragraph 166, then bring it to trial with every legal and intellectual source the *Centralverein* could make available. Picking on smaller incidents was likely to generate a reverse effect from that intended.[31]

Centralverein officials continued to read every issue of *Der Stürmer* and inform everyone who was attacked in its pages. The problem was that few of the victims chose to act on the information. Some wanted nothing to do with *Der Stürmer*, particularly in a courtroom. In other instances, the *Centralverein* itself conceded that the charges contained "a small kernel of truth," however Streicher might have exaggerated the events. Logic suggests that particularly where sex or business were involved, a certain reluctance to press matters was understandable.[32]

It is against this background that "The Great Nürnberg Ritual Murder Trial" began on October 29, 1929. The *Centralverein's* lawyers had built a case in two areas. The first charged Streicher, Holz, and *Der Stürmer* with presenting certain deaths, particularly the Gladbeck and Manau killings discussed above in chapter four, as possible ritual murders. The tone of the articles in question, the plaintiffs declared, attacked all Jews through misinterpreted or misapplied Talmudic quotations. The second category of charges involved *Der Stürmer's* assertions that Jews could commit perjury in Gentile courts and were not required to respect Gentile laws concerning property. Expert witnesses traced the origins of both of these lines of argument, demonstrating them as purely legal devices dating from previous millenia. On the other hand, it was possible to cite quotation after quotation from Jewish law prohibiting perjury and treachery under any circumstances, describing them as punishable before God and threatening one's place in the World to Come.

The trial made headlines throughout Germany. This brief summary says nothing of the massive behind-the-scenes effort required to get Streicher's parliamentary immunity suspended in order to bring him before the bar of justice in the first place. Nor does it address the question of whether Streicher's racial views received more publicity as a result of the trial than if *Der Stürmer* had been allowed to publish unchallenged. On the whole, the court acted properly throughout the trial. In their decision the judges stressed the difficulty of evaluating exact meanings of certain sections of Jewish law, particularly in translation. They agreed that it was difficult to determine the exact extent to which specific arguments in the Zohar, the Talmud, or the Torah might be considered valid in contemporary society.

The court also conceded that the defendants gave the impression of being extraordinarily well-read in Jewish law and its esoterica. These very facts, however, worked to their condemnation. Men with the specific knowledge Streicher and Holz had manifested day after day in court should be well aware that they could not hope to use material dating from the middle ages to describe behavior patterns in the Weimar Republic. In a more intellectual vein, they should be aware that the meanings of the passages they cited were by no means as plain as *Der Stürmer* asserted week after week.

The accused were, in short, guilty as charged of libeling the Jewish religion under Paragraph 166 of the Weimar Penal Code. Streicher and Holz might leave the court to the accompaniment of a cheering, singing crowd of over four hundred people, but the original verdict stood on appeal. Streicher was sentenced to two months in prison, Holz to three and a half months. This represented a sharp reduction from the prosecution's recommendation of eight months for Streicher and ten for Holz. The court justified its decision on the grounds that the defendants had not acted from reprehensible motives such as personal gain. This point was meant not to declare that Jews were fair game, but to indicate the essentially political nature of Streicher's anti-Semitism. It was possible to punish him for going too far in specific instances. The validity and acceptability of his general political position were not appropriate matters for the law to settle. That was up to the voters.[33]

The *Centralverein* had won a partial victory, which proved useful on subsequent occasions. The last major *Stürmer* banning under the Weimar Republic involved an issue whose lead article on a sensational murder in Paderborn was interpreted as repeating ritual murder allegations.[34] By this time, however, the proceedings were routine. Once the police obtained the necessary court orders and were able to raid the print shop, the type forms had already been broken. Copies of the offending issue were forwarded to Nürnberg from everywhere in Germany. Dresden, Hamburg, Zwickau, all made their contributions. But the only follow-up was the filing of charges by the Wilhelmsdorff gendarmerie against a man for displaying the issue in question after he knew its sale was banned. The *Centralverein* protested that too many towns outside the Nürnberg area received confiscation orders so late, and implemented them so lethargically, that *Stürmer* vendors learned of them in time to sell the offending paper before police arrived to collect whatever copies remained. The response was an exasperated statement that the Nürnberg police sent out banning notices by radio and informed all of the police districts of *Mittelfranken*. If the officials in a given community failed to execute a given ban promptly, this was not Nürnberg's responsibility; complaints should be filed in Ansbach. Everyone knew, after all, that *Der Stürmer* would be back on the stands in a week or a month.[35]

Attempts at fighting boycotts also ran into an increasing number of obstacles. In advising its local groups on dealing with this issue, the Bavarian *Centralverein* recommended above all careful planning. Lawyers should be chosen and evidence collected with equal care. Verbal statements were difficult to try in court; avoid depending on them. If posters of any kind appeared, make sure the responsible groups were acting legally. And above all, try to find three or four businessmen who could claim and prove economic hardship as a result of a boycott.[36]

These recommendations might be good law, but particularly for small-town organizations they were virtually useless as advice. The final point was the key. A Munich lawyer might declare that a representative *Stürmer*, DS 50/1931, included at least three invitations to a boycott. The articles "Bist du Phar," "Stürmer Leser," and "Geht nicht zum Juden" could serve as the basis for pressing charges.[37] But to what purpose? How many storekeepers would be willing to testify against their customers, particularly in the midst of a depression? And if a ritual murder trial had been worth no more than a few weeks in jail, would not a boycott trial merely provide another public forum for Streicher?

In the countryside the Jews' situation was worse. In December, 1931, the Bavarian *Centralverein* complained to the District Office of Feuchtwangen. Sections of *Der Stürmer* were being hung illegally by the Nazis; could they not be removed on the grounds that official permission was required to post placards? The local police reported that the *Centralverein* was describing a *Stürmer* showcase which included all eight sides of the paper and was changed regularly, like the display cases of any other news-paper. And since the courts had consistently decided papers were not posters, pressing charges would be a waste of everyone's time.[38]

Gareis was vigorous in his protestations that he did his best to explain to groups and individuals, specifically the *Central-verein*, what the police could and could not do in coping with anti-Jewish propaganda. Not every attack of every kind on a Jew was a self-evident crime.[39] Most scholars dismiss this as special pleading. Gareis has the image of a man all too willing to over-look such minor Nazi sins as public anti-Semitism. Local police for their part are presented as raw material for concentration-camp staffs and execution squads in the new Germany they real-ly wanted.[40]

Despite the praise bestowed on him by such notorious Nazis as Ernst Röhm, Gareis was more a conservative nationalist than a National Socialist. His right-wing sympathies did not keep him from fulfilling his duties.[41] His reports reveal more insensitivity than anti-Semitism and more cynical objectivity than insensitiv-ity. Given the problems of obtaining convictions for offenses against the press laws, or for religious libel, the attitude of local police forces also becomes clearer. Without denying the presence in their ranks of actual and potential Nazis and Nazi sympa-thizers, without denying that their reports and records often show insensitivity to the feelings and anxieties of Franconian Jews, throughout the existence of the Weimar Republic its police enforced its laws even in the heart of Streicher country.

A considerable proportion of the official complaints filed locally during the rise of Nazism in Franconia involved citizens from the comfortable middle class—the kind of people who, whatever their ethnic identity or formal political affiliation, ex-pected to be treated with deference when they walked into a sta-tion, who were always ready to go over an officer's head and complain to his superiors. It was not likely to generate much sympathy among the police when such an individual presented a set of vague charges with the demand that they be pursued im-mediately—particularly when it was increasingly plain that such charges led at best to time-consuming, inconclusive trials bring-ing no credit to any official involved and more commonly leading to mere harassment, with the accused back on the streets almost as soon as the paperwork on his case was completed.

Such harassment could, however, be effective with the strong support of public opinion, and not every Jewish protest was ignored. A man from Pfarrkirchen, for example, filed charges in May, 1932, against a newsdealer for displaying a banned issue of *Der Stürmer*. The local police informed the court that the salesman deserved no special consideration. He was regarded as an unpleasant fanatic who used his newsstand to ridicule other parties and individuals through pictures, cartoons, and photos—just the kind of public pest against whom police forces could still proceed with public applause.[42]

Courts might be reluctant to rule on the political aspects of anti-Semitism. Nevertheless, initiating legal proceedings against gross incitement to violence, or taking action against a Nazi regarded by the community at large as a nuisance, could bring enough results to encourage a man from Coburg to contact the Nürnberg Prosecutor's Office on February 15, 1933—five minutes before midnight. He argued that *DS* 6/1933 contained a statement that "every single Jew" was a sex criminal. I, the correspondent declared, am Jewish. I am also not a sex criminal, and I can prove it. Therefore I wish to press libel charges against Streicher and his paper.[43] The syllogism was worthy of a class in logic. It could not have had less relevance to the events surrounding the composition of the letter. But it also supports the conclusion that where anti-Semitism interacted with the law, the police and the legal authorities of Nürnberg and Franconia did enough to make the Weimar system work—enough, at least, to sustain the Jews' general belief that they ultimately lived under a government of justice as well as a government of laws.[44]

3

The series of attacks against Mayor Luppe mentioned in chapter seven generated one of the most familiar public political events of Streicher's career in Nürnberg: a series of trials on charges of libel and malicious mischief. Under any circumstances such trials involved the accuser's integrity. Did he deserve to have such attacks made on him? The courts also had to decide whether a given statement was actually public, and legal opinion in Weimar favored a narrow definition of "public." Then they had to determine whether the statement was actually libelous. Sarcasm, for example, was not illegal—but how was sarcasm defined?[45] Circumstances, in short, tended at best to favor the accused.

Streicher was expert at loading the dice even more heavily. In the first trial, which began in the fall of 1924, he repeated his farrago of accusations against Luppe and his administration in a courtroom crowded with a mixed bag of trial buffs and Streicher supporters, before a presiding justice who had no experience and less expertise at controlling what amounted to a public tribunal.[46] He also had a focal point, a central issue epitomizing his charges. In 1917 Nürnberg had established an old clothes center to provide cheap clothing and shoes to its poor. At war's end, the center began selling confiscated goods and purchasing new wares from its own funds, establishing itself as a kind of bargain center whose competition was particularly resented by small businessmen. Shortly after his arrival in Nürnberg, Luppe, accompanied by several officials, visited the center and was encouraged to purchase a coat. Unacquainted with the details of the center's operation, he accepted the explanation that the coat was part of a stock too expensive for ordinary purchasers, a supply of dress clothing confiscated from a profiteer.

Luppe paid 130 marks for the coat—at that time a sum only a prosperous man could afford. He seemed bewildered that such a fuss could be made five years later over a coat bought at a fair price, whose purchase did not deprive a poor man of clothing. Indeed, Luppe declared, he found little joy in his purchase, even at home—his wife scolded him for buying a coat instead of the suit he needed.[47]

Objectively, the only real impropriety in the incident was the desire of the officials involved to curry favor with the new mayor. For *Der Stürmer*, however, Luppe's "welfare coat," often described as an expensive fur diverted from stock intended for distribution to the poor, became a symbol of the corruption and favoritism National Socialism promised to eradicate.[48] This was the kind of story that could readily appeal to the little man of

Nürnberg, the man who always found himself with a month too long for his money. When Streicher requested contributions to help pay the lawyers' fees, a typical pledge sheet contained thirty or thirty-five names, with an average pledge of a mark or two. Some of the signers gave their jobs: a bookkeeper, a barber, a half-dozen bank employees.[49] Few of them were likely to feel a strong sense of sympathy for, or identity with, a man who could casually spend over a hundred marks on a coat of any kind.

In a trial which exposed the inner structure of Nürnberg's city goverment in a way unknown before or since in Weimar Germany, Luppe's administration was generally vindicated. As for Streicher, the court conceded that he acted in good faith, but described him as a previously convicted libeller whose crude attacks had damaged Luppe in the most extreme fashion. He was found guilty and sentenced to a month in prison.[50]

The sentence itself was by no means a mere slap on the wrist. To describe the court's behavior as a "scandalous failure"[51] is to misjudge the nature of the trial itself. Streicher's tactics were a clever form of legal judo. Certainly Social Democrats and the Social Democratic press had suffered in Imperial Germany from unsympathetic courts willing to use every possible twist and turn of the legal system—plus some extralegal pressures—against politicians and newspapers. Three factors, however, combined to limit the use of similar tactics against Streicher and *Der Stürmer*. While the Socialists were regarded and regarded themselves at least ideologically as outcasts, men without a country, Julius Streicher was still part of mainstream Germany. A prominent politician, a teacher, and a war hero, he enjoyed too much public credibility, especially in Nürnberg, to be treated as being beyond the pale. To say this, is not necessarily to say that Streicher merely put into words what many of his fellow citizens were thinking. It is rather to argue that he belonged to his community to an extent just sufficient to secure the treatment given to a "respectable" offender as opposed to a common felon. Violators of anti-trust legislation seldom face the same courtroom atmosphere as auto thieves.

The Weimar Republic had still not established its credibility with a broad spectrum of the German population. This point is so generally conceded that it has become a cliché. It is usually accompanied by weighty judgments on the nature of the party system, the shortcomings of specific politicians, or the antidemocratic heritage of Bismarck's Empire.[52] In this context it seems reasonable to ask a simple, perhaps a stupid question: why *should* Weimar in its early years have automatically and naturally received or expected more than the passive allegiance of the mass of its citizens? The concept of government that has evolved in the Atlantic world since the French and American revolutions denies any form of divine right to any form of political organization. Legitimacy and authority must be earned through actions perceived by the community as beneficial to the general welfare. In this context the *Vernunftrepublikaner*, the millions of Germans who adopted a reserved, show-me stance towards their new government, were acting in the mainstream of Western political behavior. The Republic was expected to perform. As a new form of government it naturally lacked a foundation of custom on which to rely when times grew hard. Its leaders could expect criticism of every kind from every source. Yet too often even a man of Luppe's caliber retained an Imperial cast of mind, in which the Streichers of the world should humbly acknowledge their superiors and accept the behavior of higher authority without question.

This leads to a third point. Had the court's judgment borne heavily on Streicher, had the punishment been draconic, it might have served notice of the Republic's determination to maintain itself in Nürnberg. However, libel legislation under the Empire and Republic alike was not politically focused. Its primary purpose was to protect the honor of decent people against inappropriate attacks by other slightly less decent people. The penalties involved were designed to modify behavior by shaming the guilty party. A short jail sentence, a stinging fine, and above all the resulting negative publicity would theoretically deter libelous words and actions, or at least destroy or diminish the credibility of the libeler. Such an approach assumes a pre-existing social consensus, one depending heavily on shame as a deterrent. It was hardly likely to be effective against men or institutions who gloried in their challenging of the establishment, and who regarded it as an honor to have enemies in certain quarters.

The sternest application of libel laws under the Empire had

not deterred the Social Democratic press from exposing scandal wherever they saw it—and even occasionally manufacturing a scandal or two.[53] In the divided Germany of the 1920s, strict enforcement was even less likely to deter a man of Streicher's character. Perhaps unfortunately, it was impossible to lock him up and throw away the key on the kinds of charges brought against him during the "overcoat trial." Instead he emerged as something of a public hero, cheered by crowds large enough to require extra security forces for their control, driving through Nürnberg in a car filled with bouquets tossed him by admirers. As the conservative *Fränkischer Kurier* aptly put it, a broad spectrum of public opinion regarded Streicher as sentenced but the city government as judged.[54]

Both parties appealed the decision, Streicher on grounds similar to that advanced by Socrates in his *Apology* and Luppe in an effort to secure a more appropriate sentence for a man he increasingly regarded as a dangerous criminal. The new trial, which began in November, 1925, essentially rehashed the material first presented a year earlier. The combination of Streicher's polished courtroom performance with the court's decision to stick closely to the letter of the law might well have broken a lesser man than Luppe.[55] The final judgement, however, upheld both Luppe's conduct as mayor and the verdict of the earlier trial. Streicher was sentenced to two months in prison. The court stated that Streicher had kept up his attacks on Luppe for over two years without being able to prove the substance of his charges. It justified its relatively light sentence on two grounds. First, Streicher's battle against Luppe was not undertaken for personal gain; Streicher honestly regarded Luppe as unfit to govern a German city. Second, the worst attacks had occurred at a time when political tensions were high on all sides— a polite euphemism for the months surrounding the Beer Hall Putsch. In effect, the court argued that it was time to mend fences.[56]

On several occasions during the second trial, Luppe's testimony had incorporated what the court described as "objective inaccuracies" and "objective falsehoods." On November 30, 1925, the Nürnberg Prosecutor's Office opened a preliminary hearing on the charge that Luppe had been guilty of perjury.

Three days later Luppe was provisionally suspended as mayor. The general consensus among republicans at the time and among historians since has been that this reflected the growing hostility of local authorities to Luppe and the system he represented. Suspending a mayor on such charges was not usual; sending him on unpaid leave was a more common solution. And since when did a libel trial end with a charge of perjury being filed against the injured party? The mayor's lawyers argued that much testimony in long-running cases involved the kind of contradictions Luppe had made. No self-respecting prosecutor confused lapses of memory with perjury, particularly when minor details of long-past incidents were being discussed. Laws, declared one discussion of the case, were of little help. What was needed were courts willing to employ "correct judicial attitudes" to end this misuse of the legal system.[57]

Parallels can be drawn between this attitude and the National Socialist insistence on the establishment of "healthy public opinion" as the key element of the legal system. One might suggest that Streicher and his enemies were making identical demands that the courts follow the law's spirit instead of its letter. On the other hand, in such an environment prosecutors and administrators were caught in a cleft stick. Streicher and his adherents were not political outlaws who could be safely ignored. Their very skill at playing on the paragraphs they professed to despise made every element of the administration cautious. Luppe's lack of popularity—which is not the same as unpopularity—among regional officials did probably encourage taking legal action against him. A related interpretation is that Luppe's very innocence made legal proceedings in this case more reasonable than they might have been if his conduct really were questionable. The bureaucrats could go through a charade. They could present themselves to their nationalist critics as doing their duty according to the law, proceeding even against Weimar's highest officals. On the other hand, since the outcome was sure to end favorably for Luppe, the decision could only further strengthen his position.

The Munich *Oberste Landgericht* did decide in Luppe's favor within two months. Luppe re-entered the Nürnberg city hall as official mayor on March 3. He was welcomed by a majority of the council, greeted ostentatiously by respectable citizens on the street, and counted as a hero and martyr of the Republic throughout Germany.[58] Streicher for his part, after exhausting his appeals, presented himself for incarceration. Jail certainly did not silence him. But Nürnberg's mayor was learning how to use some of Streicher's weapons, with mixed results.

As part of his campaign against Luppe, Streicher had introduced a new phrase. A "Luppe oath" became *Der Stürmer*'s new synonym for carelessness with the truth.[59] And now Luppe could play paragraph pinball with the legal system. Since his name had definitively been cleared of any taint of perjury, he filed suit to forbid *Der Stürmer* to use the phrase "Luppe oath." The court upheld Luppe's point. In August, 1926, *Der Stürmer* was officially forbidden to repeat its accusations under threat of an unlimited fine or six months prison sentence for the publisher and the responsible editor.[60]

Der Stürmer ignored the order, probably because Streicher hoped to goad Luppe into "defending his honor" by another trial. Instead, issues of the paper were repeatedly confiscated for violating a court order by using the prohibited phrase. In November publisher Maximilian Hardel was informed he was risking a choice between a fine of three hundred marks or a jail sentence. The next month, Karl Holz as responsible editor was fined five hundred marks for using "Luppe oath" in an article. Holz and Hardel were each sentenced to a week in jail for printing the offending prhase in another issue.[61]

Naturally the two Nazis appealed the sentences. On December 28, the Civil Section of the Nürnberg *Landgericht* denied the appeal in strong terms. Holz and Hardel argued through their attorneys that their attacks were against Luppe the politician rather than Luppe the man. They supported their position with the ingenious assertion that their accusations did not come under the libel laws because Luppe's profits and career had not in fact been damaged! If anything, the defendants asserted, Luppe's position as Nürnberg's mayor and leader of the national Democratic Party was stronger than ever.

Luppe may have been flattered by this affirmation of his endurance. But it could not be doubted, declared the judges, that *Der Stürmer* was publishing material intended to hurt Luppe personally. Calling a man a perjurer and a coat-thief had nothing to do with politics. Holz and Hardel were ordered to avoid discussing the issue in print for six months, to pay all costs of the trial, and to post a bond of 5,600 marks to insure compliance.[62]

An appellate court summarized several related decisions by declaring that no party paper had a special right to attack anyone's honor. *Der Stürmer* could ruffle Luppe's feathers only within the limits set by the courts. While it was not per se illegal to try to force Luppe's defeat or resignation, the deliberate series of personal attacks designed to diminish his credibility could no longer be allowed. And since *Der Stürmer* showed no sign of abandoning its campaign, the publisher and the responsible editor would have to take the consequences.[63]

Holz, as stubborn as he was stupid, was willing enough to continue ramming his head into the Weimar courts. In May, 1928, *Der Stürmer* published an article on "Eid der Luppe"—an attempt to evade earlier court orders by changing wording slightly. The Nürnberg *Landgericht* responded promptly. Holz was sentenced to two weeks in jail. The Aesopian language of the article, declared the court, would not deceive the simplest mind. As for Holz, his previous sentences had been meant to dissuade him, and had obviously failed. Perhaps two weeks behind bars might drive home the point.[64]

Luppe, however, scored only some of the points in his ongoing battle with Streicher. In the autumn of 1926 a *Bombe* burst in Nürnberg. It began with a "special number" featuring the "exposure" of Julius Streicher as a rapist and warning "Great Julius" not to forget that he who digs a pit for others often falls in himself.[65] In December it offered a more circumstantial story based on the statement of one Georg Schmidt, who had served in Streicher's company in 1916. According to Schmidt, while billeted in a French village, Streicher pushed his way into a schoolteacher's house, seized her, and was ready to proceed further when the woman screamed for help. Schmidt, who had been in another room of the house, promptly appeared. Streicher begged for silence; Schmidt agreed; and that was the end of the matter until one Kurt Hennch fused the explosive story.[66]

Hennch has been variously described as a Communist, a

völkist, and an agitator. Probably the last adjective is the best. He seems to have been a man who enjoyed making wheels turn for his own profit. The Nürnberg police considered him as a man of questionable reputation, and did not take his sheet seriously. Streicher, however, was too expert in the use of innuendo not to recognize the dangers involved in this kind of accusation. His position in the Nürnberg party was never unchallenged, and *Die Bombe*'s allegations were manna to his local enemies.

Three other factors encouraged Streicher to file libel charges. One was the persistent rumor that Schmidt and Hennch were being paid by certain highly placed local officials. Another was the fact that neither was a man of spotless character. A third was the strength of Streicher's defense. The situation was tailor-made for *Der Stürmer* and its editor. While Streicher fulminated against Jewish lawyers, the Elders of Zion, and the suborning of perjury, one of his lieutenants made a journey to France. He returned with all the evidence Streicher needed to press his case.[67]

The *Bombe* case kept Nürnberg talking in the summer of 1927. Such despicable accusations, declared Streicher's attorney, could not be tolerated, even if they involved events alleged to have taken place a decade ago and in another country. A man's honor was limited neither by time nor space. What was true for Hermann Luppe must hold for Julius Streicher. Streicher contributed to the process of transforming a wolf into a lamb by holding his testimony to the obvious. He admitted he had been stationed in the village named during the time in question, but he never attacked anyone. As a man with a strict sense of honor, he would have shot himself had he behaved as Schmidt alleged.

What might have been dismissed as courtroom melodrama gained credibility as Streicher's testimony was corroborated by member after member of his old company. They jeered at Schmidt's declaration that Streicher walked into a house in midday and attempted what amounted to rape without even inquiring if anyone else was present. One ex-soldier suggested the implausibility of such behavior in broadest Bavarian when he declared that he had had a woman in the same village, but when he visited her he never took company along.

More convincing was the sworn statement of the alleged victim. She declared that she had known both Streicher and a man named Schmidt in 1916, but recognized neither's picture when shown them. No one, Schmidt nor Streicher, ever lived with her. Streicher never offered violence to her, nor did she give him language lessons to camouflage an affair. She neither spoke nor understood German.[68]

Whatever its exact combination of truth, self-protective memory, and desire to avoid scandal, this account proved more credible than the character of Streicher's principal accuser. Schmidt testified that he had been initially urged to open the case by another ex-soldier. Then several of Streicher's political enemies offered to help him tell the real truth about the *Frankenführer*. They paid for a trip to France, where he met the woman and helped "refresh her memory." Apart from that, Schmidt declared, he had received no more than thirty marks, five or ten at a time, out of sympathy for his "debilitated physical condition."

The question before the court, and in the minds of more and more *Nürnberger*, was which of Streicher's enemies had financed Schmidt's travels and the publication of *Die Bombe* itself. More and more evidence pointed to Mayor Luppe. Then Hennch directly implicated the mayor. Luppe, he declared, had not only listened to Schmidt's story as told by Hennch. He had paid him to edit and print it. Luppe testified that he had in fact underwritten *Die Bombe* and given Schmidt several hundred marks in an attempt to clarify the matter of Streicher's alleged behavior in France.[69]

As Luppe's attorneys argued that it was no crime to support the publication of a newspaper, *Der Stürmer* went to work. It delighted in characterizing Hennch as a convicted thief and swindler whose charges against Streicher were so flimsy that even the *Tagespost* had ignored him. Nürnberg's mayor, on the other hand, welcomed this criminal into his office, gave him a visiting card with a handwritten reference, and finally paid him to do the dirty work to which the high-minded Luppe would not stoop himself—at least in public.[70]

The final arguments in the case depended on plausibility. Schmidt's lawyer said that a man of Streicher's well-known aggressive character might have attempted something like rape. Particularly in an occupied country, he declared, one does not say "excuse me, madam, but how about a little. . . ." Manners tend to be substantially cruder. Schmidt's silence in 1916 reflected the fact that Streicher was at that time a senior non-commissioned officer, able to retaliate by systematic harassment which might ultimately prove fatal.

The case for the plaintiff also appealed to common sense. The court was asked why a man in Streicher's position, a man under constant observation and with a great deal to lose, a man of education, a teacher, would simply walk into a house and try such a crude approach to another teacher. If he were guilty, would he have put such effort into finding the woman and obtaining her sworn statement, running the risk that she might choose to play the role of the violated heroine? Schmidt's silence had lasted for too long to be credible. The war, after all, had been over since 1918, and Schmidt did not even try to argue that he had been terrorized for eight years after being demobilized. It did not take the court long to find Schmidt guilty of libel and sentence him to a year in prison. Hennch drew eight months for an attack on Streicher the court described as underhanded, dirty, and low.

Most accounts overlook or de-emphasize the *Bombe* affair, probably because of the relatively ignoble role played by Luppe. His actions were understandable. He believed that he could destroy Streicher by exposing his true character to the public. He believed Schmidt's story, and certainly Streicher's alleged approach to the woman fit his public image. But the years of persecution had driven Luppe into a rage that blinded his judgment. Normally he was a man of too high principles and a politician of too much experience even to consider using such flimsy material against an opponent.

Luppe would have been well advised to heed the *Central-verein*'s warning against trying to undermine the *völkisch* movement with its own weapons.[71] Streicher emerged with an enhanced image as a man's man, who made war when he made war, love when he made love, and never confused the two—the kind of man who might make errors of judgment, who might at times behave a bit rashly, but whose heart and other organs were all in the right places. Without this vindication, Streicher's party enemies might well have been able to unseat him. A year later, for example, a notice to "Voters, National Socialists, SA Men" called the official Nazi list for the upcoming elections unacceptable because of Streicher's immorality.[72] But prospective Nazi voters had literally heard it all before.

The Bavarian Ministry of the Interior refused to discipline Luppe. In its opinion, the kind of attacks he had been facing required measures not to be evaluated by usual standards. Reprimanding the mayor officially would only strengthen Streicher's position and encourage further slanderous attacks. On one level, Luppe's greatest days in office were still ahead.[73] On another, however, his position in Nürnberg suffered significant damage. To his right-wing opponents he became "Luppe the *Bomb*-Maker." Pointed questions about the relationship of means to ends were raised in the city council. Burghers already wavering in their allegiance to democratic parties apparently unable to deliver either voters or results found themselves taking the high road, asking if a man who could be involved in such a dirty business was really a suitable representative of Weimar in Nürnberg.[74]

This perspective carried over into the courts as well. In 1928 Streicher was fined a thousand marks for saying in public that he could watch Luppe "croak like a sow." The same year a Nürnberg court sentenced Luppe to an identical penalty for using the legally slanderous word *gemein* in a context referring to Streicher. The latter verdict was reversed on appeal.[75] It nevertheless seems probable that the Nürnberg judiciary reflected a broad spectrum of public opinion in its belief that the conflict between Luppe and Streicher had gone on too long to benefit either the city of Nürnberg or the legal system of Bavaria. The political differences between the men were exacerbated by mutual personal hatred of a kind no legal system could resolve. It was therefore appropriate to assess fines and jail sentences, steadily increasing the penalties until the rivals either mended their ways or ceased using Nürnberg's courts as a political forum.

Der Stürmer's attacks on Luppe in fact diminished in tone and volume after 1928. But in winning this limited victory, Luppe acquired a reputation, however undeserved, as just another politician. Like the Republic he represented, Luppe functioned on constant trial before an audience regarding itself as above and uninvolved in a dubious battle.

CONCLUSION

National Socialism, like all variants of fascism, appealed to a desire to belong. It spoke to the alienated, the confused, the frightened—to people who, whatever their objective circumstances, perceived themselves as actual or potential losers. In this context the Jew served as the ideological symbol of everything that had gone wrong in Germany since the Enlightenment, the Industrial Revolution, and the Versailles Treaty. He was the principal negative image, the antitype juxtaposed to the new world the Nazis proposed to create. Mobilizing the German masses against the Jew was an important means of achieving the consensus National Socialism required not merely to take and exercise power, but to carry out its revolutionary visions of a Germany and a world reborn.[1]

A key element in this mobilization involved consciousness raising. German anti-Semitism before and after 1918 was essentially moderate. It involved unease, dislike, and distrust. It seldom, even in theory, crossed the line of actively seeking to harm Jews individually or collectively.[2] This in turn reflected its abstract nature. Direct cultural clashes and overt cultural shock were less significant in Germany than in eastern Europe or the lands of the Hapsburg Empire. Germany's Jews, though certainly not assimilated, were highly acculturated—a process encouraged by the Jewish community's relatively small size and relatively even distribution. This acculturation meant that the common sense evidence of one's everyday experience tended to work against the apocalyptic visions of the Jew projected in National Socialism.

The challenge lay in overcoming this barrier, in integrating folk tales, personal antagonisms, and individual grievances into a *Weltanschauung*. And here the essentially verbal nature of Nazi propaganda had certain limits. The orations, the rallies, the parades, were regarded by the participants as elements of a ritual experience affirming their membership in a new community. The style and rhythm of a speech were more important than its content. General impressions might remain, but very little more could be depended upon to stick.

In this context *Der Stürmer* could perform two necessary tasks. First, by its nature as a printed medium, it could reinforce the ideas expressed in the meeting halls. The very repetition critics found monotonous was part of the paper's role in a systematic propaganda offensive. More importantly, *Der Stürmer* labored systematically to create cultural antagonism where none existed. Its principal attacks were on "the Jew next door." They involved giving a sinister dimension to everyday encounters. In this sense *Der Stürmer* was a journalistic version of that most frightening form of nightmare, when the known and familiar suddenly assume malevolent forms.

Streicher used the Jew as the focal point for a broad spectrum of social, economic, and psychic anxieties calculated to evoke responses from respectable people. *Der Stürmer* played on fears of modernization, attacking anything from department stores to condom dispensers that might threaten someone's vision of the good old days. It appealed to the insecurities of people on unknown neutral ground, or required to interact with strangers in unfamiliar situations. Even its sex stories were not dominated by the *outré* or the bizarre. Many of them featured circumstances that might happen to anyone. Week after week the paper sought to convince its readers that the everyday aspects of the Jewish conspiracy were as important and as menacing as its cosmic elements.

Der Stürmer and Streicher did more than affirm Nazi myths. They challenged those of the opposition as well—particularly the myths of civilization, of decent middle class behavior. *Der Stürmer*'s style reflected Streicher's personal approach to politics, whatever its mixture of pathology and deliberate choice. But on another level *Der Stürmer* was part of an image: full-blooded mind-speaking against all odds from the old order in support of the new. Streicher's revolutionary rhetoric was not presented from the perspective of a man who has stepped outside of his society. Throughout the *Kampfzeit* he sustained his image as a crusader, not an outlaw. In a practical sense, he was expert at using his insider's position, pursuing his career as a politician and a journalist within patterns of freedom under law developed in the empire and extended by the republic. Groups and individuals could successfully challenge *Der Stürmer* in the courts. They could not destroy the paper while it functioned in a legal framework presuming just the kind of consensus that National Socialism challenged. On a political/psychological level, this allowed Streicher and his newspaper to maintain the role of critic and gadfly, attacking targets that the little man might enjoy seeing pilloried in a way he might not dare to do himself, but could admire from a distance.

With the Nazi seizure of power, Streicher became expendable. His enemies constantly kept Hitler aware of his one-man rule of Franconia, his brutality, his corruption, his inefficiency. With the fall of the Republic and the growing institutionalization of anti-Semitism, *Der Stürmer* ran short of targets. It found new ones in party rivals and party programs, thereby increasing the hostility the "Frankish Nero" already inspired. Not until 1939, however, were "Himmler's man in Nürnberg," Police President Benno Martin, and Luppe's successor, the ambitious Nazi Mayor Willy Liebel, able to take advantage of Streicher's alleged assertion that the child ostensibly fathered by Hermann Göring was the product of artificial insemination. With this as a catalyst, Hitler finally banished Streicher from Nürnberg, allowing him to retain only the empty title of *Gauleiter*.[3] He spent World War II on his country estate. By the time of his arrest and imprisonment by the Americans in 1945 he had degenerated into an object of contempt for all who came in contact with him. His execution inspired neither contemporary grief nor subsequent remorse.

What of *Der Stürmer*'s impact? The paper did exercise a demonstrable direct influence on National Socialism. "Respectable" Nazis may have made a point of distancing themselves from Streicher's brand of anti-Semitism. But *Der Stürmer* was also among the best-known and most profitable of the local Nazi newspapers, and no one could deny Streicher's success in election after election. Even Josef Goebbels as gauleiter of Berlin used Streicher's technique of personifying the weaknesses and short-comings of the Weimar system in a single individual. What Streicher did to Mayor Luppe, Goebbels and *Der Angriff* did to Deputy Police President Bernhard Weiss with even more success. On local levels, Franconian Nazis increasingly imitated Streicher and *Der Stürmer* by making scandals of alleged administrative failures or shortcomings, emphasizing the smallest details again and again, until public excitement reached a fever pitch.[4]

Der Stürmer's general effect remains debatable. Facing the gallows, Streicher and his attorneys strove mightly to downplay the paper's circulation and influence. Germans, especially *Nürnberger*, have made an understandable effort since 1945 to insist that *Stürmer* readership was confined to schoolboys and cranks, that respectable people ignored the paper or were sickened by it. As a rule party newspapers are intended less to make converts than to strengthen the faithful. *Der Stürmer*, however, was unusual in its ability to mobilize hostilities and frustrations. Many of these emotions were not specifically Jewish-centered. It is surprising how much even of Streicher's hate mail responded to incidents and events that a reasonable person could consider disturbing in themselves. It was the perceived fact of Jewish involvement that led these correspondents to voice their grievances to a man and a paper known to be sympathetic in such matters.

Publication meant recognition. It implied acceptance of one's problems and implied the possibility of their solution in the framework of a new order. One might not be able to get along with one's employer, one's neighbors, or one's fellow-workers. *Der Stürmer* at least offered an explanation for the failure of those everyday relationships involving Jews. National Socialist propaganda was essentially based on hatred; *Der Stürmer* put petty spite and everyday resentment at the service of Hitler's movement.

Experience suggests that *Der Stürmer* played an even more directly instrumental role for many of its readers. It could be a means of harassing authority figures, collecting debts, even extorting kegs of beer. The preface of the present work made the point that *Der Stürmer* did not exist in a vacuum. It was a weekly party sheet which never claimed comprehensive news coverage. Even the most committed National Socialist was likely to have access to alternative sources of information and opinion. On a day to day level *Der Stürmer*'s audience probably took the paper far less seriously than Streicher hoped during the *Kampfzeit* or the judges believed at Nürnberg. The cartoons were erotic. The sex-and-scandal stories were stimulating. And nothing was really going to happen to the Jews anyway. The soup is never eaten as hot as it is cooked.

Paradoxically, *Der Stürmer* could even reinforce these kinds of feelings. Streicher steadfastly denied during his trial that his paper ever directly advocated genocide.[5] Whatever may have been true after 1933, during the *Kampfzeit* this assertion is defensible. *Der Stürmer* proclaimed German Jews as unwelcome aliens whose only place in the Nazi new order would be behind bars, or as specimens in a criminal museum. It advocated draconic penalties for any individual Jew who might in any way offend a member of the master race. It described the solution of the Jewish question as the greatest problem of the world.[6] But the Final Solution *Der Stürmer* described between 1923 and 1933 described emigration and expulsion, not mass murder. The Jews could go to Palestine, Russia, or America—anywhere that would take them without their ill-gotten wealth, as long as Germany was freed of their presence. Those who chose to remain would get what they deserved: ghettos, yellow badges, and "appropriate" surnames, so that no German would ever again fail to recognize his enemy.[7]

Advocating collective violence of any kind against Jews was too clear a violation of the Weimar Penal Code to be lightly risked. Constant descriptions of Jews as plague bacilli and parasites can certainly be read as indirect prefigurations of the Holocaust. But verbally and in print, *Der Stürmer*'s staff insisted that they were not pogromists. A cartoon might show a Nazi pumping poison into the roots of a tree, and be captioned "when the vermin are dead, the German oak will again flourish." But the dying animals were carefully labeled "trusts," "press," and "stock exchange." Jews were not mentioned. We Nazis, declared Karl Holz, do wish to be rid of the Jews. What is necessary is to

Wenn das Ungeziefer tot ist, grünt die deutsche Eiche wieder!

"When the vermin are dead, the German oak will again flourish."

load them into freight and cattle cars as quickly as possible, and send them back where they came from: Jerusalem. Revenge, according to Streicher, was a dish best served cold. The Jews constantly proclaimed their longings to return to Zion. The National Socialists would help them go back, see that they stayed there, and enjoy watching them eat each other like rats.[8]

The sincerity of such statements is less significant than their propaganda impact. *Der Stürmer* was generally recognized as embodying the most extreme form of Nazi anti-Semitism. If the paper and its creators insisted on every occasion that their goal was the separation of Germans and Jews by legal and constitutional means, surely this must indicate that National Socialism's Jew-baiting involved more rhetoric than substance—or that repressive measures would be applied legally and quietly—or that the deportations to the east were to labor camps—or that the executions were legitimate reprisals for atrocities committed against German soldiers. At least the rationalizations may have comforted many a casual *Stürmer* reader before and after 1933.[9]

The Nazi extermination system functioned to reduce the Jews to an undifferentiated mass in the eyes of their executioners. *Der Stürmer* performed the same task for Germany's little man. The cattle dealer, the office manager, the chance acquaintance in a train compartment—all were defined by their Jewishness. And this was the connection between the Final Solution and the ordinary newspaper reader who never seriously wished to hurt anyone, who would admit to no offense more serious than a taste for soft-core pornography. Two anecdotes, reported with equal glee in *Der Stürmer*'s columns, tell the story better than any statistics. In 1925 the paper featured a news story describing a "Monstrous Transport." A trainload of Poles and Czechs had passed through Nürnberg on its way to France. Officially the passengers were listed as contract labor for rebuilding the areas devastated in World War I. The probable reality, Streicher declared, was that these unwitting victims would find themselves in the ranks of the Foreign Legion, fighting France's latest war in Morocco. Naturally, the transport was in charge of a "fat Jew" —like all of his race, a dealer in human flesh.[10]

There are many kinds of prophecy and many kinds of vision. What might Streicher's have been as he wrote that particular piece? Fifteen years later trains would run in an opposite direction, laden with people who also believed—or wished to believe —that they would be employed on public works projects. And as early as 1927 when the National Socialist movement was at its lowest ebb, an elderly Jewish woman told her neighbors that she had nightmares about Nazis, and suffered cardiac seizures when three brownshirts actually appeared in her small town.[11] Perhaps she too saw the future more clearly than either the educated, prominent, influential German Jews or the little men, the simple, ordinary common men whose twenty pfennigs a week enabled *Der Stürmer* to survive and flourish.

NOTES

Introduction

1.   Cf. *inter alia* Dietrich Orlow, "The Conversion of Myths into Political Power," *American Historical Review*, LXXII (1967), 906–924; M.v. Brentano, "Die Endlösung—Ihre Funktion in Theorie und Praxis der Faschismus," in *Antisemitismus*, ed. H. Huss and A. Schröder (Frankfurt, 1976), pp. 36–76; and Fred Weinstein, *The Dynamics of Nazism* (New York, 1980), pp. 79 passim. The best overview is Eberhard Jaeckel, *Hitlers Weltanschauung*, tr. H. Arnold (Middletown, Conn., 1972).

2.   The genesis of the Final Solution has generated an immense critical literature. The opposing poles are well represented by Lucy Dawidowicz, *The War Against the Jews, 1933–1945* (New York, 1975); and Karl Schleunes, *The Twisted Road to Auschwitz: Nazi Policy toward German Jews, 1933–1939* (Urbana, Ill., 1970). See also Uwe Dietrich Adam, *Judenpolitik im Dritten Reich* (Düsseldorf, 1972).

3.   W.S. Allen, *The Nazi Seizure of Power* (Chicago, 1963) is a good discussion of the way the process worked in one German community.

4.   Dawidowicz, 163ff; Golo Mann, *Der Antisemitismus* (Munich and Frankfurt, 1960), pp. 32–33; Sebastian Haffner, *The Meaning of Hitler*, tr. E. Osers (New York, 1979), pp. 91ff.

5.   Examples include Geoffrey Pridham, *Hitler's Rise to Power: The Nazi Movement in Bavaria, 1923–1933* (New York, 1973), pp. 237ff; Jeremy Noakes, *The Nazi Party in Lower Saxony, 1921–1933* (Oxford, 1971), pp. 209–10. H.W. Koch, *The Hitler Youth: Origins and Development 1922–45* (New York, 1976), pp. 116ff; Claudia Koonz, "Mothers in the Fatherland: Women in Nazi Germany," in

Becoming Visible: Women in European History, ed. Renate Bridenthal and C. Koonz (Boston, 1977), pp. 449–52.

6. Schleunes, 55ff. However, David L. Blackbourn suggests that anti-Semitism was sufficiently institutionalized in the Center Party to generate a homeopathic effect, countering Nazi propaganda with smaller, less virulent doses of the same medicine. "Roman Catholics, the Centre Party and Anti-Semitism in Imperial Germany," in *Nationalist and Racialist Movements in Britain and Germany before 1914*, ed. Paul Kennedy and Anthony Nicholls (London, 1981), pp. 123–124.

7. George L. Mosse, "The Image of the Jew in German Popular Literature: Felix Dahn and Gustav Freytag," in *Germans and Jews* (New York, 1970), pp. 61–76.

8. See such standard analyses as Henry Nash Smith, *Virgin Land: The American West as Symbol and Myth* (Cambridge Press, 1971); and Russel B. Nye, *The Unembarrassed Muse: The Popular Arts in America* (New York, 1973); and John G. Cawelti, "Myth, Symbol, and Formula," *Journal of Popular Culture* VIII (1975): 1–8.

9. Smith describes some of the underlying assumptions of his research methods in "Can 'American Studies' Develop a Method?" *American Quarterly* IX (1957): 197–208.

10. Gregory H. Singleton, "Popular Culture or the Culture of the Populace?" *Journal of Popular Culture* XI (1977): 254–66, is a useful introduction to this issue. See also Herbert J. Gans, *Popular Culture and High Culture: An Analysis and Evaluation of Taste* (New York, 1974).

11. Kingsley Amis, *The James Bond Dossier* (London, 1966), pp. 111–12.

Chapter 1

1. Karl Bosl, "Gesellschaft und Politik in Bayern vor dem Ende der Monarchie," *Zeitschrift für bayerische Landesgeschichte* XXVIII (1965): 1–31, is an excellent introduction by the dean of Bavarian historians. See also the massive *Bayerische Geschichte im 19. und 20. Jahrhundert: 1800–1970*, 2 vols, ed. Max Spindler (Munich, 1978); and Karl Möckl, *Die Prinzregentenzeit. Gesellschaft und Politik während der Ära des Prinzregenten Luitpold in Bayern* (Munich and Vienna, 1977). Axel Schnorbus, *Arbeit und Sozialordnung in Bayern vor dem Ersten Weltkrieg (1890–1914)* (Munich, 1969); W. Zorn, *Kleine Wirtschafts- und Sozialgeschichte Bayerns 1806–1933*, (Munich, 1962); and Ian Farr, "Populism in the Countryside: The Peasant Leagues in Bavaria in the 1890s," in *Society and Politics in Wilhelmine*

Germany, ed. R.G. Evans (London and New York, 1978), pp. 136–59, are useful for their specific subjects.

2. The Bavarian revolution's genesis, course, and aftermath are surveyed in Karl-Ludwig Ay, *Die Entstehung einer Revolution. Die Volksstimmung in Bayern während des Ersten Weltkrieges* (Berlin, 1968); Georg Kalmer, "Die Massen in der Revolution 1918–1919. Die Unterschichten als Problem der bayerischen Revolutionsforschung," *Zeitschrift für bayerische Landesgeschichte* XXXIV (1971): 357–68; and the essays in Karl Bosl, ed., *Bayern im Umbruch* (Munich/Vienna, 1969). Allen Mitchell, *Revolution in Bavaria, 1918–1919* (Princeton, 1965), remains the best and most familiar account in English.

3. For brief overviews of Franconian history, Karl Bosl, "Franken und Altbayern—Nürnberg und München," *Zeitschrift für bayerische Landesgeschichte* XXXIII (1970): 3–16, is a painless introduction to a complex situation. See also Dietrich Thränhardt, *Wahlen und Politische Strukturen in Bayern 1848–1953* (Düsseldorf, 1973), pp. 63ff, 124 passim; and Rainer Hambrecht, *Der Aufstieg der NSDAP in Mittel- und Oberfranken (1925–1933)* (Nürnberg, 1976), pp. 2ff.

4. Cf. W. Benz (ed.), *Politik in Bayern 1919–1933. Berichte des württembergischen Gesandten Moser von Filseck* (Stuttgart, 1971), p. 116; and Hans Fenske, *Koservatismus und Rechtsradikalismus in Bayern nach 1918* (Bad Homburg, Berlin, Zürich, 1969), p. 33.

5. Of the many general histories of Nürnberg, *Nürnberg—Geschichte einer europäischen Stadt*, ed. Gerhard Pfeffer (Munich, 1971) is good coffee-table scholarship. Carol Ehlers, "Nuremberg, Julius Streicher, and the Bourgeois Transition to Nazism, 1918–1924," (Ph.D. diss. University of Colorado, 1975), pp. 29ff., is an English summary of the city's evolution. Wolfgang Zorn, "Zur Nürnberger Handels- und Unternehmergeschichte des 19. Jahrhunderts," *Beiträge zur Wirtschaftsgeschichte Nürnbergs* vol. II (Nürnberg, 1967), pp. 851–64; and Werner Schultheiss, "Die Industriellisierung Nürnbergs im 19/20 Jahrhundert," *Mitteilung des Vereins für Geschichte der Stadt Nürnberg* LIV (1966): 158–64, are useful special studies. For the revolution of 1918 see especially Klaus-Dieter Schwarz, *Weltkrieg und Revolution in Nürnberg. Ein Beitrag zur Geschichte der deutschen Arbeiterbewegung* (Stuttgart, 1971).

6. For alternative interpretations of this controversial issue see Gerald Feldman, *Army, Industry, and Labor in Germany, 1914–1918* (Princeton, 1966); Gerhard Ritter, *Sword and Scepter*, tr. Heinz Nordau, vols. 3–4 (Coral Gables, Fla., 1972–73); and Martin Kitchen, *The Silent Dictatorship: The Politics of the German High Command under Hindenburg and Ludendorff 1916–1918* (London, 1976). Wilhelm Deist, *Militär und Innenpolitik im Weltkrieg 1914–1918*, 2 vols. (Düsseldorf, 1970) is an invaluable documentary source.

7. Cf. Friedhelm Mennekes, *Die Republik als Herausforderung. Konservatives Denken in Bayern zwischen Weimarer Republik und*

antidemokratischen Reaktion (1918–1925) (Berlin, 1972); W.G. Zimmermann, *Bayern und das Reich, 1918–1923* (Munich, 1953); and Falk Wiesemann, *Die Vorgeschichte der nationalsozialistischen Machtübernahne in Bayern, 1932/1933* (Berlin, 1975).

8. Hambrecht, 404ff.

9. Ehlers, 616ff.

10. The most complete demonstration is Stadtarchiv Nürnberg, Evi Rothmann "Entwicklung und Zielsetzung der NSDAP in Nürnberg von 1928–33," Schriftliche Handarbeit zur Wissenschaftlichen Prüfung für das Lehramt am Gymnasium, Juni, 1975.

11. Martha Ziegler, "The Socioeconomic and Demographic Bases of Political Behavior in Nuremberg during the Weimar Republic, 1919–1933," (Ph.D. diss., University of Virginia, 1966), esp. chapter seven.

12. Hermann Glaser, *The Cultural Roots of National Socialism*, tr. E.A. Menze (Austin, Tex., 1978).

13. Cf. in particular H.A. Winkler, *Mittelstand, Demokratie und Nationalsozialismus. Die Politische Entwicklung von Handwerk und Kleinhandel in der Weimarer Republik* (Köln, 1972); and "German Society, Hitler, and the Illusion of Restoration 1930–33," *Journal of Contemporary History* XI (1976); 1–16; Herman Lebovics, *Social Conservatism and the Middle Classes in Germany, 1914–1933* (Princeton, 1969); and Thomas Childers, "National Socialism and the New Middle Class," *Die Nationalsozialisten*, ed. R. Mann (Stuttgart, 1980), pp. 19–33.

14. Cf. Iris Hamel, *Völkischer Verband und nationale Gewerkschaft: Die Deutschnationale Handlungsgehilfen-Verband 1913–1933* (Frankfurt, 1967); Robert Gellateley, *The Politics of Economic Despair: Shopkeepers and German Politics, 1840–1914* (London, 1974); and Shulamit Volkov, *The Rise of Popular Antimodernism in Germany: The Urban Master Artisans, 1873–1896* (Princeton, 1978). David Blackbourn, "The *Mittelstand* in German Society and Politics, 1871–1914," *Social History* IV (1977): 409–33, exaggerates the *Mittelstand*'s potential for leftward development.

15. On the DDP cf. Werner Schnieder, *Die Deutsche Demokratische Partei in der Weimarer Republik, 1924–1930* (Munich, 1978): Robert A. Pois, "The Bourgeois Democrats of Weimar Germany," *Transactions of the American Philosophical Society*, vol. 66, pt. 4 (1976); Werner Stephan, *Aufsteig und Verfall des Linksliberalismus 1918–1933* (Göttingen, 1973); and Bruce Frye, "The German Democratic Party," *American Historical Review* LXXIII (1968): 1933–53. Larry Eugene Jones's brilliant "The Dying Middle: Weimar Germany and the Fragmentation of Bourgeois Politics," *Central European History* V (1972): 23–34; and David Abraham, "Constituting Hegemony: The Bourgeois Crisis of Weimar Germany," *Journal of Modern History*

LI (1979): 417–33, deal from variant perspectives with the general failure to integrate Weimar's *Mittelstand* into a stable political bloc.

16. Wilhelm Hoegner, *Der Politische Radikalismus in Deutschland, 1919–1933* (Munich, 1966), pp. 46ff.

17. For introductions to the issue of religious anti-Semitism, see the essays in *Judenhass—Schuld der Christen?!*, ed. Wm. Eckert and E.L. Ehrlich (Essen, 1964); and *Judenfeindschaft. Darstellung und Analysen*, ed. Karl Thieme (Frankfurt, 1962). Hermann Greive, *Theologie und Ideologie. Katholizismus und Judentum in Deutschland und Österreich, 1918–1935* Heidelberg, 1969), Hans-Joachim Kraus, "Die Evangelische Kirche," in *Entscheidungsjahr 1932*, ed. W.E. Mosse and Arnold Paucker (Tübingen, 1966), pp. 249–69: and Richard Gutteridge, *The German Evangelical Church and the Jews 1879–1950* (New York, 1976), are useful case studies.

18. Of the voluminous literature on this theme, cf. especially Elonore Stirling, *Judenhass. Die Anfänge des politischen Antisemitismus in Deutschland 1815–1850)*, 2nd. ed. rev. (Frankfurt, 1969); Uriel Tal, *Christians and Jews in Germany*, tr. Noah Jacobs (Ithaca, N.Y., and London, 1975); Alfred D. Low, *Jews in the Eyes of the Germans* (Philadelphia, 1979); and the essays in Reinhard Rürup, *Emanzipation und Antisemitismus. Studien zur "Judenfrage" der bürgerlichen Gesellschaft*, (Göttingen, 1975).

19. Fritz Stern, *The Politics of Cultural Despair*, (New York: Anchor, 1965), pp. 5ff.

20. An excellent discussion of this issue is Klaus Bergmann, *Agarromantik und Grosstadtfeindschaft* (Meisenheim, 1970). Cf. also Karlheinz Rossbacher, *Heimatkunstbewegung und Heimatroman* (Stuttgart, 1975).

21. Cf. Shalom Adler-Rudel, *Ostjuden in Deutschland 1880–1940* (Tübingen, 1940); and Jack. L. Wertheimer, "German Policy and Jewish Politics: The Absorption of East European Jews in Germany (1868–1914)," (Ph.D. diss., Columbia, 1978).

22. Cf. Peter Pulzer, *The Rise of Political Anti-Semitism in Germany and Austria* (New York, London, Sydney, 1964); and the convincing analysis in Richard S. Levy, *The Downfall of the Anti-Semitic Political Parties in Imperial Germany* (New Haven, Conn., 1975).

23. The best monographic treatment of this subject is Egmont Zechlin, *Die deutsche Politik und die Juden im Ersten Weltkrieg* (Göttingen, 1969). *Deutsches Judentum in Krieg und Revolution 1916–1923*, ed. W.E. Mosse and Arnold Paucker (Tübingen, 1971), includes several outstanding essays. Werner Angress, "Das deutsche Militär und die Juden im Ersten Weltkrieg," *Militärgeschichtliche Mitteilungen* XIX (1976): 77–146, is definitive on the *Judenzählung* of 1916. Cf. also David Engel, "Organized Jewish Responses to German Anti-Semitism during the First World War," (Ph.D. diss., UCLA, 1979). For evidence

of the role of cultural shock in generating anti-Semitism, see the material in Stadtarchiv Nürnberg, *Stürmer-Archiv* VIII, "Kriege,"and such letters as "Der Jude im Weltkrieg," *Der Stürmer* 21/1927 (Hereafter cited as *DS*).

24. The memo and Westarp's reply in *Nachlass Westarp* are quoted in Annelise Thimme, *Flucht in den Mythos. Die Deutschnationale Völkspartei und die Niederlage von 1918* (Göttingen, 1969), pp. 48–49.

Chapter 2

1. Cf. Bradley Smith, *Reaching Judgment at Nuremberg* (New York, 1977), pp. 200ff; and Klaus Kipphan, "Trial of Julius Streicher: Justice Denied?" (Paper delivered at the American Historical Association, December, 1974).

2. For Streicher's early life, see the information in the decision of the *III Strafkammer, Landesgericht Nürnberg*, 14.3.24., included in "Julius Streicher im Kampf um sein Recht. Gesammelt und Überreicht von einem Namenslosen aus der Schar seiner Getreuen" (n.p., n.d.), in Bundesarchiv Koblenz, *Nachlass Streicher*, AL 10; the copy of his birth certificate in Hoover Institution, Stanford, Calif., NSDAP Hauptarchiv, Microfilm Reel 85, Folder 1735 (hereafter cited as HA); Staatsarchiv Nürnberg, *Regierung von Mittelfranken, Kammer das Innern* XIII, 5686a, 5686b, *Personalakten Julius Streicher*; and Stadtarchiv Nürnberg, Otto Fischer, "Der Braune Zar," (unpublished ms., 1969), pp. 4–5.

3. This interpretation takes issue with the conclusions of W.P. Varga, "Julius Streicher: A Political Biography, 1885–1933" (Ph.D. diss., Ohio State University, 1974), pp. 3–5. For background, see Manfred Messerschmidt, "Militär und Schule in der wilhelmischen Zeit," *Militärgeschichtliche Mitteilungen* XXIII (1978): 51–76; and Karl Demeter, *Das deutsche Offizierkorps in Gesellschaft und Staat*, 2nd ed. rev. (Frankfurt, 1962), pp. 37 passim.

4. For Bavaria's and Nürnberg's school systems see Pfeifer, p. 423; and Ehlers, pp. 63–64.

5. For Streicher's wartime career, see Stadtarchiv Nürnberg, Manfred Rühl, "Der Stürmer und sein Herausgeber," Diplomarbeit, Institut für Politik und Kommunikationswissenschaft der Univ. Erlangen, Nürnberg, 1960, pp. 37ff; and Ehlers, pp. 78 passim.

6. Report of 23.8.26 in *Nachlass Streicher*, AL18; Rühl, p. 87.

7. HA 84/1730; 98/19; *Trial of the Major War Criminals before the International Military Tribunal, Nuremberg, 14 November–10*

October 1946, 42 vols., (Nürnberg, 1947–49), XII, 307–09 (hereafter cited as *IMT*).

8. Streicher's view of his entry into politics is in Heinz Preiss, *Die Anfänge der völkischen Bewegung in Franken* (Nürnberg, 1937), pp. 48–49. This work, originally an Erlangen dissertation written by one of Streicher's followers, must be used with caution. Nevertheless, it contains much useful first-hand information on Streicher's early years.

9. Ibid, pp. 50ff; Jay W. Baird, ed., "Das politische Testament Julius Streichers," *Vierteljahrshefte für Zeitgeschichte* XXVI (1978): 670, 672; and *IMT*, XII, 308–9, embody Streicher's memory of these events. See also the discussion in Robin Lenman, "Julius Streicher and the Origins of the NSDAP in Nuremberg, 1918–1923," in *German Democracy and the Triumph of Hitler*, ed. A.J. Nicholls and Erich Matthias (London, 1971), pp. 129–59.

10. "Das politische Testament Julius Streichers," pp. 663–64; G.M. Gilbert, *Nuremberg Diary*, Signet ed. (New York, 1961), pp. 14–15. Florence A. Meale and Michael Selzer, *The Nuremberg Mind*, intro. G.M. Gilbert (New York, 1976), is a recent example of the limits of psychiatric techniques in this context.

11. Cf. Hermann Luppe, *Mein Leben*, ed. W. Lehnert and M. Heinsen-Luppe (Nürnberg, 1977), p. 141; and Varga, pp. 3 passim.

12. George E. Vaillant, *Adaptation to Life* (Boston, 1977).

13. Jaeckel, p. 22; and James M. McRandle, *The Track of the Wolf* (Evanston, Ill., 1965), pp. 124ff; develop this point in the case of Adolf Hitler. It seems to apply to Streicher as well.

14. A copy of Sven Hedin's article in *Nija Baglit Alleshanda*, March 11, 1937, is in *Nachlass Streicher*, AL 28.

15. Streicher's sex life is evaluated in Rühl, pp. 88ff, 117–18; and Fischer, pp. 6, 45–50.

16. For Streicher's political career between 1919 and 1922, see the accounts in Preiss, pp. 65ff; Ehlers, pp. 330 passim; Hambrecht, pp. 20 passim; Uwe Lohalm, *Völkischer Radikalismus. Die Geschichte des Deutschvölkischen Schutz-und Trutz-Bundes 1919 bis 1923*, (Hamburg, 1970), pp. 113 passim; and Lenman, 135ff. His activities as a speaker are described in the police reports of this period collected in HA 84/1730.

17. George Franz Willing, *Die Hitlerbewegung. Der Ursprung 1919–1922* (Hamburg, Berlin, 1962), p. 92.

18. Cf. Kurt Ludecke, *I Knew Hitler* (London, 1938), p. 100; Konrad Heiden, *Geschichte der Nationalsozialismus* (Berlin, 1932), p. 101. Perceptive treatments of leadership patterns in National Socialism include W. Horn, *Führerideologie und Parteiorganisation in der NSDAP (1919–1933)* (Düsseldorf, 1972), pp. 26ff; and Albrecht Tyrell, *Vom "Trommler" zum "Führer." Der Wandel von Hitlers Selbstverständnis zwischen 1919 und 1924 und die Entwicklung der NSDAP* (Munich, 1975), passim.

19. The most detailed discussion of this complicated period is Hambrecht, pp. 43 passim. Lenman, pp. 143ff., is brief and perceptive.

20. *DS* 1/1923.

21. Klaus Kipphan, "Julius Streicher und der 9. November 1923," *Zeitschrift für bayerische Landesgeschichte*, XXXIX (1976), 277–88, is the definitive account of Streicher's role in the putsch. Cf. also *Schutzhaftanstalt* Landsberg to *Polizeidirektion Nürnberg-Fürth*, 25.2.24, HA 86/1742; letter to Streicher of 28.1.24, *Nachlass Streicher*, AL 15: Streicher to *Generalstaatskommissariat*, 12.2.24, ibid. Streicher's diary for the period of his imprisonment in ibid. is uninformative.

22. Ronald Rogowski, "The Gauleiter and the Social Origins of Fascism," *Comparative Studies in Society and History* XIX (1977), pp. 399–430; Peter Merkl, *Political Violence under the Swastika* (Princeton, 1975), pp. 62ff.

23. Cf. the critical letter of 9.12.23 in *Nachlass Streicher*, AL 124 with the fulsome flattery of 18.3.24 in ibid., 13, and 21.5.24 in ibid. 124; or the letter of *Völkisch-Sozialistische Freiheitsbewegung, Ortsgruppe Sonnenberg*, 28.3.24, in ibid. AL 124 contains much similar correspondence.

24. Cf. the police reports in HA 17A/1731, especially those of 7.3.24, 16.6.24, 17.6.24, 4.7.24 and 29.7.24. *Nachlass Streicher*, AL 16 contains several drafts and revisions of speeches. AL 103 includes a copy of his corrections of errors from earlier speeches, with the remark that speeches must carry the audiences with them from the beginning. George Mosse, *The Nationalization of the Masses* (New York, 1975), discusses the roots and nature of this "new politics."

25. Horn, pp. 180ff; Peter Hüttenberger, *Die Gauleiter: Studie zum Wandel das Machtgefüges in der NSDAP* (Stuttgart, 1969), pp. 10–11.

26. This is clearly demonstrated in Reinhard Kuhnl, *Die Nationalsozialistische Linke 1925–1930* (Meisenheim, 1966), pp. 34ff, 134 passim.

27. The post-putsch conflicts within the Franconian *völkisch* movement are analyzed in Hambrecht, pp. 70ff.

28. See the correspondence of 11.11.24 and 11.24.24 in HA 17A/1731.

29. "Das Volksbuch vom Hitler," *DS* 19/1924; "Nach der Wahl," *DS* 38/1924, "Nach seiner Heimkehr," *DS* 40/1924.

30. Directive to *Ortsgruppen*, 21.9.25, in Bundesarchiv Koblenz, Schumacher Sammlung, *Ordner* 373; Report of 18.2.26, HA 84/1732; Dinter to Streicher, 19.4.26; *Nachlass Streicher*, AL 124; Request from *NSDAP Bremen*, 23.5.26, in ibid.

31. "Die 'Psychopathen' an der Arbeit," *DS* 1/1925.

32. Cf. inter alia "Unser Vormarsch," *DS* 15/1926; "Adolf Hitler

zum Geburtstag," *DS* 7/1926; "Dr. Arthur Dinter zu seinem 50. Geburtstag," *DS* 27/1926; "Die Hitlerfahne," *DS* 34/1926; "Mei löiba Stürmer," *DS* 10/1927; "Aus der Bewegung," *DS* 8/1927; "Wie Nationalsozialisten Sterben," *DS* 1/1927; "Allbayerischen Maitanz," *DS* 18a/1927.

33. Staatsarchiv Nürnberg, *Polizeidirektion Nürnberg-Fürth*, report of 23.3.27 (Hereafter cited as LPN).

34. Report of 4.3.27, HA 85/1732.

35. "Deutschland Erwache," *DS* 33/1927; "An Alle," *DS* 33/1927; "Der Tag der Nationalsozialisten," *DS* 35/1927; LPN, 22.11.27.

36. Statement of Ludwig Käfer, 9.11.25, HA 86/1744.

37. Pfeffer to Streicher, 14.2.28, Bundesarchiv Koblenz, NS 22 (Reichsorganisation der NSDAP). Cf. Eric A. Reiche, "The Development of the SA in Nürnberg, 1922–1934," (Ph.D. diss., University of Delaware, 1972); and Hambrecht, pp. 122ff.

38. *NSDAP Nürnberg* to *Reichsleitung München*, 16.12.27, *Reichsleitung München* to *Fränkische Kurier*, 19.12.27; Hitler to Käfer, 15.12.27, Bundesarchiv Koblenz, NS 22; LPN, 15.2.28; police report of 21.5.28, HA 85/1733.

39. Letter from *Ortsgruppe Forchheim*, 5.3.28, NS 22.

40. LPN 2.4.28, 5.12.28; Charges of 30.5.28 and *Protokoll* of 9.10.29, HA 85/1733.

41. Hambrecht, pp. 129ff.

42. "Die Geschichte der Ortsgruppe St. Johannis;" and *Führer* Carl Weiner, "Ortsgruppe Reichelsdorf," *Nachlass Streicher* AL 113; "NSDAP Ortsgruppe Nürnberg, Sektion Maxfeld," ibid., AL 114. This material was collected after the seizure of power for a history of *Gau Franken*.

43. See the report of Streicher's speech in Altdorf 11.11.28, in HA 86/1743, and the letters of 5.5.28 and 11.5.28 in *Nachlass Streicher* AL 124.

44. "Propaganda," ibid., AL 102.

45. "Prosit Neujahr," *DS* 46/1928; "Der Brief eines Unbeugsamen," *DS* 23/1929; "Ein deutsches Mädchen," *DS* 33/1929; and "Der Held von Brzezeny," *DS* 4/1930.

46. LPN 31.1.29, 6.6.29, 31.5.30, and 29.7.30; Hambrecht, pp. 162ff; Hüttenberger, p. 63.

47. Contrast the tones of "Macht dem Skandal ein Ende," *DS* 36/1930: "Der Schicksalstag," *DS* 37/1930; and "Der Sieg ist Unser," *DS* 38/1930. For the 1930 election in Franconia and its implications, see Hambrecht, pp. 190ff., and 309ff; and Varga, pp. 211ff.

48. Report of 9.9.30, HA 85/1734.

49. "Die Schande am Hesselberg," *DS* 27/1931; "Die Woche," *DS* 11/1931; "Trommelfeuer über Franken," *DS* 30/1931; "Pg. Ludwig Berthold Tot," *DS* 32/1931.

50. Johannes Schwarze, *Die bayerische Polizei und ihre histor-ische Funktion bei der Aufrechterhaltung der öffentlichen Sicherheit in Bayern von 1919–1933* (Munich, 1977), pp. 197 passim, presents the problem of maintaining order from the perspective of the *Landes-polizei*. J.H. McGee, "The Political Police in Bavaria, 1919–1936" (Ph.D. diss., University of Florida, 1980), is less sympathetic.

51. Reports of 13.10.29, HA 85/1733, and 27.11.29, HA 86/1744; *KdI to Polizeidirektion Augsburg*, 17.12.29, Stadtarchiv Nürnberg, *Regierung von Mittelfranken, Kammer des Innern*, II, 688 (Hereafter cited as KdI II).

52. Report of 29.5.30, KdI II, 689.

53. Report of 8.9.31 in ibid., 691.

54. Communication of 23.7.32 and accompanying reports in ibid., 694.

55. Reports and statements on the incident are in ibid.

56. Letters in *DS* 46/1931, *DS* 42/1931, and *DS* 37/1931.

57. Communication of 30.10.31, HA 85/1734.

58. Hambrecht, pp. 336–37.

59. Cf. "Die Todesangst," *DS* 11/1932; and "Der zweite Sturm;"and "Das Ergebnis des 10. April in Mittelfranken," *DS* 15/1932. Hambrecht, pp. 339ff, is the most complete analysis of regional voting patterns and their significance.

60. "Hundert Meter vom Ziele," *DS* 23/1932; "Freie Bahn dem neuen Deutschland," *DS* 24/1932; "Hitler über Deutschland," *DS* 30/1932; "Ein Gedenkmünze," *DS* 31/1932; "Her mit den Hitlerblät-tern," *DS* 38/1932.

61. Report of 11.11.32, KdI II, 694.

62. For detailed analyses of the Streicher-Stegmann conflict, see Hambrecht, pp. 370ff; and Reiche, pp. 179ff. "Werdegang und Kampf der SA Standarte Nürnberg," an unpublished unpaged essay written in 1936, in *Nachlass Streicher*, AL 73, also contains some useful informa-tion.

63. List of party members in *Gau Mittelfranken* sent to *Reichs-leitung* NSDAP, 23.4.34, *Nachlass Streicher*, AL 102. Cf. Wiesmann, 160ff.

64. Heinz Preiss, "Der 9. März 1933 in Gau Franken," *Nachlass Streicher*, AL 138.

Chapter 3

1. A good introduction to the scholarly value of German news-papers is Wilhelm Mommsen, "Die Zeitung als historische Quelle," in *Beiträge zur Zeitungswissenschaft. Festgabe für Karl D'Ester*

(Münster, 1952), pp. 165–72.

2. Among the references consulted in preparing the above discussion, the best general history is Kurt Koszyk, *Deutsche Presse im 19. Jahrhundert. Geschichte der deutschen Presse* vol. II (Berlin, 1966). Modris Eksteins, *The Limits of Reason. The German Democratic Press and the Collapse of Weimar Democracy* (London, 1975), pp. 70–86, is a good summary. Emil Dovifat, *Die Zeitungen* (Gotha, 1929); and Heinrich Walter, *Zeitung als Aufgabe. 60 Jahre Verein Deutscher Zeitungsverleger* (Wiesbaden, 1954), are useful sources of technical information. André Banuls, "Das völkische Blatt "Der Scherer," *Vierteljahrshefte für Zeitgeschichte* XVIII (1970): 196–203, is a good analysis of a turn-of-the-century paper whose format was similar to that of *Der Stürmer*.

3. Roland V. Layton, "The *Völkischer Beobachter*, 1925–1933, A Study of the Nazi Party Newspaper in the *Kampfzeit*" (Ph.D. diss., University of Virginia, 1965), passim. This dissertation also contains useful general material on local and party papers.

4. Larry Dean Wilcox, "The National Socialist Party Press in the *Kampfzeit*, 1919–1933," (Ph.D. diss., University of Virginia, 1970), is definitive. Cf. the anonymous essay "Geschichte und Entwicklung der Partei-Presse im Gau Franken," in *Nachlass Streicher*, AL 114.

5. *Nachlass Streicher*, AL 9, contains a wealth of material on the day-to-day operations of the *Deutsche Sozialist*. See the letters of H. Liebel, 14.14.21, and *Buchdruckerei Bellmann*, 13.8.22, in *Nachlass Streicher* AL 9 and AL 19, for financial information. Rühl, pp. 100ff., offers a general survey of *Der Stürmer*'s direct forerunners.

6. "Aus der Redaktionssitzung eines gekannten Wochenblattes," *Nachlass Streicher* AL 2.

7. The statement of purpose is in *DS* 6/1923. For summaries of the eighteenth-century heritage cf. Jacob Katz, *From Prejudice to Destruction: Anti-Semitism, 1700–1933* (Cambridge, Mass., 1980), pp. 13ff; and Richard D. Hecht, "Four Recent Studies of Anti-Semitism, A Review Essay," *Modern Judaism* I (1981), 236–38. Eckhardt's style of journalism is discussed in Margarete Plewnia, *Auf dem Weg zu Hitler: der "völkische" Publizist Dietrich Eckart* (Bremen, 1970), pp. 30 passim.

8. Rühl, pp. 98ff.; Pressl, pp. 98–99.

9. See Cornelia Berning, *Vom "Abstammungsnachweis" zum "Zuchtwart"; Vokabular des Nationalsozialismus* (Berlin, 1964);and Streicher to *Oberste Landgericht Nürnberg*, 9.8.24, *Nachlass Streicher*, AL 74. Cf. J.J. Gann, *Der braune Kult. Das Dritte Reich und sein Ersatzreligion* (Hamburg, 1962).

10. Rühl, pp. 188ff.

11. Uncaptioned cartoon, *DS* 11/1924.

12. For information on Ruprecht see "Das politische Testament Julius Streicher," 681–82; Kuhn to Hardel, 20.7.28, in *Nachlass*

Streicher, AL 76; the report of 22.9.26 in HA 85/1732; and a list of payments for cartoons 22.2.26 in *Nachlass Streicher*, AL 42.

13. Letter of 24.1.27, ibid., AL 42.

14. Rühl, pp. 139.

15. Testimony of 24.7.27, 15.3.27, and 10.7.27 in *Nachlass Streicher*, AL 75.

16. Eduard Fuchs, *Die Juden in der Karikatur* (Munich, 1921) remains the best historical survey of this subject from a German perspective.

17. "General Dawes" *DS* 1/1928; cartoon, *DS* 3/1926.

18. Judgment of 3.8.28 in *Nachlass Streicher*, AL 79; "Der Floh, *DS* 37/1932; "Koschere Betrachtung des Falles Bauernfreund," *DS* 9/1929; "Halunkenangst," *DS* 33/1932.

19. "In der Sommerfrische," *DS* 35/1932; "Jüdische Kultur," *DS* 35/1929.

20. "Für wen die Opfer," *DS* 23/1928; cartoon, *DS* 10/1926; "Im Kleinen wie in Grossen," *DS* 29/1930; "Zweierlei Menschen," *DS* 24/1928.

21. "Der Kampf geht weiter," *DS* 43/1930.

22. Cartoons, *DS* 41/1928; *DS Sondernummer* 1/1929; *DS* 7/1930.

23. *Stürmer-Archiv*, XIII, "Antisemitismus." Most of the material included here was published after the 1880s.

24. Copy of contract (undated) in *Nachlass Streicher*, AL 41.

25. The technical details of publication are summarized in Rühl, pp. 105ff.

26. Letter of 19.12.25 in *Nachlass Streicher*, AL 41.

27. The undated originals of "Jüdische Gemeinderäte reissen Plakate ab!," *DS* 26/1924; and "66/70er Kriegsveteranen wegen Bettels verhaftet," *DS* 29/1924, are in *Nachlass Streicher*, AL 63.

28. Rühl, pp. 106 passim.

29. Essay dated 5.8.30; and *Der Stürmer* to the essay's author, 7.8.30, in *Nachlass Streicher*, AL 40.

30. Cf. LPN 6.3.26, 27.6.31, and 24.10.31. A copy of *Die Kanone* is included in HA 17A/1882.

31. "Paul Klury," *DS* 36/1932.

32. Report of Leutershausen *Gendarmerie*, 1.9.31, HA 58/1407. Cf. the report of Kitzingen police of 6.12.31 in ibid., 85/1734; and a request of 17.1.27 for permission to sell *Der Stürmer* in Eisenach in *Nachlass Streicher*, AL 42.

33. Letter of February, 1933 in ibid., AL 41.

34. Report of 1.3.27 in HA 91/1885.

35. Letter in *DS* 22/1932.

36. Letter of 9.4.25 in *Nachlass Streicher* AL 41.

37. Reports of 10.10.32, 10.10.32, and 3.10.32 in HA 92/1891.

38. Letters of 21.5.24 and 21.2.27 in *Nachlass Streicher*, AL 41.

39. Reports of 13.9.27 and 22.11.27, HA 91/1885.

40. Report of 26.3.32; Holz's statement of 9.4.32, HA 86/1744.

41. Cf. the general discussion in Rühl, pp. 179–80; with the letter in *DS* 7/1932; and "Wie die Usinger Juden den *Stürmer* hassen," *DS* 24/1932.

42. *DS* 2/1924.

43. *DS* 40/1924; *DS* 16/1926.

44. *DS* 35/1927.

45. Notice "To All Comrades," undated, in Schumacher Sammlung, *Ordner* 260.

46. *DS* 9/1932, *DS* 41/1932. Cf. the directives of *Gau* Munich-Upper Bavaria, 15.9.31 and 17.9.31, HA 8/176.

47. *DS* 50/1929.

48. *DS* 25/1925; *DS* 7/1926; *DS* 52/1929.

49. *DS* 17/1924.

50. *DS* 14/1926.

51. "Wer kann Helfen?" *DS* 14/1926.

52. *DS* 35/1927.

53. Rühl, pp. 155ff.

54. Ibid., 147; *IMT*, XII, 342; and XVIII, 202.

55. See the order to the Nürnberg police and their reports of 8.12.27 and 12.12.27, HA 85/1732.

56. Letter of 13.7.24 in *Nachlass Streicher*, AL 17.

57. *Rundschreiben* to *Gauleiter*, 12.9.25; Hitler to *Gauleitungen, Bezirksleitungen, Nazi-Zeitungen*, 2.11.32, in Schumacher Sammlung, *Ordner* 227.

58. *Rundschreiben* to *Gauleiter*, 24.10.28; *Rundschreiben* to NS *Presse*, 26.11.30 in ibid., *Ordner* 373, 227.

59. Adolf Hitler to *Schriftleitung NS Presse*, 27.6.28; Memo to *Der Stürmer*, 14.10.29, in ibid., *Ordner* 260.

60. Albrecht Tyrell, "Gottfried Feder and the NSDAP," in *The Shaping of the Nazi State*, ed. Peter Stachura (New York and London, 1978), p. 73; Wilcox, p. 145.

61. Streicher to *Flamme*, 18.6.27; *Flamme* to Streicher, 20.6.27 in Schumacher Sammlung, *Ordner* 260.

62. Communications of 17.9.28 and 2.11.28 in ibid; Police report of Feder's discussion of the issue in a meeting of 14.2.30, HA 85/1734; LPN 20.3.30; 31.10.32.

Introduction —Part II

1. Jonathan Sarna, "Anti-Semitism and American History," *Commentary* LXXI (March, 1981): 44.

2. Dorothea Hollstein, *Antisemitische Filmpropaganda. Die Darstellung des Juden im nationalsozialistischen Spielfilm* (Munich-Pulloch, Berlin, 1971), p. 113; "Die Rassenmerkmale der Juden," *DS* 38/1928.

Chapter 4

1. As in Hambrecht, pp. 250–51.
2. Report of speech, 15.3.24, in HA 17A/1731; "Rassenschande," *DS* 21/1927; "Die Fälschung des Blutes," *DS* 6/1929.
3. "Jüdische verhöhnung deutscher Frauen in einem sogennanten Arbeiterblatt," *DS* 10/1926.
4. *DS* 15/1928.
5. Letter in *DS* 11/1931; "Der 71-jährige Moses," *DS* 20/1928.
6. "Die verführte Jüdin," *DS* 32/1930; "Die Tochter des Rabbiners Vogelstein," *DS* 49/1928; "Er kann kein Vieh heiraten," *DS* 38/1928.
7. "Frauenarzt Dr. ———," *DS* 5/1923; "Tot gemacht," *DS* 47/1932.
8. "Judenbastarde in grosser Auswahl zu beziehen . . ." *DS* 22/1927; Letter, *DS* 12/1932: "Der Judenbastard," *DS* 1/1930; "Zwei Judenbastarde," *DS* 49/1930; cartoon, *DS* 15/1928.
9. "Marie Juster. Wie sie zur Kindsmörderin wurde," *DS* 19/1926.
10. Regensburg Prosecutor's Office to NSDAP, 29.9.27, *Nachlass Streicher*, AL 114.
11. "Vom Juden verseucht," *DS* 44/1930.
12. "Der Leidensweg der 74-jährigen Witwe Mössmang," *DS* 34/1929; "Tot gemacht. Das Drama des Trudel Gross," *DS* 51/1928; "Das Opfer eines Talmudjuden," *DS* 5/1928; "Der jüdische Kindsvater," *DS* 32/1928.
13. In *Nachlass Streicher*, AL 4.
14. Letter of 29.9.24 in ibid.
15. Letter of 23.8.28 in ibid., AL 43.
16. "An den Schandpfahl," *DS* 3/1927
7643—73 Shoe String—Little Man, What Now

13. In *Nachlass Streicher*, AL 4.
14. Letter of 29.9.24 in ibid.
15. Letter of 23.8.28 in ibid., AL 43.
16. "An den Schandpfahl," *DS* 3/1927.
17. "Liebesstürme in Bürgermeisteramt," *DS* 25/1924.
18. "Der Jude und die deutsche Frau," *DS* 42/1931.

19. *DS* 11/1925; "Das Attentat im Keller," *DS* 11/1927; "Rassenschande," *DS* 17/1928; "Moses Reich," *DS* 31/1931.

20. "Der Jude im Wartezimmer," *DS* 41/1930; "Der Schänder von Suderwich," *DS* 30/1928; "———. Sein Verbrechen und sein Freispruch," *DS* 10/1928.

21. "Im Bahnhof," *DS* 51/1927.

22. "Der Uffenheimer Kinderschänder vor Gericht," *DS* 33/1929.

23. Letter of 20.4.26 in *Nachlass Streicher*, AL 42.

24. "Der Fuchs geht um," *DS* 39/1927.

25. "Der Kuss," *DS* 38/1929; "———aus der Bultmanstrasse," *DS* 47/1931.

26. Siegfried Kracauer, *From Caligari to Hitler: Psychological History of the German Film* (Princeton, 1947).

27. "———und sein Mädchen für alles," *DS* 38/1931. Cf. such articles as "Moses Eckman," *DS* 50/1927; "So will es der Talmud," *DS* 14/1927; and "———. Der Dienstbotenschänder von Kitzingen," *DS* 35/1929.

28. "Das Mädchen für alles," *DS* 37/1925.

29. "Das Dienstmädchen des Juden ——— verschwunden," *DS* 10/1929: "Das Drama des Dienstmädchens von Ottensoos," *DS* 11/1929; "Das verschwundene Dienstmädchen von Ottensoos," *DS* 14/1929.

30. Report of 25.3.29 in HA 58/1407.

31. "Rosele," *DS* 29/1927.

32. Representative examples include letters of 30.7.24 and 2.12.25 in *Nachlass Streicher*, AL 4 and AL 41; "Jüdische Vergewaltigungsversuch am einem Fürther Mädchen," *DS* 25/1924; "Jüdischer Überfall auf ein Lehrmädchen," *DS* 40/1925; "Der Notzuchtsversuch des ———," *DS* 9/1927; "Hartwig Lewin," *DS* 18/1928; "Der Rassenschänder," *DS* 15/1931; "Viehisches Sittlichkeitsverbrechen in Altdorf," *DS* 31/1931; "Schuhjude ———," *DS* 47/1931; "Jud ———," *DS* 37/1932. Renate Bridenthal, "Beyond *Kinder, Küche, Kirche*: Weimar Women at Work," *Central European History*, VI (1973), 148–66, is an excellent survey.

33. "Gallinger und Kohn," *DS* 37/1925: decision of 14.10.25 in HA 17A/1731.

34. "Jud Schäfer als Sittlichkeitsverbrecher," *DS* 34/1926; "Rudolf Schäfer und sein Verteidiger Josef Kahn II," *DS* 48/1927; "Ein neuer Rudolf Schäfer Prozess," *DS* 6/1929.

35. "Jüdische Sexualverbrecher und ihre Verteidigungssystem," *DS* 24/1928; "Das Geheimnis im Büro des Juden ———," *DS* 45/1929; cartoons in *DS* 15/1931 and *DS* 44/1928.

36. "Mädchenfleisch Handel," *DS* 30/1926; "Ins Bordell verkauft," *DS* 29/1928; "In den Lasterhöhlen," *DS* 27/1929; "Handel mit Mädchen," and cartoon in *DS* 30/1930. It is ironic that Streicher

obtained much of his material on Jewish involvement in the white slave traffic from the work of Jewish' reformers. See Marion A. Kaplan, *The Jewish Feminist Movement in Germany* (Westport, Conn., 1979), pp. 114ff.

37. "Judenfutter," *DS* 40/1930; "Das Inserate des Juden ———," *DS* 25/1931.

38. "Ein besserer Herr," *DS* 25/1929; "Menschenhandel," *DS* 10/1924.

39. "Mädchenfleisch Handel," *DS* 30/1926.

40. Undated memo of 1928 in *Nachlass Streicher*, AL 46; "Synagogenvorbeder ———," *DS* 1/1926.

41. Fritz Ertl, "Homosexuelle Judenparagraphen," *DS* 10/1928.

42. "Der homosexuelle Rabbiner von Ansbach," *DS* 36/1925.

43. "Mädchenmörder Schwarz von Gerolshofen," *DS* 11/1925; "Der Mädchenmörder von Gerolshofen," *DS* 13/1925; "Die Bürgermeisterede von Gerolshofen," *DS* 15/1925; "Jude und Justiz," *DS* 44/1925.

44. For *Der Stürmer*'s view of the Schloss case, see especially "Entsetzliches Verbrechen," *DS* 52/1925; "Das Geheimnis in der Bauerngasse," and "Ganz Israel burgt für einander," *DS* 53/1925; "Louis Schloss vor dem Schwurgericht," *DS* 16/1926; "Folterjude Schloss," *DS* 27/1926.

45. Letter of 8.4.26, *Nachlass Streicher*, AL 42.

46. "Alfred Guckenheimer und sein Kindermädchen," *DS* 14/1926; "Warum wird Guckenheimer nicht verhaftet?" *DS* 17/1926; "Jud Guckenheimer und sein Verbrechen," *DS* 26/1926; "Jud Guckenheimer," *DS* 27/1926; "Alfred Guckenheimers Glück und Ende," *DS* 32/1926; "Jude und Nichtjude vor Gericht," *DS* 38/1926.

47. "Otto Mayer, der Kreuzigungsjude vom Spittlertorgraben 39," *DS* 15/1926; "Das Urteil," *DS* 5/1927; "Die Kreuzeschändung des Juden Mayer," *DS* 7/1927; "Die Verbrecherhöhle am Spittlertorgraben," *DS* 16/1927; "Die Zeugen und der Staatsanwalt," *DS* 16/1927. The police considered *Der Stürmer*'s treatment of the Schloss and Mayer cases generally accurate and that of Guckenheimer "still unclear"—probably because of the hints of a coverup. Report of 20.4.26 in KdI II, 687.

48. "Das Mädchenmord von Paderborn," *DS* 14/1932; "Judas Angst," *DS* 16/1932; "Der Mord von Paderborn," *DS* 17/1932; "Kurt Meyer. Der Mädchenmörder von Paderborn," *DS* 38/1932; "Kurt Meyer, 1. Fortsetzung," *DS* 39/1932; "Kurt Meyer, 2. Fortsetzung," *DS* 40/1932. For the legal actions see "Gewaltmassnahmen gegen den Stürmer," *DS* 19/1932; "Die Gewaltmassnahmen gegen den Stürmer," *DS* 20/1932; "Der Stürmer beschlagnahmt," *DS* 40/1932; and the court orders of 29.9.32 and 13.10.32, HA 91/1889 and 92/1891.

49. *DS Sondernummer* 1/1934. A full copy is in HA 91/1887. The front page has been frequently reprinted in popular books such as

Kurt Zentner, *Illustrierte Geschichte des Dritten Reiches* (Munich, 1965), p. 179.

50. "Blutmord von Dobrzyn," *DS* 5/1927.

51. "Der Blutmord in Tirol," *DS* 44/1928; "Die Blutskapelle," *DS* 16/1932; "Kindermorde der Juden in Mittelalter," *DS* 36/1932; "Der Blutmord auf der Judenstein," *DS* 44/1929; letters of 15.5.29 and 1.12.30 in *Nachlass Streicher*, AL 81, AL 40.

52. "Das Purimfest," *DS* 7/1924; "Luftschiff und Purimfest," *DS* 14/1929.

53. "Enthülling der Jüdischen Geheimgesetz," *DS* 28/1928; "Gibt es Jüdische Ritualmorde?" *DS* 38/1928; "Ritualmord in Lichte der Wissenschaft," *DS* 27/1929.

54. "Ritualmord?" *DS* 28/1926; "Ritualmord?" *DS* 43/1926.

55. "Blutmord von Gladbeck," *DS* 19/1928; "Gladbecker Blutmord," *DS* 39/1928.

56. "Der Mord im Schwarzwald," *DS* 27/1928; "Der Jude ——— und der Blutmord im Schwarzwald," *DS* 34/1928.

57. "Der Blutmord in Manau," *DS* 13/1929; "Der Mord von Manau," *DS* 19/1929; "Der Kampf um die Blutmordfrage," *DS* 21/1929; "Der Rehbock als Mörder," *DS* 22/1929; Würzburg police report of 11.5.29 in HA 86/1744.

58. "Schachtjude ———," *DS* 40/1927.

Chapter 5

1. "Juda der Geldteufel," *DS* 26/1932; "Jüdische Hochstapelei," *DS* 1/1927; "Der Parasit," *DS* 19/1927; "Silberberg und Duisberg. Die Industriejuden," *DS* 40/1926; cartoon, *DS* 46/1930.

2. Letter of 13.7.23 in *Nachlass Streicher*, AL 6; Streicher's speech of 22.2.29 in Bavarian *Landtag* in ibid., 134; "August Bauernfreund," *DS* 41/1925; "Wurstjud Bauernfreund," *DS* 8/1929; "Bauernfreundliche Bohnen," *DS* 37/1929.

3. "Das Geheimnis der Fürther Suppenvergiftung," *DS* 30/1931; "Der Bauernfreundsche Vergiftungskandal," *DS* 34/1931; Poem, "Die Wurstsuppe," *DS* 35/1931; Police order of 27.8.31, HA 91/1889.

4. Report of the Fürth Prosecutor's Office, 27.8.31, HA 58/1407.

5. Appeal of 28.8.31 in ibid.

6. Decisions of 20.8.31 and 27.8.31 in ibid.

7. Letter in *DS* 6/1931.

8. "In Sonneberg," *DS* 49/1927; "Jüdischer Reklametrick," *DS* 1/1929; "Nothilfe Lotterie," *DS* 11/1929; "Der Weinachtsküchen," *DS* 31/1929.

9. "Jüdische Geschäftsreklame," *DS* 1/1930; "Die Juden-spende," *DS* 22/1931; "Jud —,——," *DS* 49/1931; "Conitzereien in Nürnberg," *DS* 50/1931; "Die Nothilfe," *DS* 48/1931.

10. Letters of 8.9.24 and 28.1.31 in *Nachlass Streicher*, AL 41.

11. See particularly the analysis in Marlis Steinert, *Hitler's War and the Germans*, ed. and tr. T.E.J. DeWitt (Athens, Ohio, 1977), pp. 132ff, 334–35.

12. Cartoon, *DS* 22/1932; "Die Judenpresse," *DS* 40/1925; "Die Agfa," *DS* 42/1928; "Die Schlotbarone," *DS* 14/1928; "Kunert und Levy," *DS* 26/1932.

13. "Der Konkurs des Juden ———," *DS* 38/1932; "Verhaftung wegen einer Restschuld von Mark 12.30," *DS* 23/1929; "Der Jude ——— von Bielefeld," *DS* 24/1932.

14. "Der Woll-und Strumpfjude ———," *DS* 12/1924; "Der geprellte Goi," *DS* 45/1929.

15. "Das Drama in der Hirschelgasse," *DS* 35/1928; "Das Drama in der Hirschelgasse," *DS* 37/1928; "Die Verderben Wilhelm Baldaufs," *DS* 45/1928.

16. "Bankkrach in Regensburg," *DS* 42/1928; "Die Vermögens-Schutzbank," *DS* 17/1930; "——— Der Felljude von Windesheim," *DS* 43/1931; "Abhandeln," *DS* 18/1930; "Der Guttmannskandal," *DS* 33/1932; cartoon, *DS* 34/1928.

17. "——— innere Laufergasse 2," *DS* 2/1927; "Der Guttman Flieger," *DS* 29/1927; "Beinparade," *DS* 27/1927.

18. For a typical use of this quotation see *DS* 51/1925.

19. Cartoon, *DS* 53/1925 and a similar one in *DS* 51/1928; cartoon, *DS* 50/1927.

20. Notice in *DS* 49/1928; "Goi, kauf ein," *DS* 50/1927; "Christusfest und Christusmörder," *DS* 51/1929.

21. "Die Firma Soldau," *DS* 23/191931; "Fort mit der Ausländerei," *DS* 27/1931; "Die Sowjetbleistifte des Warenhausjuden Tietz," *DS* 19/1932.

22. Letter of 6.5.27 in *Nachlass Streicher*, AL 42; letter in *DS* 12/1932.

23. Letter of 17.3.28 in *Nachlass Streicher*, AL 43.

24. "Streikbrecher," *DS* 7/1924; "Juden als Lohndrücker," *DS* 32/1924; "Der Sklavenhändler," *DS* 17-18/1931; "Direktor ———," *DS* 9/1924; "——— als Sklavenhalter," *DS* 8/1925; "Das Geheimnis des Bayreuther Warenhauses," *DS* 6/1927; "Die vornehme Firma," *DS* 25/1928.

25. "Die Schloss AG," *DS* 45/1929.

26. "In den Tod gegangen," *DS* 46/1927.

27. "Der Abortgrube des Alteisen-Juden ———," *DS* 31/1924. Cf. "Der Kaufmannsgehilfe und seine Ausbeuter," *DS* 20/1930.

28. Letters of 26.3.24, 25.4.24, and 6.5.24 in *Nachlass Streicher*, AL 41, AL 5 and AL 5.

29. "———, der Pinseljude und das Fabrikmädchen," *DS* 12/1929.

30. Letter of 22.9.32 in *Nachlass Streicher*, AL 40; "Der Jammer der Arbeitssklaven," *DS* 23/1931.

31. H. Uhlig, *Die Warenhäuser im Dritten Reich* (Köln/Opladen, 1956), pp. 5 passim, is a good summary of the evolution of department stores in Germany.

32. Ibid., p. 38.

33. As in "Juden Reklame," *DS* 27/1926.

34. Letter of 23.7.26 in *Nachlass Streicher*, AL 42.

35. "Das Warenhaus," *DS* 42/1926; "Das neue Lied vom Warenhaus," *DS* 43/1926; "Luppe und der Warenhausjude," *DS* 43/1926; "Jud Schocken und seine Knechte," *DS* 46/1926; "Kaufhaus Schocken," *DS* 42/1926.

36. "Warenhäuser," *DS* 21/1928; "Das verurteilte Warenhaus," *DS* 21/1928.

37. "Salman Schocken der Judenkönig," *DS* 13/1927; "Das Schocken Attentat," *DS* 10/1927; "Das Warenhaus," *DS* 27/1927.

38. Johannes Bartelmas, "Nürnberger Spaziergang," *DS* 3/1930; "Der Warner am Bodensee," *DS* 16, 17/1930; *DS* 2/1932.

39. "Betrug und Wucher im Saison-Ausverkauf," *DS* 24/1924; "———. Der Fruchtsaftjude . . ." *DS* 43/1929.

40. "Der Saustall im Warenhaus," *DS* 29/1932; "Ein Todesurteil über das deutsche Warenhaus," *DS* 26/1932; "Unglaubliche Zustände in den Jüdische Einheitspreisgeschaften," *DS* 33/1932; "Chape in Fürth," *DS* 34/1932.

41. "Der Jude Woolworth verteilt 70 Prozent Dividend," *DS* 6/1932; "Der Jude Woolworth und die Kehlfadenlampen," *DS* 2/1932.

42. "Woolworth," *DS* 16/1930.

43. Advertisement in *DS* 36/1930.

44. "Das Johannismännchen," *DS* 25/1930; "Die Bescherung im Sommer," *DS* 27/1930; "Der Feuerwehrmann als Affe," *DS* 48/1930; "Der Nichtjude als Kettenhund," *DS* 33/1931.

45. Uhlig, p. 53.

46. Letter in *DS* 38/1931; Letter in *DS* 40/1931; "Das neutrale Entwicklungspapier," *DS* 32/1931.

47. "Israelowitsch Friedmann," *DS* 13/1927; Letter in *DS* 21/1931; "Beamtenfängerei," *DS* 47/1928; Letter in *DS* 20/1932.

48. Letter of 18.1.27 in *Nachlass Streicher* AL 47.

49. Letter of 16.2.28 in ibid., AL 5.

50. Letters of 7.3.24, 5.4.24, and 24.3.24 in ibid., AL 5.

51. "Was uns Nottut," *DS* 4/1924; "Judenspiegel," *DS* 18/1923; "Jud ——— hat Ausverkauf," *DS* 21/1928; Reports of 18.11.28 and 27.12.28 in HA 86/1743.

52. Letters of 22.12.25, 4.2.28, 21.3.28, 19.2.31 in *Nachlass Streicher*, AL 41, 43, 43, and 40.

53. Letters of 28.11.27 and 12.11.25 in ibid., AL 43 and 41.
54. See *DS* 12/1924, and the letters of 24.6.24 and 16.7.24 in *Nachlass Streicher*, AL 41.
55. Cited in Schleunes, p. 167.
56. "Verzeichnis deutscher Geschäfte in Nürnberg." A total of 127 firms are listed in this undated brochure. *Nachlass Streicher*, AL 114.
57. Letter of 21.8.28 in ibid., AL 43.

Chapter 6

1. "Die Juden und die Wanzen," *DS* 15/1925; "Das gelöste Rätsel," *DS* 44/1926; "Judenblut," *DS* 35/1926; "Warum keine Judenleichen," and "Die tote Juden," *DS* 47/1927.
2. Letters in *DS* 30/1931 and *DS* 9/1930.
3. "Der Goi ist unrein," *DS* 32/1931; "Der Fettschöpfer als Nachtgeschirr," *DS* 18/1929; "Benno Worms," *DS* 53/1931.
4. "Der besudelte Brunnen," *DS* 49/1928; "Streng vertraulich," *DS* 24/1928. Cf. the brief discussion of the historical connection between Jew and filth in L.K. Little, *Religious Poverty and the Profit Economy in Medieval Europe* (Ithaca, N.Y., 1978), pp. 52–53.
5 *Judische Schweinerein. Stenografischer Bericht über den grossen Fleischbesudelungs-Prozess in Würzberg am 28. März 1901*, 8th ed. (Würzburg, 1901) in *Stürmer-Archiv*, IV, "Der Jude als Verbrecher."
6. "Der Judenbäcker von Meillrichstadt," *DS* 11/1931; "Die Säue von Meillrichstadt," *DS* 33/1932.
7. "Wenn Juden alt werden," *DS* 37/1926; Heimdal, "Der Hund," *DS* 43/1927; Letter in *DS* 6/1932; cartoon *DS* 34/1932.
8. "Pfiffi und Der Talmudjude," *DS* 9/1931.
9. "Der Sportrummel eine Judenmache," *DS* 25/1932; "Der Musterjude," *DS* 3/1930; "Im Suddeutschen Fussballbund herrscht der Jude," *DS* 32/1932; "Der 1. Fussballklub Nürnberg geht am Juden zu Grunde," *DS* 31/1932.
10. "Schützenfest in Köln," *DS* 24/1930; "Ein Schützenbrief," *DS* 25/1930; letter in *DS* 28/1932.
11. "Deutsche Türner," *DS* 42/1931; "Das jüdische Weinachtsfest," *DS* 3/1931; "Der verrätene Turnvater Jahn," *DS* 8/1932; "Bar Kochba," *DS* 3/1930; "Die deutsche Türnerschaft stirbt am Juden," *DS* 35/1931; "Der Staffellauf," *DS* 32/1931.
12. "Der Judenhochzeit und der Männergesängverein Cham," *DS* 16/1930; "——— der Fidelio Jude von Roth," *DS* 48/1930.

13. "Faschingsmützen," *DS* 7/1927; "Judenfasching in Würzburg," *DS* 7/1929; "Der Judenhohn," *DS* 15/1930; "Juden und
Fasching," *DS* 8/1932.

14. Letter in *DS* 8/1932.

15. Letter in *DS* 22/1931; "Der Jude ———," *DS* 23/1924.

16. "Erlebnisse mit Juden," *DS* 6/1931; "Juden in der Strassenbahn," *DS* 40/1927.

17. "Jüdische Frechheit," *DS* 31/1924.

18. "Ein Jude aus der Strassenbahn hinausgeworfen," *DS*
23/1925; "Der verbogene Synagogenschlussel," *DS* 45/1926.

19. Letter in *DS* 10/1932; "Juden als Hausherren," *DS* 31/1924;
"Das Herrenlose Gut," *DS* 35/1924; "Unglaublicher Tierschinderei
einer Juden," *DS* 6/1926,

20. " Obdachlos," *DS* 31/1927; "Wie der Jude Dr. ———
Deutsche verhöhnen darf," *DS* 11/1931.

21. "Die Jüdin ———," *DS* 25/1931; letter in *DS* 13/1932.

22. "——— attackiert einen Greis," *DS* 41/1929; "Der ———
von Burgpreppach," *DS* 14/1929; "Die Ohrfeige des Juden," *DS*
9/1924.

23. The best analyses of Jewish attitudes are Carl Rheins, "German Jewish Patriotism, 1918–1935," (Ph.D. diss., SUNY Stony Brook,
1978); and Ulrich Dunker, *Der Reichsbund jüdischer Frontsoldaten
1919–1938* (Düsseldorf, 1977).

24. "Jüdische Denkmalsenthüllungen," *DS* 6/1925; "Jüdischer
Frontsoldatentag," *DS* 26/1925; "Die jüdischen Frontsoldaten," *DS*
40/1928; "Die Juden im Krieg," *DS* 10/1926; "Die Juden im Krieg," *DS*
3/1928.

25. "Die Juden und die Weltkrieg," *DS* 2/1930. Cf. H.
Baumann, "Das Märchen von der zwölftausend gefallenen Juden," *DS*
5/1931.

26. "Deutsche und jüdische Töchter," *DS* 23/1925; "Eine neue
Gemeinheit des Juden ———," *DS* 32/1932; "Judenwirtschaft der
Erlanger Universität," *DS* 26/1925; "Der Zweikampf," *DS* 52/1927.

27. "Das entweihte Heldendenkmal von Gostawitz," *DS*
26/1926; "Garnisonstag in Fürth," *DS* 21/1925; "Die Vorstandschaft,"
DS 45/1930.

28. Dahlhelm, "Herunterschiessen," *DS* 32/1932; Letter in *DS*
9/1931; "Der Verkehrsposten in Regensburg," *DS* 5/1929; correspondence of 13.3.28 and 16.5.28 in *Nachlass Streicher*, AL 76.

29. "Jud ——— von Ansbach," *DS* 36/1927; "Die Büsse des
Juden ———," *DS* 45/1927; and letter of 26.8.27 in *Nachlass
Streicher*, AL 43; "Unterm Judenauto," *DS* 31/1928.

30. "Der Juden Nächstenliebe," *DS* 48/1928; "Jud ———," *DS*
6/1932; "Talmud und Meineid," *DS* 9/1930; cartoon in *DS* 29/1929.

31. "Der Tiere Qual," *DS* 29/1927; "Die Neustädter
Viehschächtung," *DS* 11/1927; letter from TSV in *DS* 19-20/1931; "Die

Tierschutzversammlung," *DS* 23/1929; "Tierquälerei," *DS* 1/1930; "Der Henkersknecht," *DS* 6/1930; "Im Schlachthof," *DS* 27/1930; "Gegen die Tierquälerei," *DS* 50/1931.

32. "Wucher am Fremden," *DS* 34/1930.

33. "Deutsch-jüdische Wandersäue," *DS* 37/1931; "Der Skandal an der Pegnitz," *DS* 39/1931.

34. "Aus einem Badebrief," *DS* 9/1932; "Der Jud in Familienbad," *DS* 37/1926; Letter in *DS* 27/1931; "Österreichs Badeplage," *DS* 46a/1931.

35. Letter in *DS* 10/1932; "Juden im Gartenkaffe" *DS* 27/1930; "Jüdische Frechheit," *DS* 23/1931; letter in *DS* 25/1932; "Juden in der Wirtschaftgärten," *DS* 21/1932.

36. "Antisemitismus der Tat," *DS* 25/1924; "Den C.V. Jude als Mitarbeiter der Stürmer," *DS* 30/1927.

37. Cartoon in *DS* 38/1927.

38. "Schulausflug und Juden," *DS* 30/1930; "Schabbes und Zeppelin," *DS* 35/1930; "Der Oberlängermeister," *DS* 3/1932.

39. "Der Rote Volksbetrug," *DS* 30/1932; "Reichshilfe für Juden und Judenknechte aus den Steuergeldern des Volkes," *DS* 26/1932.

40. "Der Bilderdiebstahl in der Cadolzburg," *DS* 3,4,5/1929.

41. "Strafferei Lumperei," *DS* 13/1925; "Sonderbarer Justiz," *DS* 14/1925; "Das Urteil von Chicago," *DS* 25/1924.

42. "Goi und Rechtsanwaltjude," *DS* 35/1928; A. Zimmerman, "Der Jude als Richter," *DS* 48/1927.

Chapter 7

1. "Marxistisch jüdischer Saustall aufgedeckt," *DS* 36/1926; "Otto Hamberger," *DS* 26/1932; "Das Freudenhausparlament in Genf," *DS* 9/1932; "Die Juden in der Schweiz," *DS* 36/1932.

2. "Ein König heiratet seine Sekretärin," *DS* 33/1931; "Der Weltausbeuter," *DS* 41/1931; "Samuel und Reading," *DS* 42/1931; "Der Judenhass in Frankreich," *DS* 4/1927; "Judengift in Frankreich," *DS* 39/1931; "Die Judenangst," *DS* 22/1932; "Die Legion der Schande," *DS* 46/1930; "Der Marokkokreig: ein Judengeschäft," *DS* 24/1926.

3. "De Metz," *DS* 34/1924; "Der Armeebefehl des Juden Levi," *DS* 15/1929.

4. "Lindbergh," *DS* 23/1927; "Die Herren der Welt," *DS* 14/1926; "Der Untergang der deutschen Industrie," *DS* 7/1927; "In New York," *DS* 34/1927; "Um des Geldes willen," *DS* 34/1925.

5. "Jüdischer Kampf gegen die Einehe," *DS* 36/1928; "Der Stürmer in Brasilien," *DS* 17/1930.

6. "Der Bluthund," *DS* 22/1928; "Antisemitisch Studenten-Kundgebungen in Rumänien," *DS* 9/1929; "Selbsthilfe in Polen," *DS* 15/1930; "Polnische Grosstat," *DS* 2/1928; "Volksjustiz," *DS* 41/1928; "Die Entlarvung des Blutbundes," *DS* 51/1928; "Anti-judischer Boykott in Polen," *DS* 1/1932.

7. "Russen," *DS* 4/1923; "Das sterbende Volk," *DS* 36/1928; "Die Luge von der Leichenschandung," *DS* 4/1931; "Bauernelend in Sowjetjudäa," *DS* 36/1932; "Brief aus Russland," *DS* 40/1931; "Der Auslander in der Sowjetindustrie," *DS* 25/1932; "Ein Kreuzzug nach Sowjet Judäa," *DS* 5/1931.

8. "Religion oder Nation," *DS* 47/1925; "Jud oder Bauer," *DS* 42/1929; "Der Jude in Palästina," *DS* 3/1930; "Der Bauernaufstand in Palästina," *DS* 36/1929.

9. "Verlumpung in der Republik," *DS* 6/1923; "Die Republik," *DS* 33/1930; "Opfer des Systems," *DS* 46/1930; "Die Verräter des Achtstundentages," *DS* 9/1924; "Beamtenbesoldung," *DS* 16/1924; "Republikanische Pensionisten," *DS* 9/1932.

10. "Verlorene Heimat," *DS* 45/1930; "Warum wird das Rheinland geräumt?" *DS* 11/1927; "Die Besatzung am Rhein," *DS* 27/1930.

11. "Die Hand Juda ruht schwer auf dem deutschen Volke," *DS* 39/1927.

12. "Die Goja," *DS* 21/1928; "Wer trifft die Schuld," *DS* 24/1928; "Die Eisenbahn," *DS* 35/1928; "Dawes Bahn," *DS* 26/1928.

13. "Young Sklaven," *DS* 22/1930; Albert Forster, "Der Youngplan," *DS* 51/1929.

14. A. Wolf, "Briefe aus dem Landtage," *DS* 11/1924; "Judengeld für die Deutschdemokraten," *DS* 22/1924; "Die grosse Lumperei," *DS* 26/1928; "Präsident Hindenburg," *DS* 50/1927.

15. "Alljuda im Not," *DS* 16/1931.

16. "Ungeheuerliche Beschimpfung Hindenburgs," *DS* 12/1932; "Die Judenfront," *DS* 13/1932; "Regierung Papen und die Juden," *DS* 29/1932; "Einen Besseren findst Du nicht," *DS* 30/1932; "Hindenburg und die Juden," *DS* 34/1932.

17. This attitude is reflected throughout the previously cited works of Hambrecht, Lenman, and Ehlers; it also mars the definitive study of Luppe's years in Nürnberg, Hermann Hanschel, *Oberbürgermeister Hermann Luppe: Nürnberger Kommunalpolitik in der Weimarer Republik* (Nürnberg, 1977).

18. Ehlers, pp. 311ff; Lenman, pp. 117–18.

19. Dr. Hermann Luppe, "Mein Leben war Kampf für Demokratie und Reichseinheit. Selbstbiographie dis Nürnberger Oberbürgermeisters und Kämpfers gegen bayerischen Separatismus und Nationalsozialismus." The manuscript, consulted in the Bundesarchiv Koblenz as part of the *Nachlass Luppe*, consists of four volumes with pages consecutively numbered. The edited version, *Mein Leben*, cited

as fn. 11, chapter 2, includes page references to the original. It is therefore the only version cited unless the manuscript, cited as "Mein Leben," is more complete.

20. Cf. "Luppe in Trommelfeuer," *DS* 3/1923; "Der Judensystem in Rathaus," *DS* 17/1923; "Es lebe Luppe in Maybach-Wagen," *DS* 33/1924; "Gibts für Luppe keine Gesetze?" *DS* 4/1924; "Der Hereinfall," *DS* 2/1925; "Grosser Seiltanzer Akt," *DS* 40/1927; "Das Oberhaupt," *DS* 42/1927; "Diogenes Streifzüge durch die Stadt Nürnberg," *DS* 28/1927.

21. Stadtarchiv Nürnberg, Hermann Busch, "Geschichte der Nationalsozialistischen Kommunalpolitik 1925–1933," unpub. ms., Nürnberg, 1936–1942, is detailed on the behavior of the Nazi city councilmen.

22. Letters of 10.1.26 and 16.1.26 in *Nachlass Streicher*, AL 78.

23. For Luppe's evaluations of Streicher and Hitler see particularly Luppe, pp. 111, 118–119, 219, 246. Cf. Hanschel, pp. 190 passim.

24. "Die Proletarier Kanzler Süssheim," *DS* 5/1925; "Ein neues Extrahonorar für Dr. Süssheim," *DS* 2/1926; "Süssheim verteidigt den Betrug," *DS* 11/1923; "Süssheim und der Spucknapf," *DS* 48a/1925; "Pistolenforderung auf dem Juristentag," *DS* 40/1928.

25. For examples of Süssheim's successes, cf. the court decision of 21.3.22, reprinted in *Julius Streicher im Kampf um sein Recht, Nachlass Streicher*, AL 10; Süssheim's statement of 20.10.28 in ibid., AL 79; and the account of Streicher's 1928 disciplinary hearing before the Nürnberg Disciplinary Court for Non-Judicial Officials in Varga, 179–180. Cf. Luppe, p. 54.

26. Luppe, p. 51; "Die Wohnungsgeschichte des Nürnberger Stadtrats . . . Dr. Heimerich," *DS* 3/1924; "Heimliches und Unheimliches . . . Herrn Dr. Heimerich," *DS* 4/1924; "Dr. Heimerich hat Nürnberg satt," *DS* 8/1924; "Der Heimerich wieder durchgefallen," *DS* 26/1924; "Dr. Heimerich nimmt Abscheid," *DS* 12/1925.

27. "Dr. Julius Fleischmann," *DS* 19/1925; Karl Holz, "Der Einbruchdiebstahl des städt. Oberfinanzrates Dr. Julius Fleischmann," *DS* 21/1925; "Der Sockenmauser Prozess," *DS* 43/1925; court decisions of 5.3.26 and 8.3.26 in *Nachlass Streicher*, AL 76; "Sockenmauser-Prozess," *DS* 11/1926.

28. "Die Rathauswirtschaft," *DS* 15/1923; "Verjudung des Krankenhauses," *DS* 16/1923; "Ein Schandfleck Nürnbergs," *DS* 15/1925; L. F. Gengeler, "Die Volkshochschule," *DS* 9/1931; "Der Antrag in der Brieftasche," *DS* 7/1931.

29. Hanschel, pp. 77ff. and 251ff., is the best general analysis of Luppe's administration. Ehlers, pp. 142ff. is extremely useful for the early years.

30. "Neuer Luppe-Skandal," *DS* 18/1925; "Spezialpädagoge Dr. Baege enthaftet," *DS* 22/1925; Luppe, "Mein Leben," p. 433.

31. "66/70er Kriegsveteranen wegen Bettels verhaftet," *DS* 29/1924; and report of 4.11.24 in HA 17A/1731; "Die Polizeiwache in der Pfannenschmiedsgasse unter der Luppe-Peitsch," *DS* 11/1923; "Der Skandal in der Landwirtschaftsamt," *DS* 37/1924; "Aus der Luppe'schen Sklavenkolonie Mittelburg," *DS* 32/1925; "Die Staat als Preistreiberin," *DS* 36/1926; "Die Schande im Südfriedhof," *DS* 17/1924; "Ein brutaler Regierungsakt des Luppe-Stadtrats," *DS* 18/1924.

32. "Der Überfall auf Karl Holz," *DS* 4/1927; council resolution of 15.1.30 in Busch, III, 6-7; council resolution of April, 1925, in ibid., II, 143; council meeting of 26.5.26 in ibid., II, 249; "Das Festessen," *DS* 36/1927; "Der Kampf ums Festessen," *DS* 37/1927.

33. "Luppes Rathauswirtschaft," *DS* 53/1929.

34. "Skandalöse Zustände in der Nürnberger Ortskrankenkasse," *DS* 27/1925; Fritz Ertl, "Allgemeine Ortskrankenkasse," *DS* 30/1925; "Krankenkassenbetrug," *DS* 36/1930.

35. Luppe, pp. 72ff. Ehlers, pp. 172 passim analyzes Nürnberg's housing problem in the early 1920s. Dan P. Silverman, "A Pledge Unredeemed: The Housing Crisis in Weimar Germany," *Central European History* XII (1970): 112-39, puts the subject in a general context showing the relative effectiveness of Luppe's approach.

36. "Wohnungsbau ist Luxus," *DS* 8/1923; "Geheime Diktatur im Rathaus," *DS* 12/1923; "Republikanische Wohnungsfürsorge," *DS* 12/1923; "Nürnberger Wohnungsfürsorge," *DS* 13/1923.

37. "Dokumente der Schande," *DS* 8/1924; "Schwarz-rot-gold Roheit," *DS* 8/1924; "Ein kriegsbeschädigter Fabrikarbeiter wohnt im Waschhaus," *DS* 6/1924; "Nürnberger Schande," *DS* 13/1924; "Alle menschen sind irgendwo untergebracht," *DS* 36/1924; Karl Holz, "Mit Beil und Revolver rationiert das Wohnungsamt beim Arbeiter," *DS* 7/1925; " Aus dem Luppeparadies," *DS* 36/1925; "Wieder eine Scheibung," *DS* 41/1925.

38. "Jud im Palast. Wohnung des Arbeiters im Ziegenstall," *DS* 51/1926; letter of 6.3.27 in *Nachlass Streicher*, AL 42; "Nürnberger Wohnungslupperei," *DS* 43/1928; cartoons, *DS* 37/1928; and *DS* 2/1931.

39. Cf. "Die gebotene Eile halber," *DS* 29/1932; and "Der Volksentscheid," *DS* 31/1932; with the analyses in Hänschel, pp 314ff., and Luppe, pp. 252-53.

Chapter 8

1. "Schildbürgerstreiche," *DS* 25/1925. The column appeared in several other issues of the paper, with different themes.

2. "Gefühlslosigkeit," *DS* 8/1923; "Süssheim verteidigt den Betrug," *DS* 11/1923.

3. "Der Bauer. Der Nazionalsozialismus seine Rettung," *DS* 41/1926; "Der Schulschluss," *DS* 9/1928.

4. K. Roth, *Schmelscher für Landwirte* (n.p., n.d.) in *Stürmer-Archiv*, V, "Berufe."

5. Cf. such articles as "Die Kuh des Georg Dürnberger," *DS* 16/1927; Letter in *DS* 32/1932; "Judenmethoden," *DS* 14/1927; "Der Fellheimer Viehjude," *DS* 9/1927; "Der Bauernwürger," *DS* 29/1932.

6. "Bauer, hab acht," *DS* 10/1924.

7 "Sigmund Strauss," *DS* 34/1926; "Der Tauschhandel," *DS* 48/1927; "Nathan Frank," *DS* 39/1927; "Der Jude von Heilbronn," *DS* 13/1928; "Der Talmudschwur," *DS* 34/1928..

8. General analyses of the Nazis' growing impact on the German farmer include J.E. Farquharson, *The Plough and the Swastika* (London, 1976), passim; and Werner Angress, "The Political Role of the Peasantry in the Weimar Republic," *Review of Politics* XXI (1959): 530–49. Varga, pp. 190–91, discusses Streicher's initial problems in speaking to rural audiences.

9. "Ein Riesenskandal auf dem Nürnberger Hopfenmarkt," *DS* 14/1929; "Die Hopfenjuden," *DS* 17/1929; "Der Kuhhandel von Hopfenpreppach," *DS* 16/1929; "Der Hopfenhandel von Gericht," *DS* 31/1929; "Der Skandal auf dem Hopfenmarkt," *DS* 32/1929; "Der Sonderbar Ausgange des Hopfenjudenprozess," *DS* 36/1929.

10. "Wurstjud Bauernfreund," *DS* 8/1929; "Bauernfreundskandal," *DS* 9/1929; "Bauernführer Dr. Fehr," *DS* 10/1929; "August Bauernfreund klagt," *DS* 13/1929. Varga, pp. 191ff., and Busch, III, pp. 6ff., summarize the incident and its aftermath.

11. "Der Staat als Bauernschlachter," *DS* 5/1930; "Der Bauernmord," *DS* 10/1930; "Bauernbetrug," *DS* 31/1930; Albert Foerster, "Bauernelend," *DS* 12/1931; "Der Untergang der Milchbauern," *DS* 21/1931.

12. "Jakob Regensburger," *DS* 23/1929; "———, der Viehjud von Ellwangen," *DS* 4/1930; "Siegfried Regensburger," *DS* 24/1930; "Hugo Eichberg," *DS* 26/1931; "Der Judenkonkurs," *DS* 23/1931; "Judenpest in der Hallertau," *DS* 32/1931; "Grosser Judenskandal in Dinkelsbühl," *DS* 53/1932.

13. "Der Halsabschneider," *DS* 4/1932; "Jud ———, der Bauernpeiniger aus Straubing," *DS* 40/1932; cartoon, "Auf der Gant," *DS* 42/1930; cartoon "German Harvest," *DS* 26/1931.

14. Cf. Rudolf Heberle, *Landbevölkerung und Nationalsozialismus* (Stüttgart, 1963); and Gerd Stoltenberg, *Politische Strömungen im Schleswig-Holsteinschen Landvolk* (Düsseldorf, 1962).

15. Reports of 18.7.26 and 2.3.30 in HA 86/1743/1744.

16 Cf. Holz's comments at a *Landbund* speech of 28.6.31 in ibid., 1744; "Landbundschurkereien," *DS* 37/1930; "Der Landbun-

daufmarsch," *DS* 19–20/1931; "Die Flucht aus dem fränkischen Landbund," *DS* 7/1932; and Horst Gies, "NSDAP und landwirtschaftliche
Organisationen in der Endphase der Weimarer Republik," *Vierteljahrshefte für Zeitgeschichte*, XV (1967), 341-76.

17.   "———Der Wechselfälscher und Bauernwurger, "*DS*
12/1932. The issue was banned for inciting violence. Order of 23.3.32
in HA 81/1889.

18.   "Der Überfall im Kuhstall," *DS* 37/1930; Cf. also such pieces
as "Der verprügelte Jude," *DS* 47/1928; "Das Strafgericht im
Kuhstall," *DS* 51/1928; "Judenfirmung und Judentaufe," *DS* 24/1930;
"Das Bad in der Mistgrube," *DS* 21/1931.

19.   "Der Engel aus Berolzheim," *DS* 24/1930; "Der Rote Max,"
DS 41/1930; "Waldmann als deutscher Michel," *DS* 10/1929; "Der
abgewimmelte Viehjud," *DS* 21/1927.

20.   "———aus Volkerleier," *DS* 39/1929.

21.   "Jud Aal und die Bauern von Herreden," *DS* 2/1932; "Der
Bauernaufmarsch von Herreden," *DS* 5/1932.

22.   Reports of *KdI* to *Bez. Feuchtwangen*, 5.2.32, and of Herreden gendarmerie, 5.2.32 in KdI II, 692.

23.   "Der Versteigerung von Windsheim," *DS* 5/1932.

24.   Edward N. Peterson, *The Limits of Hitler's Power* (Princeton, 1969), pp. 404ff., describes the difficulties National Socialism
faced after 1933 in penetrating institutionally, particularly the
Catholic villages of Bavaria. Studies of those Protestant Franconian
villages which voted heavily for the Nazis before 1933 would be useful.

25.   Max Kele, *Nazis and Workers* (Chapel Hill, N.C., 1972), is
the best general study.

26.   Georg Gärtner, *Mit Uns zieht die neue Zeit* (Nürnberg,
1928).

27.   "Übung macht den Master," *DS* 20/1929.

28.   "An die deutsche Arbeiterschaft," *DS* 39/1929;
"Grosskapital und Kapitalistenfresser," *DS* 47/1928; "Der Staat der
Verheissung," *DS* 1/1930; "Proletarierführer Dr. Müller im Grand
Hotel Berlin," *DS* 31/1924; "Die entlarvten Sozibonzen," *DS* 26/1932;
"Die Schutztruppe der Hochfinanz," *DS* 34/1928; "Es lebe die
Gleichheit," *DS* 36/1926; "Die grosskapitalistischen Konsumvereine,"
DS 48/1932; "Konkursparade," *DS* 24/1927.

29.   Albert Forster, "Der Verrät der Sozialdemokratie," *DS*
49/1930; "Der Verrät der SPD," *DS* 42/1931; "Die Eiserne Front," *DS*
9/1932; "Das Hakenkreuz und die drei Pfeile," *DS* 30/1932; "Die
Mistgabel als Jüdische Reklamezeichen," *DS* 40/1932. Good brief
surveys of SPD policy in this period include Robert A. Gates, "German
Socialism and the Crisis of 1929–33," *Central European History* VII
(1974): 332–59; and Erich Matthias, "German Social Democracy in the
Weimar Republic," in *German Democracy and the Triumph of Hitler*,
pp.47–57.

30. "O Herr, lass mich gesund bleiben; O Herr mach uns frei," *DS* 2/1924; "Diktator Fentz," *DS* 12/1930; "Warum?" *DS* 14/1927.
31. "Die Tagespost als jüdisches Familienblatt," *DS* 17/1923; "Der Tagespostjude und seine Ahnenreihe," *DS* 43/1930; cartoons in *DS* 18/1926; and *DS* 7/1926; "Was der 'Tagespost'—Jude verschweigt," *DS* Extra/1924;"Meine Antwort an den Plakatjuden der Tagespost," *DS* Extra/1924.
32. "Was man Arbeitern zu bieten wagt," *DS* 49/1925; "Vergiftung in Roth," *DS* 29/1924; "Zweierlei Mass in der Tagespost," *DS* 6/1923; "Die Tagespost in Verlegenheit," *DS* 1/1924; "Die Presse," *DS* 36/1927; "Riesenblamage des Tagespostjuden," *DS* 32/1929; Gert Rückel, *Die Fränkische Tagespost. Geschichte einer Parteizeitung* (Nürnberg, 1964), is a good study of the paper.
33. Karl Rohe, *Das Reichsbanner Schwarz-Rot-Gold* (Düsseldorf, 1966), pp. 224ff, 289-90.
34. "Blutschande eines Reichsbannerführers," *DS* 16/1926; "Heldentum eines Reichsbanners," *DS* 38/1928; "Der Grab des Genossen," *DS* 45/1926; "Auf dem Friedhof," *DS* 37/1929.
35. "Die Meute und ihr Opfer," *DS* 35/1929; "Aufreizung zum Klassenhass," *DS* 31/1929; "Judenknechtsaufmarsch," *DS* 33/1926; "Die Reichsbannertage—eine Niederlage Alljudas," *DS* 34/1926; "Fasching in November," *DS* 49/1930.
36. "Arbeiterjugend," *DS* 11/1923; "Der Kinderkreuzzug," *DS* 30/1929; "Frau Blöth," *DS* 30/1931; "Rotsport," *DS* 32/1931; "Arbeitersportfest," *DS* 27/1925.
37. "Der Skandal in Behringersdorf," *DS* 46/1930; "Der socialisierte Baum," *DS* 29/1928; "Ein rotes Schwein," *DS* 24/1927.
38. "Geburstag des Kontrolleurs," *DS* 6/1930; "Der Schwarzjäger," *DS* 2/1932; "Das Urteil des Amtgerichts," *DS* 27/1929; "Bürgermeister Huber von Treuchtlingen," *DS* 35/1925; "Der Rote Amtsvorsteher," *DS* 41/1928; "Vom Klasse 4 in Klasse 9," *DS* 21/1924; "Mit dem Parteibuch in der Hand," *DS* 20/1932.
39. Cf. Donald L Niewyk, *Socialist, Anti-Semite, and Jew: German Social Democracy Confronts the Problem of Anti-Semitism 1918–1933* (Baton Rouge, LA., 1971); Hans-Helmuth Knütter, *Die Juden und die deutsche Linke in der Weimarer Republik* (Düsseldorf, 1971); Werner Angress, "Juden im politischen Leben der Revolutionszeit," *Deutsches Judentum in Krieg und Revolution*, 137–315; and George L. Mosse, "German Socialists and the Jewish Question in the Weimar Republic," *Yearbook of the Leo Baeck Institute* XVI (1971): 123–51.
40. "Es gibt keine Partei, deren Programm nicht von Juden gemacht wurde," *DS* 21/1924; Karl Holz, "Was ist der Kommunismus," *DS* 12/1924; "Der rote Trompeter," *DS* 47/1931; "Wie die Juden wählen," *DS* 37/1930; "Die Hammel," *DS* 39/1940.

41. "Der Judengenosse," *DS* 48/1931.
42. "Verjudung der Hochschulen," *DS* 11/1930; speech of 26.6.25 in Bavarian Landtag in *Nachlass Streicher*, AL 130; Letter of 4.3.30 in ibid., AL 40; "Der Jude in der Elternvereinigungen," *DS* 9/1932; "Schulprüfrung in Mossbach," *DS* 14/1930; "Schulprüfung in Treutlingen," *DS* 17/1930; "Der Judenlehrer in Hof," *DS* 30/1931.
43. Speech in the Bavarian *Landtag* of 23.3.26 in *Nachlass Streicher*, AL 131; and speech of 23.2.28 in ibid., 133.
44. "Judenknechtsgeist in der *Allgemeinen Deutschen Lehrzeitung*," *DS* 24/1931; Letter in *DS* 29/1932; "Die Lehrerzeitung," *DS* 25/1932; "Eine Unerhörte Herausforderung der Lehrerschaft," *DS* 4/1930; "Der Prügelpädogoge vom Hakenkreuz," *DS* 9/1931.
45. *Regierungsrat* Kuntze, "Der Nationalsozialismus und die Schule," 2.3.31, in HA 71/1537, is a perceptive contemporary discussion of the issue. Cf. Rainer Bölling, *Volksschullehrer und Politik: Der Deutsche Lehrerverein, 1918–1933* (Göttingen, 1978).
46. Cf. especially Michael Kater, *Studentenschaft und Rechtsradikalismus in Deutschland, 1918–1933* (Hamburg, 1975); Michael Steinberg, *Sabers and Brown Shirts: The German Students' Path to National Socialism, 1918–1935* (Chicago, 1977); and Jürgen Schwarz, *Studenten in der Weimarer Republik. Die deutsche Studentenschaft in der Zeit von 1918 bis 1923 und ihre Stellung zur Politik* (Berlin, 1971).
47. "Deutsche Ärzte verhungern," *DS* 3/1931; "In zwei monaten sechs Juden," *DS* 28/1929; "Stadtrat Schäffer bestraft die Armut," *DS* 49/1931.
48. Manfred Franze, *Die Erlangen Studentenschaft, 1918–1945* (Wurzburg, 1972), pp. 53 passim, 91–92.
49. "Der deutsche Akademiker geht unter," *DS* 1/1929; "Numerus Clausus," *DS* 8/1929; "Numerus Clausus," *DS* 11/1929; "Numerus Clausus auch in Würzburg angenommen," *DS* 11/1929; Schwarz, pp. 362ff.
50. As in Louis Bondy, *Racketeers of Hatred* (London, 1946), pp. 42ff; and Rühl, pp. 180ff.
51. "Julius Streicher und unsere Jugend," *Nürnberger Zeitung*, 8.10.25; speech of 20.4.26 in Bavarian Landtag in *Nachlass Streicher*, AL 131.
52. "Wie die Mönschrother Schuljugend den Juden das Leben sauer macht," *DS* 35/1932.
53. "Auf der Volkschochschule," *DS* 15/1932; Professor ———aus Nördlingen," *DS* 6/1932; "Der Jude in der Mittelschule," *DS* 15/1931.
54. Paraphrase from letter of 18.3.24, *Nachlass Streicher*, AL 49. Claudia Koonz, "Nazi Women before 1933: Rebels against Emancipation," *Social Science Quarterly* LVI (1976): 553-63, is a good introduction to the perceptions of the party faithful during the *Kampfzeit*.

55. Statement of 20.4.26, in KdI II, 687.
56. Reports of 15.1.32 and 14.3.30 in HA 85/1734 and 86/1744; cartoon in *DS* 23/1929.
57. Jill Stephenson, *Women in Nazi Society* (New York, 1975).
58. "Eine ernste Mahnung an die deutschen Mädchen . . ." *DS* 8/1930.
59. "Frauen und Politik," *DS* 2/1924; "Aufruf der deutschen Frau," *DS* 35/1930; "Zigarette und Frau," *DS* 9/1924; Maria Fontaine, "Aus dem Kochbuch der jüdischen Modeindustrie," *DS* 34/1931; "Puder und Farbstift," *DS* 42/1926; "An alle deutschen Frauen und Mädchen," *DS* 16/1924.
60. "Bubikopf," *DS* 13/1924; "Der Lausbubikopf," *DS* 35/1925; "Der Bubikopf im der Kleinkinderschule," *DS* 17/1926; "Hermine Maas," *DS* 27/1926; letter of 24.4.26 in *Nachlass Streicher*, AL 42.
61. "Seelenmord," *DS* 33/1926; "Der Paragraph der Unzucht und des Verbrechens," *DS* 47/1929; "Freiheit des Blutschande, der Notzucht und der Homosexualität," *DS* 25/1929.
62. The most graphic—or pornographic—essay on this theme is Fritz Sauckel, "Schutzt die deutsche Frau vor dem Tier im Juden," *DS* 48/1925. See also the set of verses, "Der Bastard," in *DS* 13/1927.
63. "Mord im Mutterleib," and cartoon, "Krieg dem keimenden Leben," in *DS* 27/1931; and order in HA 58/1409. Stephenson, 57–61, discusses Nazi opposition to abortion.
64. "Dr Hirschfeld und Dr. Hodann," *DS* 13/1930; "Der Judensaustall in der Städischen Volkhochschule," *DS* 49/1929.
65. Speech of 20.4.27 in HA 85/1732.
66. Letter of 12.6.33 in *Nachlass Streicher*, AL 17.
67. Letter of March, 1931, in ibid., AL 40.

Chapter 9

1. Alex Hall, *Scandal, Sensation, and Social Democracy: the SPD Press and Wilhelmine Germany* (Cambridge, 1977).
2. Cf. particularly Emil Gumbel, *Vom Fememord zur Reichskanzlei* (Heidelberg, 1962); H. and E. Hannover, *Politische Justiz 1919–1933* (Frankfurt, 1966); Gotthard Jasper, *Der Schutz der Republik. Studien zur staatlichen Sicherung der Demokratie in der Weimarer Republik 1922–1930* (Tübingen, 1963); and *Die Justiz in der Weimarer Republik. Eine Chronik*, ed. Thilo Ramm, (Neuwied, Berlin, 1968). Hans Hattenhauer, "Zur Lage der Justiz in der Weimarer Republik," in *Weimar: Selbstpreisgabe einer Demokratie*, ed. K-D Erdmann and Hagen Schulze (Düsseldorf, 1980), pp. 169–76, is a brief defense of the Weimar judiciary.

3. "Julius Streicher in Kampf um sein Recht. Gesammelt und überreicht von einem Namenlosen aus der Schar seiner Getreuen," *Nachlass Streicher*, AL 10.

4. Speeches in the Bavarian *Landtag*, 12.6.25 and 29.1.30, *Nachlass Streicher*, AL 130, 135.

5. Rühl, pp. 186–87; statement of 28.12.31, HA 58/1407; statement of 11.5.32, HA 85/1734.

6. Recommendation of KdI of 26.6.23 and police report of 20.7.23, HA 91/1884.

7. List in HA 91/1889.

8. Correspondence of 2.8.24, 9.8.24, and 22.8.24, ibid;. 91/1884.

9. Report of 23.9.24; directive of 29.9.24; and statement of 1.10.24 and decision of 7.10.24, ibid., 91/1884.

10. Reports and correspondence, ibid., 86/1742.

11. Order of 11.9.25; statement of 11.9.25, ibid., 91/1884; "Die Beschlagnahme," *DS* 38/1925.

12. Reports of 22.4.25, 5.6.25, and 28.5.25, KdI II, 685.

13. Reports of 23.4.25 and 5.6.25, ibid.

14. Reports of 28.4.32 and 10.5.32, HA 91/1889, 92/1889.

15. Hall, pp. 15ff., discusses the cat-and-mouse nature of this conflict.

16. Typical examples include the court order of 4.7.23 in *Nachlass Streicher*, AL 77; and the letters of 17.3.28, 16.9.24, 30.1.25 in ibid., AL 43, 79, 41.

17. "Das Sektgelage des Juden Bernheim," *DS* 34/1928; "Judenprozess in Passau," *DS* 3/1929; "Warum Karl Holz 6 Wochen Gefängnis Bekam," *DS* 6/1929; "Der Passauer Judenprozess," *DS* 23/1929.

18. English-language studies of the evolution of Jewish self-defense include Ismar Schorsch, *Jewish Reactions to German Anti-Semitism* (New York and Philadelphia, 1972); Marjorie Lamberti, "The Attempt to Form a Jewish Bloc. Jewish Notables and Politics in Wilhelmian Germany," *Central European History* III (1970); 73–93; and Jehuda Reinharz, *Fatherland or Promised Land: The Dilemma of the German Jew, 1893–1914* (Ann Arbor, Mich., 1975). Sanford Ragins, *Jewish Responses to Anti-Semitism in Germany, 1870–1914* (Cincinnati, 1980), is a useful critical survey. Stefan Schwarz, *Die Juden in Bayern im Wandel der Zeiten* (Munich/Vienna, 1963); and Arndt Müller, *Geschichte der Juden in Nürnberg, 1146–1945* (Nürnberg, 1968) are good on the evolution of the regional Jewish community. Cf. also Max Freudenthal, *Die Israelitische Kultusgemeinde Nürnberg 1871–1924* (Nürnberg, 1925).

19. Arnold Paucker, *Der jüdische Abwehrkampf gegen Anti-Semitismus und Nationalsozialismus in den letzten Jahren der Weimarer Republik* (Hamburg, 1968); W.J. Cahnmann, "The Nazi

Notes

Threat and the Central Verein—A Recollection," *Conference on Anti-Semitism, 1969*, ed. H.A. Strauss (New York, 1969), pp. 27–36.

20.   Varga, pp. 26–27; decision of 10.11.22 in HA 84/1730 and *Julius Streicher im Kampf um sein Recht, Nachlass Streicher*, AL 10.

21.   Decision of 10.17.24 in ibid.; and HA 17A/1731, which also includes much related information on the trial.

22.   Josef Eichmann, *Coburg, Bayern und das Reich* (Coburg, 1969), is a useful introduction.

23.   Letters of 24.5.25 and 27.6.29, HA 91/1889 and 25/499; letter of 27.8.29, HA 58/1409.

24.   Correspondence in HA 85/1733.

25.   Reports of 19.9.25 and 29.6.26, KdI II, 686, 687.

26.   "Rote Arbeitvertreter," *DS* 37/1924; and decision of 12.8.25 in *Nachlass Streicher*, AL 11; judgment of 4.5.26 in ibid., AL 75; "Kipperjuden," *DS* 8/1930; "Das Urteil von Ansbach," *DS* 23/1930; "Der Leutershausen Judenprozess," *DS* 42/1930.

27.   Paucker, pp. 75ff. is a good survey of the general problem. Cf. also Donald L. Niewyk, "Jews and the Courts in Weimar Germany," *Jewish Social Studies* XXXVII (1975): 99–113.

28.   *Centralverein* communications of 24.9.26, 4.10.26, and 5.10.26, HA 91/1884.

29.   Reports of 24.9.26, 25.9.26, and 26.10.26, ibid., report of 11.1.29, HA 86/1744. A report of 5.11.28 in HA 91/1884, discusses the problem of making a case against a newspaper under Paragraph 130.

30.   "Der Jude und die Deutsche Frau," *DS* 3/1928; "Vor dem Schwurgericht," *DS* 22/1930.

31.   Communication to *Centralverein Bayern*, 29.10.28, HA 91/1885.

32.   Undated *Centralverein* report from sometime in 1929, copy in *Nachlass Streicher*, AL 6.

33.   Copy of decision in HA 3A/498; report of 4.11.29 in HA 24/499. *Der Stürmer*'s accounts in "Der grosse Nürnberger Ritualmordprozess," *DS Sondernummer* 2/1929; Ritualmordprozessstürmer," *DS* 50/1929; "Juden und Germanen," *DS* 51/1929; can be compared with the material on the trial in HA 24 and 25/499.

34.   See above, pp. 103–104.

35.   Reports of 13.10.32., charges of 1.11.32, *Centralverein Nürnberg* to *Polizeidirektion Nürnberg-Fürth*, 8.12.32, and reply of 19.12 in HA 92/1891.

36.   Bavarian *Centralverein* to all *Ortsgruppen*, October, 1931, copies in *Nachlass Streicher*, AL 6.

37.   Letter of 12.12.31 in KdI, 692.

38.   Correspondence and reports of 4.12.31, 14.12.31, 17.12.31 in ibid.

39.   Gareis's report of 16.4.31 in ibid., 690.

40.   Utho Grieser, *Himmlers Mann in Nürnberg* (Nürnberg,

1971), pp. 1ff; 275ff., Rothmann, pp. 22ff., Hanschel, pp. 200ff., Hambrecht, pp. 275ff.

41.　Cf. Ernst Röhm, *Die Geschichte eines Hochverräters*, 2nd ed. (Munich, 1930), pp. 162–63; and Preiss, pp. 62, 81, with Hambrecht, p. 43; and Luppe, p. 185.

42.　Report of 17.5.32 in HA 91/1891.

43.　Letter of 15.2.33 in ibid., 1886.

44.　Donald L. Niewyk, *The Jews in Weimar Germany* (Baton Rouge, La., 1980); and Sidney M. Bolkosky, *The Distorted Image: German Jewish Perceptions of Germans and Germany, 1918–1935* (New York, 1975), are significant recent treatments of this issue.

45.　Jasper, pp. 198ff., offers a brief discussion of the problem of defining libel in the Weimar Republic.

46.　One of the best ongoing accounts of the trial is the daily report of the *Fränkischer Kurier*, 3–11.5.24, copies in *Nachlass Luppe*, 45. Their author was hostile to Luppe, but was nevertheless an observant reporter. See also the material in *Nachlass Streicher*, AL 48 and 91; and the file clippings in HA 1731. Hanschel, pp. 204ff., and Ehlers, pp. 123ff., are good secondary analyses.

47.　Luppe, pp. 141–42.

48.　As in "Wohlfahrtsfürsorge," *DS* 17/1923.

49.　Form in *Nachlass Streicher*, AL 91.

50.　Copy of decision of 14.3.24 in *Julius Streicher im Kampf um sein Recht*, *Nachlass Streicher*, AL 10.

51.　As in Hanschel, pp. 212ff.

52.　A good brief statement of this viewpoint, which dominates current scholarship, is Erich Matthias, "The Influence of the Versailles Treaty on the Internal Development of the Weimar Republic," in *German Democracy and the Triumph of Hitler*, pp. 13–28.

53.　For the SPD's approach to scandalmongering, see Hall, pp. 143ff.

54.　*Fränkischer Kurier*, 15.3.24.

55.　For the second trial see the *Fränkischer Kurier*'s reports from 16.11.25 to 17.12.25 in *Nachlass Luppe*, 45—a source once again described by Luppe as objective—the material in *Nachlass Streicher*, AL 78; and the accounts in Luppe, pp. 151ff., Hanschel, pp. 217ff.

56.　Copy of judgment of 16.2.25 in *Julius Streicher im Kampf um sein Recht*, *Nachlass Streicher*, AL 10.

57.　"Dienstsuspendierung, Einleitung und Einstellung des Verfahrens gegen Dr. Luppe wegen Meineid bezw. Falscheid," *Nachlass Luppe*, 48; Luppe, 156–57. The quotation is from *Die Justiz in der Weimarer Republik*, p. 58.

58.　Luppe, p. 157.

59.　"Luppes Eid?" *DS* 11/1925; "Lügt der Nürnberger Oberbürgermeister?" *DS* 11/1925; "Luppe der Wahrhaftige," *DS* 31/1925; "Wer ist der Lügner?" *DS* 33/1925.

60. Decision of 30.8.26 in *Nachlass Luppe*, 49.

61. Court orders of 29.10.26, 15.11.26, 1.12.26, 16.12.26 in ibid.

62. Decisions of 28.12.26, 1.3.27, and 8.4.27 in ibid.

63. Decision of 15.10.27 in ibid.

64. Decisions of 19.6.28, and 28.7.28 in ibid.

65. "Die Bombe," copy in HA 17/1882, LPN 16.10.26.

66. Statement in *Nachlass Streicher*, AL 75. Unless otherwise indicated, all material relative to the *Bombe* case is drawn from this file.

67. Report of 16.10.26 in LPN; speech of 1.4.27 in HA 85/1732.

68. Statement of 26.12.27 in HA 85/1733. Streicher's enemies and opponents, particularly the Luppe-founded *Nürnberg-Fürther Morgenpresse*, advanced hypotheses that the woman was bribed or threatened, or the statement simply forged. No effort seems to have been made, however, to substantiate these allegations by direct investigation.

69. Luppe, p. 186, and the more detailed version in "Mein Leben," pp. 462ff. Cf. Busch, II, pp. 283ff.

70. Letter of 25.10.27 in *Nachlass Luppe*, 46; "Dr. Hermann Luppe und Kurt Hennsch," *DS* 30/1927; "Bombenfabrikant Luppe," *DS* 43/1927; "Was geht im Nürnberger Justizpalast vor?" *DS* 23/1928.

71. Letter of 18.1.26 in *Nachlass Luppe*, 46.

72. Notice of 17.10.28 in Schumacher Sammlung, *Ordner* 374.

73. Hanschel, pp. 227-28; Luppe, pp. 187 passim.

74. Busch, II p. 287.

75. Report of Streicher's speech of 14.10.27 and related statements in HA 85/1732; statements of 9.9.27, judgments of 30.11.27 and 24.3.28 in *Nachlass Luppe*, 46.

Conclusion

1. See particularly Wolfgang Sauer, "National Socialism: Totalitarianism or Fascism?" *American Historical Review* LXXIII (1967): 404-24; and James M. Rhodes, *The Hitler Movement* (Stanford, Cal., 1980).

2. For development of this point see Niewyk, *Jews in Weimar Germany*, pp. 43 passim.

3. Martin, pp. 147ff., is the best description and analysis of Streicher's fall from power. Cf. also Peterson, pp. 274ff.

4. Hsi-Huey Liang, *The Berlin Police Force in the Weimar Republic* (Berkeley, Cal., 1970). pp. 153, 158ff; Josef Goebbels, *Das Buch Isidor* (Munich, 1930); Horst Matzerath, *Nationalsozialismus*

und Kommunale Selbstverwaltung (Stuttgart, 1970), pp. 42ff., Hanschel, pp. 226-27.

    5.   IMT, XII, 318 passim.

    6.   Cartoon *DS* 10/1932; "Zukunftsbild," *DS* 28/1932; "Die Lösung der Judenfrage ist das grösste Problem der Welt," *DS* 19/1927.

    7.   "Der Weg ins Ghetto," *DS* 25/1930; "Die Judennamen," *DS* 5/1930.

    8.   Cartoon in *DS* 48/1927; report of 20.8.29 in HA 86/1744; "Das Judenprogram der Nationalsozialisten," *DS* 17–18/1931.

    9.   Steinert, pp. 140 passim, 334–35, argues for limited public knowledge and awareness of the nature of the Final Solution. Lawrence D. Stokes, "The German People and the Destruction of the European Jews," *Central European History* VI (1973): 167–91, asserts that much of the fate of the Jews was generally known, and vaguely unpopular, but fear inhibited public response.

    10.   "Unheimlicher Transporte," *DS* 8/1925.

    11.   "Die Angst des Judin ———," *DS* 15/1927.

SELECTED BIBLIOGRAPHY

Unpublished Sources

Stanford, Cal., Hoover Institution on War, Revolution, and Peace
    NSDAP Hauptarchiv

Bundesarchiv Koblenz
    Nachlass Luppe
    Nachlass Streicher
    Schumacher Sammlung
    NS 22 (Reichsorganisationsleiter der NSDAP)

Staatsarchiv Nürnberg
    KdI II (Regierung von Mittelfranken)
    KdI XIII (Regierung von Mittelfranken)
    Polizeidirektion Nürnberg-Fürth

Stadtarchiv Nürnberg
    Stürmer-Archiv
    Hermann Busch, "Geschichte der nationalsozialistischen Kommunalpolitik 1925–1933." unpub. ms., 1936–1942
    Otto Fischer, "Der braune Zar," unpub. ms., 1969.
    Evi Rothmann, "Entwicklung und Zielsetzung der NSDAP in Nürnberg von 1928–33," Schriftliche Handarbeit zur Wissenschaftlichen Prüfung für das Lehramt am Gymnasium, June, 1975.
    Manfred Rühl, *"Der Stürmer* und sein Herausgeber," Diplomarbeit, Univ. Erlangen, 1960.

Published Documentary Sources

Trial of the Major War Criminals before the International Military Tribunal, Nuremberg, 14 November–10 October 1946. 42 vols. (Nürnberg, 1947–1949).

Secondary Sources

Most references to works integrating Streicher and *Der Stürmer* into the history of Weimar Germany and National Socialism are in the footnotes. The only published study of *Der Stürmer*—Fred Hahn, *Lieber Stürmer! Leserbriefe an das NS-Kampfblatt 1924 bis 1945. Eine Dokumentation aus dem Leo-Baeck-Institut, New York*, ed. G. Wagenlehner (Stuttgart, 1978) —has neither the research base not the analytical structure to satisfy scholarly requirements. On the other hand, Manfred Rühl's often-cited "Der Stürmer und sein Herausgeber" remains a basic source. Larry Dean Wilcox, "The National Socialist Party Press in the *Kampfzeit*, 1919–1933," (Ph.D. diss., University of Virginia, 1970), puts *Der Stürmer* in its journalistic context. William Paul Varga, "Julius Streicher: A Political Biography, 1885–1933," (Ph.D. diss., Ohio State University, 1974), is a better narrative than analysis. His *The Number-One Nazi Jew-Baiter: A Political Biography of Julius Streicher, Hitler's Chief Anti-Semitic Propagandist* (New York, 1981), appeared too late for consideration. Heinz Preiss, *Die Anfänge der völkischen Bewegung in Franken* (Nürnberg, 1937), originated as an Erlangen dissertation by one of Streicher's followers, and contains useful first-hand information on Streicher's early career. Otto Fischer's "Der Braune Zar" is an after-the-fact journalistic critique. Streicher's own apologia is in Jay Baird, "Das politische Testament Julius Streichers," *Vierteljahrshefte für Zeitgeschichte* XXVI (1978): 660–93. Peter Hüttenberger, *Die Gauleiter: Studie zum Wandel des Machtgefüges in der NSDAP* (Stuttgart, 1969); and Ronald Rogowski, "The Gauleiter and the Social Origins of Fascism," *Comparative Studies in Society and History* XIX (1977): 399–430, provide background.

The best general histories of the *Kampfzeit* in Streicher country also began as doctoral dissertations. Rainer Hambrecht,

Der Aufstieg der NSDAP in Mittel-und Oberfranken (1925–1933) (Nürnberg, 1976); and Hermann Hanschel, *Oberbürgermeister Hermann Luppe: Nürnberger Kommunalpolitik in der Weimarer Republik* (Nürnberg, 1977), are indispensable for an understanding of the local atmosphere in which Streicher and his newspaper flourished. Both tend, however, to be hectoring in tone and overgenerous with hindsight. Carol Ehlers, "Nuremberg, Julius Streicher, and the Bourgeois Transition to Nazism, 1918–1924," (Ph.D. diss., University of Colorado, 1975), is detailed on the early years but exaggerates the depth of direct middle-class commitment to National Socialism. Robin Lenman, "Julius Streicher and the Origins of the NSDAP in Nuremberg, 1918–1923," *German Democracy and the Triumph of Hitler*, ed. A.J. Nicholls and Erich Matthias (London, 1971), pp. 129–59, is concise and informative. Martha Ziegler, "The Socioeconomic and Demographic Bases of Political Behavior in Nuremberg during the Weimar Republic, 1919–1933 (Ph.D. diss., University of Virginia, 1966), analyzes the growth of the Nazi vote. Eric A. Reiche, "The Development of the SA in Nürnberg, 1922–1934," (Ph.D. diss., University of Delaware, 1972), covers the local history of the storm troopers.

The memoirs of Hermann Luppe, Nürnberg's greatest mayor and Streicher's most determined opponent, have been published as *Mein Leben*, ed. W. Lehnert and M. Heinsen-Luppe (Nürnberg, 1977). Arnold Paucker, *Der jüdische Abwehrkampf gegen Anti-Semitismus und Nationalsozialismus in den letzten Jahren der Weimarer Republik* (Hamburg, 1968), puts the Jews' fight against *Der Stürmer* in context. Arnd Müller, *Geschichte der Juden in Nürnberg 1146–1945*, (Nürnberg, 1968) and Donald L. Niewyk, *The Jews in Weimar Germany* (Baton Rouge, La., 1980) are useful for background information. Jacob Katz, *From Prejudice to Destruction: Anti-Semitism, 1700–1933* (Cambridge, Mass., 1980), is the most distinguished treatment of the development of modern anti-Semitism in western Europe. George L. Mosse, *Toward the Final Solution: A History of European Racism* (New York, 1978) is also useful.

Utho Grieser, *Himmlers Mann in Nürnberg* (Nürnberg, 1971), has the best analysis of Streicher's decline and fall after 1933. Edward N. Peterson, *The Limits of Hitler's Power* (Princeton, 1969), is also useful despite some factual and interpretive errors. Bradley Smith, *Reaching Judgment at Nuremberg* (New York, 1977), includes a balanced evaluation of Streicher's trial and sentencing. Eugene Davidson, *The Trial of the Germans* (New York, 1966), contains a less satisfactory narrative treatment.

INDEX

Index

Index

DATE DUE

FEB 1 5 2009			

#47-0108 Peel Off Pressure Sensitive